John Bell Bouton

Roudabout to Moscow

An Epicurean Journey

John Bell Bouton

Roudabout to Moscow
An Epicurean Journey

ISBN/EAN: 9783744753449

Printed in Europe, USA, Canada, Australia, Japan

Cover: Foto ©Andreas Hilbeck / pixelio.de

More available books at **www.hansebooks.com**

ОКОЛЬНЫМЪ ПУТЕМЪ

ВЪ

МОСКВУ

ЕПИКУРЕЙСКОЕ ПУТЕШЕСТВІЕ

ИВАНА НАѲАНАИЛОВИЧА БУГОНА

Автора „За Угломъ"

НЬЮ-ІОРКЪ

Д. Аппльтонъ и Ко.

1887

See pages 203 and 317.

ROUNDABOUT TO MOSCOW

AN EPICUREAN JOURNEY

BY
JOHN BELL BOUTON
AUTHOR OF "ROUND THE BLOCK"

NEW YORK
D. APPLETON AND COMPANY
1887

PREFACE.

If any reader of this book happens to be carrying about a heavy pack of fine old English prejudices, I beg that he or she will drop it before entering upon the eleven chapters relating to Russia. The best preparative for crossing the Russian frontier is to throw out of the carriage-window every English volume with which the tourist has beguiled the way in the vain hope of forming correct impressions of the country ahead.

Englishmen can not be trusted to treat Russia fairly. John Bull hates Ivanovitch. With him the Russian is always a Tartar or a Cossack. Though these terms are not, in fact, opprobrious—since the Tartar of to-day is the model business man of Russia, industrious, faithful, highly respected, and the Cossack preserves none of his ancient traits but an excessive fondness for horses, a martial spirit, and fervent patriotism—they are slurring words in the English sense.

Americans have no cause of quarrel with Russians. There is no Turkey on this continent which we feel bound to save from the jaws of the Russian bear in order to devour her ourselves. We have no distant province with 200,000,000 inhabitants of an alien race, retained by a tenure so precarious that the approach of a rival within 500 miles of the border throws us into a panic. We have no India for Russia to invade. Americans are in a position to do what their English friends have never done—see and report Russia as she is.

If a sense of gratitude for the touching sympathy shown by Russia to the United States at a time when the offensive interference of England in our affairs was strongly feared, shall prepossess the American traveler in favor of that great country and people, there is little danger that he will paint them in colors too bright for truth. For, with his best efforts, he will find it impossible to dismiss all the false anti-Russian ideas with which English literature has filled him. So clinging and powerful is their effect, that he will at times question the evidence of his own senses, and be tempted to discard his personal experience as exceptional and misleading.

I saw no drunken priests reeling through the streets of St. Petersburg and Moscow, and not a single case of intoxication, even among the *mujiks*. Tea is the national beverage of Russia. Beggars drew but lightly upon the little pocketful of kopecks which I had set apart for them. I lost nothing by theft, and was not defrauded, to my knowledge, under cover of overcharges at the shops or the hotels. Government officers are considerate, polite, and do not seem to be in pursuit of bribes. Russians of the lowest class are not more unclean in appearance than the corresponding grade in England. The "rough" who infests London and Liverpool is unknown in St. Petersburg and Moscow.

If external indications are any guide, I should call the Russians the most religious people in Europe. They build more churches, adorn them more sumptuously, attend service oftener and in greater numbers, repeat more prayers, and perform more devotional rites every day, than the men and women of any other land. There are shrines at almost every street-corner, and every house has its Icon. The Russian type of face is serious. Unfriendly critics note this as an infallible sign of national despair, the overt manifestation of which is that revolt against God and Man called Nihilism. But it is only the characteristic gravity of semi-Orientals, for such are the Russians. They are not down-trodden; and, out of their 100,000,000 free souls, there is a proportion of Nihilists no larger, probably, than that of Socialists in Germany, Communists in France, "Dynamiters" in London, or Anarchists in Chicago. The Tsar enjoys the confidence and love of the vast majority of his people. Russia may safely challenge the rest of Europe to exhibit a parallel to the comparative progress, social and political, which she has made in the past thirty years. When the Cossack waters his horse in the Bosporus, and looks down into India from his outpost in the Solyman Mountains, jealous powers will lament his irresistible advance. But Americans can not share their regrets, believing that civilization and liberty may be borne in his train as surely as in that of any other aggressive member of the great European family.

The record of "An Epicurean Journey" is not a place for the discussion of controverted matters. And my sole object in writing this preface is to explain to the possibly surprised reader why I can not echo that censure of Russian institutions and aims which is the burden of so many English books and magazine and newspaper articles. But I have not gone out of the way to praise Russia, or to do her more than simple justice. That a far greater number of Americans annually may include her in their European rounds, and count their stay in Russia as among the most agreeable episodes of their lives, is the sincere wish of

J. B. B.

NEW YORK, *May, 1887.*

CONTENTS.

CHAPTER I.
By *train de luxe* from Paris to Nice—The Monte Carlo games . 1

CHAPTER II.
Oldpaint, Cockspur, and North Adams at the Casino . . . 14

CHAPTER III.
A bad night in Genoa harbor 27

CHAPTER IV.
Rome—Good-Friday and Easter 39

CHAPTER V.
Cutting a King—Margherita, Queen of Hearts 50

CHAPTER VI.
Naples—Sorrento—Capri—Pæstum 57

CHAPTER VII.
Fresh diggings at Pompeii—Vesuvius "working"—The tell-tale seismograph—Solfatara 68

CHAPTER VIII.
Italian beggars—A neglected grave—The blue-gum tree and malaria—Perugia—Etruscan tombs 80

CONTENTS.

CHAPTER IX.
Florence—Bologna—Como 91

CHAPTER X.
Peasant-girls—Nightingales—Isola Bella—San Carlo Borromeo in copper 104

CHAPTER XI.
The Simplon Pass in June—Vispach to Zermatt—The Matterhorn—A fine view from the snows of Gorner Grat . . . 113

CHAPTER XII.
Early Alpine flowers—A wedding-feast—The Rhône Valley and glacier—The Furca Pass 126

CHAPTER XIII.
Avalanches on the Jungfrau—The guides of Grindelwald . . 136

CHAPTER XIV.
Excelsior and the maiden 145

CHAPTER XV.
An English admirer of the "American language" . . . 158

CHAPTER XVI.
Prehistoric lake-dwellers—An island inn and its memories . . 168

CHAPTER XVII.
Carlsbad—Prague—Dresden 177

CHAPTER XVIII.
Berlin—Its military atmosphere 188

CHAPTER XIX.
St. Petersburg in July 203

CHAPTER XX.

The first droschky-ride—Sunset at the islands—Early morning views of the Nevskoi Prospekt 215

CHAPTER XXI.

Grand-Duke Alexis—The American minister and his chasseur—Russian press censorship—An indignant Briton—Undiscoverable Nihilists 233

CHAPTER XXII.

The holy city of Russia 250

CHAPTER XXIII.

The Moscow Foundling Asylum 262

CHAPTER XXIV.

Russian epicurism in tea—The Joltai-Tchai, or yellow-flower brand 275

CHAPTER XXV.

A hunt for malachite and lapis-lazuli in the Gostinnoi Dvor . . 282

CHAPTER XXVI.

The peacock-feather mystery—Manayunk and the old masters—His fruitless search for the Kremlin—The Moscow rag-fair—Petrovsky Palace—Dining in the grounds 296

CHAPTER XXVII.

A comedy of passports—Mythical police espionage . . . 313

CHAPTER XXVIII.

Summer weather in Russia—St. Petersburg and Moscow enough for sight-seers—M. Katkoff and his "Gazette"—Tsar and people—Republican possibilities of the Cossack . . . 328

CHAPTER XXIX.

Russian Finland—Stockholm—The largest known meteorite—
The Djurgarden 342

CHAPTER XXX.

By rail to Christiania—Fare on the road—Norway's capital—The
Viking-ship—An inland tour 353

CHAPTER XXXI.

A baby kudsk—Tyri-Fiord—Hönefos—Lake Spirellen—Dinner
at a Sanitarium 364

CHAPTER XXXII.

Omnipotent kroner—The family parlor at Odnæs—Rands and
Christiania Fiords 383

CHAPTER XXXIII.

The Gothenburg whale—Three kings in a bunch—Northern
out-door life—A study of windmills 394

CHAPTER XXXIV.

Diamond-cutting at Amsterdam 406

APPENDIX.

Constitutional government for Russia 419

ROUNDABOUT TO MOSCOW.

CHAPTER I.

BY TRAIN DE LUXE FROM PARIS TO NICE—THE MONTE CARLO GAMES.

BEFORE leaving America, in the spring of 1886, I read in the London "Times" a slashing attack on the celebrated *train de luxe* which runs twice a week from Paris to Nice. The writer—an Englishman—had missed a connection which he should have made by that train. So he relieved his mind —as traveling Britons are apt to do—by pitching into the delinquent through the columns of a journal still supposed to be powerful for warning and chastisement. I observed that in all his fury he did not declare that the train lacked comforts or even the luxuries claimed in its high-sounding name. Therefore we determined to try it, as it offered a passage from Paris to Nice in nineteen hours; and we did not regret the choice.

The whole distance is 675 miles. Two first-class fares paid to the P. L. M. ("short" for Paris, Lyons and Mediterranean Railway) amount to $53.68. Add to this $41.45 as special charges for the *train de luxe*—run by a separate company—and you have $95.13 as the joint first outlay for the trip. If any railway-riding in the United States is more than half as expensive as this, I have yet to discover it. The sleeping-cars do not seem to be either Wagner or Pullman; they more nearly resemble the Mann Boudoir. They are not quite as large as those in America, and are more solidly built. The compartments are designed for parties of two or four each, and have doors which make a desired privacy for the inmates. These little rooms occupy the whole width of the car, except a narrow passage for common use running lengthwise. The beds are exceedingly comfortable, and are metamorphosed into handsome sofas for the daytime. A restaurant-car accompanies the train; and in this good fare may be had *à la carte*, at all hours, and an elaborate *table d'hôte* twice a day. The attendants are alert and polite. Everybody on the *train de luxe* seems to feel a personal responsibility in keeping up its reputation and reconciling passengers to their large disbursement of money. It was my good fortune—as an American—to enlist at once the kindest sympathy of the Paris agent of the sleeping-car company, as also of the conductor. By the courtesy of those officials we were allowed to tenant a room for four, though paying only for two persons. This gave us plenty of space, and perhaps accounts in part for the general satisfaction I experienced.

Though the rate of speed averaged thirty-five miles an hour, there was little vibratory motion and no jarring whenever the train stopped or started again. If the P. L. M. does not use the Westinghouse air-brake and Miller platform, it has equivlent contrivances of its own just as good.

A better night's rest could not be asked for than the one I enjoyed till the *train de luxe* pulled up in the Lyons station at 6.25 A. M. on time. The Paris we had left at 9.25 Wednesday night, April 14th, was anything but gay. A cold rain swept the deserted streets and deepened the gloom everywhere observable on the faces of hotel-landlords, shopkeepers, and cabmen. Trade had been stagnant there all winter, and the spring season— with its promises of better times—was deplorably backward. But I must not omit to mention that it was further along than in America, or even England. The trees which line the Champs-Elysées were in full leaf, and the Bois de Boulogne was thick with shade. But a keen north wind came down upon Paris while we were there, and we were glad to quit it.

Next morning as we entered Lyons I raised the curtain at the foot of my little bed, and lo! a sight of enchantment. An unclouded sun lighted up the great manufacturing city and its environs and glorified everything. The general impression was that of an entrance to Italy. The roofs of all the houses wear the peculiar earthen tiles which one sees in Italian towns. The church-steeples begin to resemble *campaniles*. Olive-trees are possible in the soft climate of this part of Southern France. The natives, who swarm about the station at an early hour and gaze wonderingly at the *train de luxe*, are swarthy of face and profuse of gesture — more Italian than French in outward appearance. But our greatest delight was in the increasing warmth of the outer air, for the car had required heating on that cold night of a northern spring. A dainty breakfast—served on the snowiest of linen—at a table from which we could study the sunny landscape as we whirled along, completed the prelude of a lovely day. Our next stop was at Marseilles, where we changed locomotives. There the Mediterranean came into view, but a cloud over the sun prevented that full revelation of its beauties which we saw later on. What a glamour genius throws over common things! The Château d'If is nothing but a square-built tower, standing on a little island in the harbor of Marseilles. It is neither grand nor picturesque. I should not have glanced at it a second time if Dumas had not forever linked it in my mind with the imprisonment and daring escape of his Count of Monte Cristo. There may be much to see and admire in Marseilles, but I could only think of Edmond Dantes and his wonderful adventures.

Nice, into the station of which we punctually rolled amid a crowd of staring spectators, was then out of season. As a winter resort much beloved by consumptives and tired-out people, it deserves its fame. Orange and lemon trees, aloes, palms, oleanders, acacias, and many other tropical plants, thrive there in the months that are coldest elsewhere. Nice faces the Mediterranean toward the south, and is sheltered from every rude wind by the towering Maritime Alps. The fashionable season proper had already terminated with the opening of Parliament — which is the invariable signal for the resumption of social gayeties in London. The richest patrons of Nice, as of all this coast, are Englishmen. And as they leave, the great hotels begin to close in the very month when Nature is most actively renewing herself and looking her best. Even Nice, with all her tropical proclivities, is capable of being chilly upon occasion. Snow had visited the place within a month, and we found a fire comfortable in our chamber. It seemed strange to be toasting one's feet at the hearth, and looking out of window upon gardens golden with oranges and bristling with gigantic palms, or thick-set with monstrous specimens of that vegetable devil-fish known as the agave or century-plant. The arms or tentacles of these are twelve or fifteen feet long and two or three feet thick at the butt. Fill in this rough outline with lilacs, daisies, geraniums, heliotropes, and tea-roses, and the reader may realize what was seen from every hotel window and balcony on the *Riviera di ponente*.

We took the Corniche road by private carriage from Nice to Mentone, about nineteen miles. It is a marvelous piece of engineering skill, gaining a height of 1,500 feet by a bold succession of zigzags. As its name implies, this road is a mere cornice. It is cut into the sides of mountains, and in places overhangs frightful precipices. During the first hour of our journey I frequently jumped out of the carriage to pick the strange and exquisite wild flowers which grew along the road-side. But we soon reached the altitude where these attractions ceased, and we were called upon to admire the beetling rocks which towered far above us. This rugged scenery was in the ascendant most of the time. It makes the Corniche route grand in its savage loneliness, but beautiful I can not call it. But beauty flashed upon us in the distance whenever a turn of the road brought the Mediterranean into view. Under a brilliant sun that sea looks like a limitless stretch of changeable silk, full of graceful wrinkles. Near the shore its predominant color is light blue. Toward the horizon, this deepens into a darker shade. Purples and greens may also be descried in larger masses and clearer tints than one observes in the broad Atlantic in any of its moods.

We lunched at a little hamlet—Turbi—perched high up in the mountains. The landlord of the Grand Hotel at Nice had advised me to try ham and eggs, as the least objectionable dish to be obtained off-hand at the Turbi inn. The landlady accepted the order in the most accommodating spirit, and after a little delay brought in some slices of raw ham and boiled eggs. I then described to her as well as I knew how the American process of cooking ham and eggs. Her face lighted up with intelligence, and she retired to try again. Fifteen minutes later she came back with the eggs stirred up in a mess at the bottom of a skillet and the raw ham reposing beneath them, where it had been slightly warmed in the new operation. But the *vin du pays* was honest and palatable. Bread and cheese are always good to a hungry man. We stayed our appetites, if we did not lunch exactly to our liking. From Turbi to Mentone the road is mostly down-hill, and the scenery a repetition of what we had seen in the first half of the Corniche. As for Mentone itself, it is Nice over again, with a slight difference of location, but much smaller.

I have seen the notorious games at Monte Carlo (five or six miles from Mentone), strictly as an outsider. There is no lovelier spot under the whole heavens. Nature and the art paid for out of the enormous gains of the greatest gambling-hell on earth have done everything to make a paradise of Monte Carlo. The Casino is a palace in size and splendor. The surrounding gardens are full of the choicest flowers and musical with birds and waterfalls. Mountains exclude every biting wind. Three hundred feet below the promontory lies the matchless Mediterranean. All around are beautiful villas and large and elegant hotels and restaurants worthy of Paris. The season at Monte Carlo lasts the year round, and is always prosperous. Admission to the *salle de jeu* is not to be had for the asking. No one under twenty-one years of age can enter. As no resident—but only the stranger —is allowed access to the Casino, the local population is not hurt by the game. I was obliged to present my visiting-card at the bureau and write my name on the back of a ticket. Then, after surrendering my umbrella, the great doors of the den were thrown open to me. I had read of so many suicides committed at this place that I quite expected, when I entered, to interrupt some ruined gambler in the act of blowing out his silly brains. Instead of confronting such a tragedy, I found myself in the presence of a large company of quiet people, sitting around long tables, watching a revolving wheel in the center, and listening to the click of the little ivory ball as it slackened and fell into a numbered compartment of the wheel and determined the gain or loss of the players. There are four of these roulette-tables, and two others in an adjoining room, at which only *trente et quarante* is played, the latter a game of cards. No game lasts over a minute, so that the suspense is not long and agonizing. The London illustrated papers have lately represented the gamesters of both sexes as uniformly hideous. Their countenances were made infernal with avarice. As for the *croupiers*, who rake in or pay out the money, they were depicted as fiends incarnate.

Speaking of suicides, I learned that, only two days before my visit, a man who had lost all at one of the tables suddenly whipped out a pistol and shot himself. He was quietly removed, and the *roulette* and *trente et quarante* went on without interruption. A lady, who had been watching the play on one occasion, told me that she saw a person seize from the table a little pile of money which had been won by another. He appealed for redress to the superintendent of the Casino. The latter did not stop to inquire into the justice of the claim, but immediately paid over to the second player the sum which he said had been thus publicly stolen from him. This little incident proves the constant anxiety of the "administration" to avoid disagreeable scenes and scandals. But the suicides can not be stopped, as men, acting under the sudden impulse of despair, will kill themselves before the "bank" can solace them with the donations it is always ready to make for the relief of ruined gamesters. The French Government could, if it would, in the capacity of protector and powerful neighbor, suppress the monstrous evil of Monte Carlo. But Prince Charles manages to keep in favor at Paris, not merely by his personal residence there, but by a full-blown legation, which he maintains at the French capital for diplomatic purposes, just like a first-class sovereign.

Describing people as I find them, I must say that the male players seemed an average lot of human beings. The females were more mixed and questionable. The *croupiers* were evidently wearied and bored, but on the whole good-looking and certainly amiable. Most of the players were of frugal mind. The usual stake was a five-franc piece; napoleons were scarce. One reckless man who put up ten of them at a time, turned pale when he lost them all, and hauled out of the game. No one lost much at any table under my observation, and in not a single case did a player gain the possible maximum of thirty-five times the amount of his stake. To a looker-on the spectacle was monotonous in the highest degree. Perhaps it is livelier toward midnight than in the afternoon when I saw it. But, whether slow or swift, it is none the less to be condemned as demoralizing in its far-reaching influences, productive of thefts and embezzlements, as well as the undoubted cause of many suicides. How any person can turn his back on all these beauties of nature and art, and give himself up to such a sordid and destructive vice, is a puzzle to every well-regulated mind.

After seeing the games at Monte Carlo, I visited the palace of Prince Charles at Monaco. Careless writers use the two names interchangeably. Be it understood, then, that Monte Carlo is part of the diminutive principality of Monaco. The less is included in the greater. The prince's palace is situated at the other end of his possessions, about a mile from the Casino. He never occupies it. He lives in luxurious retirement at Paris on the large revenues derived from a lease of the gambling monopoly. But he is cut off from many of the pleasures of this life, as he is stone-blind. His ample income enables him to remit all taxes to his few thousand subjects, and to keep a really beautiful palace on show for all comers. Not to be wanting in any of the outward signs of sovereignty, he maintains an "army" of fine fellows—sixty-five strong—and has a park of highly burnished artillery pointing seaward. Hundreds of cannon-balls are piled up symmetrically in his palace yard. At the great gates of the edifice, as I approached it, stood two good-looking soldiers. One rested gracefully on his shining musket, and the other played with a tame crow which hopped about in the grass. Seeing me, he recovered his erect position and dignity, and returned my courteous salute. I asked permission to enter the palace. With a gesture he referred me to a gorgeous personage, looking like three major-generals rolled into one, who suddenly appeared in a doorway. I took him for the commander-in-chief; but he was only the *concierge*. With a profound bow he requested my visiting-card, which I gave him. Then, after registering my name, I was turned over to another less splendid but still imposing official, who showed me through the long galleries and suites of rooms. They are full of costly pictures and statues, and magnificently upholstered. But they have the cold, cheerless atmosphere and stuffy smell of all uninhabited houses however grand. I was glad to escape from the wearisome round into the open air.

The blind prince not only exempts his subjects from taxes, but he provides for several good schools, and is a liberal supporter of the Roman Catholic Church. A fine cathedral is now rising at Monaco.

Public morals are so deeply concerned in the suppression of the Monte Carlo games that I do not yet feel like quitting them. I will take a fresh start in Chapter II, and isolate for description a few types of character among the many that may be seen at the Casino. We will watch them at work (for it is no "play" to them save in name), amid seductions difficult to be withstood by any will that does not rest on principles.

I now beg leave to introduce the reader to Oldpaint, Cockspur, and North Adams.

CHAPTER II.

OLDPAINT, COCKSPUR, AND NORTH ADAMS AT THE CASINO.

OLDPAINT was a fellow-traveler of ours from Mentone to Monte Carlo. Not knowing her real name, I call her Oldpaint for sufficient reasons. She was wrinkled with age, and excessively painted. Turner, in his moments of divinest frenzy, would not have laid on the red more boldly. It blazed through her veil. Her cheeks were hollow, her eyes sunken, with deep black marks scored beneath them which she had vainly attempted to whiten. The whole expression of her face was desperate. I observed in her hand a ticket stamped Monte Carlo. Then I guessed she was a veteran devotee of roulette. And I was right. For, when I entered the *salle de jeu* a few hours later, she was already there, comfortably seated at the *croupier's* elbow, and evidently at home. It was by closely watching her play that I first came to understand the horrible fascination of the game for its votaries.

Cockspur is another name I was obliged to invent for an Englishman—also a confirmed gambler—whom we first encountered lunching in the Restaurant de Paris at Monte Carlo. This establishment is worthy of its imposing title. There is no better on the Boulevards. It is famous for game in season, and good wines all the year round. When we entered this paradise of *gourmets*, and dropped quietly into two chairs at a table not far from the door, we did not instantly attract attention. No waiter appearing for a moment, we fell to studying some brilliant frescoes on the ceiling, and noting the sumptuousness of the furniture, the fineness of the linen, the exquisite fragility of the cut-glass. Still no *garçon*. I turned my head impatiently, and then saw what was the matter. At the third table behind us sat a tall young man, with light, curly hair and mustaches, and by his side a showy woman, who looked like a queen of burlesque in walking-suit. There was an indescribable something in the frizzling of her hair, the look of her eyes, her stereotyped smile, which betrayed the professional winner of applause from crowded parquettes. The man was evidently under her dominion, and was testifying to his complete surrender by ordering on the costliest meats and wines. They did not seem desirous to excite public curiosity, for they spoke low and behaved decorously enough. But the lunch was prodigal, even for that place of extravagances. To serve it had required two waiters, who now, in a moment of pause, hovered about "milord's" table, wondering what he would condescend to order next. It was plain that they were all expecting liberal *pour boires* from this spendthrift of a patron. Still other waiters had gathered in the vicinity, as if to pick up some stray crumbs of his bounty. All eyes being focused on this couple, we had apparently escaped observation. I gave notice of my presence by a slight cough, and, to the lasting credit of the Restaurant de Paris, am happy to say that it provoked a prompt response. A smart waiter dutifully detached himself from the little group and bent before me with an apologetic expression of face. I hastily consulted the *carte du jour*, and gave my order.

The lunch was quickly served, and proved to be excellent. The sweetbreads, *omelette soufflé*, and some Pontet Canet of 1872, were particularly interesting. But I did not forget to look over my shoulder occasionally to see how the Englishman and his companion were getting on. They soon finished their repast; the bill, which might have been a washer-woman's for length, was delivered and paid without verification. He only looked at the total, and produced from a great roll of French bank-notes one which he placed upon the salver extended to him. Then he opened a rouleau of gold, and gave a bright-yellow piece to each of the two waiters who stood near him. As the salver was borne past me to the *caisse*, I noticed that the bill was of the denomination of 100 francs. The Englishman did not stop for his change (if any), but hurried off with his stylish enslaver; so I inferred that 100 francs was not far from the price of their lunch. Remarking this extraordinary lavishness, I said to myself, "That man has been winning a pot of money over at the Casino."

Now it happened that he had placed his new Derby hat in the embrasure of the window, just behind my chair. As one of the waiters reached over for it, I inadvertently glanced into the hat, and there chanced to see the illegible name of somebody, "maker, Cockspur St., London." So this extravagant Englishman became "Cockspur" to me henceforth and forever. We shall soon see more of him.

From our luncheon at the Restaurant de Paris we went direct to the Casino, and there, while I was hunting up my card for the inspection of the chief inquisitor, I observed an innocent-looking youth standing near me. He wore the dog-collar, the pointed shoes, the tight-fitting, single-breasted coat of the London swell, and he gripped his little silver-headed cane in the middle, like a shillalah. But I know my dear fellow-countrymen under all their disguises. A single glance at his face convinced me that he was a good young American on his first trip. His dissipation was obviously confined to clothes. He had just handed in his card, and an official personage was making an entry of the name in a book.

"*Quel pays, monsieur?*" he asked, courteously.

The good young man turned to me and said, with surprise: "Is there anything to pay here? I thought it was a free show."

"There is no charge. He only wants to know where you are from, as we would say in America," I answered.

His ingenuous cheeks colored. "I can speak French a little myself," said he; "but somehow I don't catch it when they speak it at me."

I assured him kindly that we all had the same trouble, more or less.

"*Quel pays, monsieur?*" repeated the ever-amiable *greffier* of the administration.

"Beg pardon," said the good young man, flushing again. "I'm from North Adams, Massachusetts."

"*Nort-a-darm — Massa-Massa — n'importe — Angleterre,*" murmured the *greffier*, and down it went.

The benighted Frenchman had supposed the

name of the glorious old commonwealth to be that of some obscure shire in England. It is the most flagrant piece of geographical distortion on record.

The good young man was so flustered by all this that he did not wait to exchange cards with me, but hurried off to the gambling-hall. So I was compelled to label him in my mind "North Adams." He was number three among the strangers in whose actions that day I took a deep interest. Without their presence, indeed, the game of roulette would have been tiresome to me as a mere spectator.

If Oldpaint had not been one of the large company of gamblers in that magnificent apartment, I should have been much disappointed; for I felt a profound curiosity to see how her withered features would stand the wear and tear of the game. There she was, as if by agreement, and I at once stationed myself behind her chair. Her seat was well chosen for a general survey of the table. She was just opposite the wheel, and the *croupier* who set it whirling at intervals was her nearest neighbor.

Oldpaint still wore her veil closely drawn over her face. But I could see the varying expression of her features through the gauze, as I looked down at her while she played. At one time her dull eyes would light up with a gleam of avaricious joy. Again they would become fishy. The pinched mouth would contract slightly at the corners, bringing out new wrinkles on her rouged cheeks, or her thin, vermilion-tinted lips would curve downward, just as she happened to win or lose—more commonly the latter. Her gloved hands, which terminated in skeleton wrists, trembled equally as she put up her stakes or piled her occasional winnings in little round towers before her.

By her side stood a small open bag, through the steel jaws of which I saw silver five-franc pieces and little rolls of gold, like packages of lozenges, with one coin visible at the end as a sample. Below was a thin foundation of French bank-notes. Oldpaint was one of those who play on a system. She had before her a large pasteboard card divided into many squares, and a pencil with a sharp point. Whenever the wheel slowed up so as to permit the ivory ball to drop into a compartment and decide the game, she threw a lightning glance at the winning number and color, and pricked certain entries on her card. By the time the human parrot at her side called out, "*Faites vos jeux,*" she was ready with a fresh stake, generally a small one. In no instance did she go over ten francs.

As for Oldpaint's system, it was too complicated for me to understand. But the results were plain enough: *rouge* was generally turning up when she had bet on *noir*. Her money, as a rule, stood on *pair*, when it should have been on *impair*. When other players were doubling their stakes on *passe*, Oldpaint was almost sure to have five francs on *manque*. Occasionally she would haul in something substantial. Once she bagged eight times the amount of her stake. It had been put at the intersecting lines of four numbers, one of which had won. As the *croupier* scooped them in for her with his little rake, I could see the enamel on her cheeks crack open in new places, she smiled so broadly; and then, on the strength of this bit of luck, the poor old woman would go on losing again. It made me sick to see her throwing away good money on a system which ought to have been turned round end for end. A gambler, if he had been in my place, would have made a good thing just watching Oldpaint and playing against her every time.

My attention was now called off by the sudden appearance of Cockspur on the scene. As there was no spare seat for him at the table, he stood up in the second row of players and spectators. His face was flushed, and he reached forward between two other persons to rest his hand on the back of a chair, as if to steady himself. I wondered if the man would be foolish enough to play in that half-drunken state. It was a great pity that such a free-hearted fellow should be a victim of the dreadful vice of gambling, and perhaps be reduced to beggary by his rashness before night.

Cockspur took a napoleon from a side-pocket which audibly jingled with coins. Waiting till the wheel started, he pitched the gold-piece carelessly on the table. It rolled on its edge, making a circle on the cloth and finally laid down at the junction of two lines which intersect six numbers. "*Rien ne va plus,*" droned the human parrot, when the speed of the wheel was much reduced, and a moment later the ball dropped with a little thud. "*Vingt-cinq rouge,*" said the same monotonous voice. I looked at the square on the table, and lo! it was one of the six numbers covered by Cockspur's napoleon. He had won five times the amount of his stake. One of the servitors whose duty it is to assist in placing money on the table or handing over winnings, passed the six napoleons up to Cockspur, who slipped them into the yawning side-pocket. His face expressed no pleasure. Some men, under the belief that they had struck a run of luck, would, in Cockspur's place, have risked a sum larger than twenty francs on the next round. In his condition I expected him to do something rash. But he only produced another napoleon from his store and let it fall. After wobbling about a moment it came to rest on the division marked *manque*. Again a whirl of the wheel and a fall of the ball, and the *croupier* proclaimed "*Quinze noir*," and Cockspur doubled his stake, because 15 is *manque*, or less than 18. All numbers over 18 up to 36 are *passe;* and all the players who had put their money on the part of the table so labeled, were losers to the bank.

The same good fortune pursued Cockspur as he pitched his gold pieces at random into the section *Rouge* or *Noir*, *Pair* or *Impair*. He won six or seven times running while I looked on. And then he and all the players together fell prey to the bank's single advantage. Besides the thirty-six numbers, there is a zero (o), and, when that catches the ball, all the stakes on the board are raked in by the bank, with the solitary exception that any person who has staked on the zero (thereby backing the bank) gains thirty-five times the amount of his wager. But, in the case under notice, the zero symbol was uncovered. As the bank plays nine or ten hours every day in the year, and must, according to the law of probabilities, win once in every thirty-seven games (requiring about a minute each) on the average, one can understand how the administration makes all its money without the necessity of cheating. No player is allowed to stake more than six thousand francs at a time, and the enormous capital of the bank enables it to continue the game against any conceivably probable run of bad luck.

Cockspur continued to drop his money, always the one prudent napoleon, on the table, and letting it take the chances. Sometimes he lost, but more often he won. It would have been amusing, but for the sadness of their long and hungry faces, to see Oldpaint and some others who were losing steadily on systems, look up at Cockspur who was discarding all methods and trusting blindly to luck, and showing so much judgment even in his folly, taking only small risks at a time. As I gazed across the table at him, I foresaw with prophetic eye the time, and not far off, when his luck would turn, and he would then become frenzied and reckless; perhaps put up his last napoleon, and lose it, and then the siren with the frizzled hair would drop her penniless lover, and the comedy of real life would tragically close with a pistol-shot and a newspaper paragraph.

I was dwelling on this dismal ending of the handsome fellow opposite, when a new cause of anxiety threw him quite out of my mind.

There was North Adams, fluttering around the table like a moth about a candle. He had been spending his time watching the other groups of players, I suppose, and had now come to see what our set was doing. Like most persons who look on at the game for the first time, he watched only those who won. The equal numbers who lost at every fall of the ball seemed to escape his observation. Every time a player raked in a goodly pile, North Adams's eyes would bulge out with astonishment. He would thrust his hand into a pocket and partly draw it out, and then thrust it back again. A storm of conflicting feelings swept over his smooth, beardless face. One could easily read avarice, covetousness, the love of illicit gain, struggling with the generous sentiments of youth and the good principles of New England training. I tried to catch his eye, but in vain. He was totally absorbed in the contemplation of all that money so easily won. Once he elbowed his way through the double row of outsiders, and I thought he was about to place money on the table. But just then the bank again scored zero (0), and all those yellow and white pieces down there disappeared in an instant! This was a warning for North Adams. He drew back, and I saw a look as of shrewd reflection pass across his face. He wiped his damp brow, and resolutely buttoned up the pocket into which his hand had so often dived without bringing up anything.

That one decisive hit for the bank seemed to

banish the doubts that had evidently troubled North Adams. He did not look like a person of severe moral principles; he may have had no nice scruples upon the subject of gaming; but when his mind, such as it was, still bearing the impress of his early schooling and severe discipline, realized that the bank had a "sure thing" in the long run, then he hesitated to jump at the gilded bait. Some grains of hard common sense inherited from level-headed ancestors, along with the high cheek-bones of his Scotch face, came to his rescue in the nick of time. Blood will tell, even when thinned down in the veins of a harmless dude; and while I looked at him, still questioning his firmness against temptation, he deliberately turned his back upon the game and walked straight out of the room.

I soon followed him into the open air, better pleased with that spectacle of conflict and victory than with all else I had seen in the gambling-palace of Monte Carlo.

CHAPTER III.

A BAD NIGHT IN GENOA HARBOR.

A MAN not in a hurry to reach Southern Italy before hot weather, might find happiness and contentment in three or four days of Genoa. The old city has churches and palaces worth visiting. Some of the drives in the environs are charming, and I should not soon tire of views of the Mediterranean to be had from the Acqua Sola. But, when the tourist is burning up with a desire to pass early May in Rome, Naples, and Sorrento, and hopes to see the glorious Greek ruins of Pæstum without fear of a sunstroke, he willingly leaves over Genoa to the chance of another visit. My real object in breaking the journey at that point was to take boat thence to Naples direct, and avoid the rail route to Rome, which I had traversed in 1883.

I had gathered from books the impression that, for unalloyed pleasure, nothing in the line of travel was quite equal to the steamship trip from Genoa along the coast, touching at Leghorn, Città Vecchia (port of Rome), passing in full view of Elba and Corsica, and entering the glorious Neapolitan bay by daylight. The view of Naples from the sea, with the long curve of coast, the white houses of the city piled high in terraces, smoking Vesuvius in the background, and the islands of Ischia and Capri deep blue in the offing, like sapphires in a setting of lapis-lazuli, is the identical view to which the much-quoted proverb refers. We had looked forward to this trip with the greatest pleasure, and now I must tell the reader how the cup was dashed to the ground even before it had been raised to our lips.

We thought we were in great luck when we found, on arriving at Genoa, that a steamship would start for Naples, and take in all the wonderful sights along the coast, the following night at 9 P. M. precisely. Even before I had made a tour of the city, I went to the office of the steamship company to secure the best cabin left. I greatly feared that all the accommodations had been snapped up by other more fortunate travelers. When I reached the office I was quite alarmed to see crowds of people standing before the heavy wire network which separated them from the cashier and clerks. These people were all thrusting their money through small open wickets, and receiving in exchange slips of paper that looked like tickets. I annexed myself to one of these anxious crowds, and after a delay of ten minutes, and a little firm but still polite working of my elbows into the ribs of others all about me, found myself face to face with a nervous and overworked young man.

I told him in French what I wanted, and asked him the price of two first-class tickets. Like most intelligent Italians, he understood a little French. His face expressed great surprise, as if my application for a first-class cabin on a Naples steamer was something unheard of. He begged me to excuse him a moment, and he would find out the price. I thought this very strange, when I considered the great demand that must exist for the best berths. I was curious for an explanation, but forbore to seek it when I looked at that poor young man's tired face. He sat down, with one hand partly covering his forehead, in which I could see the distended veins, while with the other hand he ciphered on a blotting-pad, meanwhile looking hard at some columns of printed figures on a placard before him. He was immersed in deep calculations for five minutes. One would have thought he was working out an eclipse of the sun.

The pack of Italians behind me was increasing, and there were murmurs of dissatisfaction on account of their delay, while the young man was performing prodigies in arithmetic. I was beginning to feel very uncomfortable under the pressure in the rear, when he suddenly footed up his elaborate computations, and told me what two first-class tickets from Genoa to Naples—table-fare included, without wine—would cost. I was surprised to learn that the fares were much higher than those by rail all the way; but, *per contra*, there was the escape from a dreary land-ride, and, better yet, the sea-view of Naples, cheap even at the price of death. So I paid over the money and received my tickets, with the accompanying injunction that I must be on board at 8 P. M., one hour before sailing, without fail. The exhausted young man also gave me directions about reaching the steamship, which was then anchored in the harbor. I thanked him, and forced myself through the ever-growing throng of Italians to the open air. I deemed myself truly fortunate to have secured that prize of a cabin, and reveled in the fondest anticipations.

The next night, a few minutes before eight o'clock, we descended from a carriage to the quay, where small boats could be obtained to put us on board. The driver blew a shrill whistle, to which several boats near by responded. The one that reached us first, and thereby became entitled to our patronage, looked like the relic of an Arctic whaler.

Its sides were worm-eaten; its bottom was covered with water. It exhaled a rank smell of fish. The rower was as unpleasant to the eye as the craft he slowly propelled with two oars that looked as if they would snap off in the middle with the least strain. My first intention was to reject the services of this boat and man; but when I glanced at the others heading for me, I saw that, if possible, they were worse. So I accepted the situation, and in a few minutes we, with our trunks, were on board, keeping our feet out of the water by resting them on the spare seat before us. Then he struck out for the steamship, and he had not made ten strokes of the oars before I had forgotten all about the disagreeable sight and smell of the boat. For in that part of the harbor, in that tide, we were initiated into the mysteries of the old sewage system of Genoa. In this respect the city is probably better off than any other along the Italian coast; but, during that little boat-ride, I ceased to wonder why the cholera, which thrives on filth and stenches, is so fond of Mediterranean towns. If I had not known the ride to be a short one, and that we should weigh anchor in an hour and be off for the open sea, I should have felt like abandoning the expedition at that early stage of it.

When we reached the goal at last, after making the circuit of several other sea-going craft, steam and sail, anchored close together, we found a large, handsome boat. She was freshly painted, and I shall always remember how nice the paint smelt in contrast with the unpleasant odors all around her. We could see men on deck hoisting in the cargo from a lighter alongside, and hear their cheery cries as they tugged at the ropes. They were so very busy that not one of them could lend a hand to us. But our boatman, with all his dirt, was not lazy. He lost no time in putting our two trunks aboard, shouldering them with ease, and bounding up the flight of wooden steps which hung precariously from the deck to the water's edge. We followed quickly, and I inquired at once for *il capitano*. One of the sailors pointed me to a wiry little man, who was sharply watching the hands as they swung the barrels and boxes on board and lowered them into the hold. I stepped up to him and handed him my ticket. He looked it over twice carefully, scratched his head in evident perplexity, and murmured words in Italian unintelligible to me. I tried him in French, but he only shook his head. His astonishment at something was even greater than that of the young man in the company's office the day before. Finally, in despair, he called to a subordinate of some rank and put us in his charge, significantly shrugging his shoulders at the same time. This man's manner expressed surprise, mingled with amusement, I should say. He also could not speak French, but he made signs that we were to follow him. We did so, and, descending the companionway, found ourselves in a small but neat saloon, off which six or eight cabins opened on either side. The one assigned to us was well situated and commodious enough, but the two beds in it were not made up, and it had a musty smell, as if it had not been aired through the port-hole for some years. But this stuffiness was more tolerable than the stench which would soon have permeated the cabin if the dead-light had been open. Of washing arrangements there were none in the cabin, but we were shown a place outside which would have supplied that deficiency, if there had been any jug for water, or stopper at the bottom of the basin to keep the water from running out, or towel or soap-dish. These discoveries were dampers, but we were inclined to be philosophical. The worst, however, was yet to be learned, and, thanks to the scrappy French of the captain's cook, whom we interviewed upon the subject of a little hot supper, we soon found it out.

It appears that this boat, and others of the same line, no longer made a business of carrying first-class passengers; the railways do all that now. Once in a while an officer of the Italian army or navy presents himself with a government pass, and some provision is made for him, but yet he must rough it. Just before nine o'clock a gentleman with a long, trailing sword and spurs, appeared with a pass, and took a cabin next to ours. He was the only first or even second class passenger aboard besides ourselves. There were a few persons in the steerage, who furnished their own food. Being out of the habit of taking saloon-passengers, the officers of the boat had made no suitable preparations for them. They were just as much amazed to see us there as the company's agent had been to receive my order for a cabin. To the former we also represented a certain amount of extra trouble and care.

"But how about the rush for tickets?" I asked the cook.

"Oh, that was only for freight-receipts," he replied.

All this intelligence, and much more of the kind, especially relating to the lean larder, and the cook's inability to get a hot supper for us, with some uncertainty as to breakfast next morning, were vexatious and even distressing. Still, we knew we should not starve on board; and, after all, the privations, whatever they might be, would last only thirty-six hours, the time required for the whole trip, including a stoppage at Leghorn, so we were told. Besides, it was almost nine o'clock now, and too late to go ashore. So we decided to put the best face on our disappointment. Meanwhile, the stewardess had come aboard, and she had fished out of the lockers enough sheets, blankets, and pillows to equip our two berths. A pair of towels were also discovered after much search and hung up on nails above the mockery of a wash-stand. Toward ten o'clock matters were becoming slightly more endurable. But the boat had not started. The men were still hoisting in the cargo, as we knew from their droning songs and the creaking of the windlass. Eleven o'clock came and went, and yet no sign of departure.

So we went to bed, hoping that we might soon fall asleep, and wake in the morning to find the boat far on her way across the Gulf of Genoa. But sleep was impossible while those interminable choruses rang in our ears. Twelve, one, two, three, four o'clock!—and our craft was still at her anchorage and the operation of loading progressing as noisily as ever. As dawn stole through the dead-light, I arose and opened it to get a whiff of fresh air as a change from the stifling atmosphere of the cabin, which had only a lattice-work opening on the saloon for ventilation. But a mephitic odor arose from the water, and compelled me to close the bull's-eye. Dressing myself, I went on deck, and there saw that the work of loading had in fact only just begun. A second lighter, with a towering pile of merchandise, had been brought alongside during the night, and the transfer of her cargo to the hold I knew would be the work of many hours. I resolved to hail a boat, go ashore with my trunks, trust to getting my passage-money refunded by the company, and leave for Rome *via* Pisa on the ten-o'clock train.

We carried this resolve into instant execution. The officers, who were then on deck, beamed with delight as they saw us preparing to leave. One hailed a boat for us. Another brought our two trunks in his strong arms from the room where they had been stored overnight. The cook bustled around ecstatically and made us a cup of good coffee, with sugar and milk. I never saw a man so pleased; for our presence on the boat had been a cause of the greatest solicitude to him, in the impoverished state of his supplies. The stewardess grinned with unspeakable satisfaction. Even the captain found time to quit his post at the hatchway to see us over the ship's side in safety. None of us said a word, but our hearts swelled with thankfulness at the thought that we were parting with each other forever.

The *battello* which put us ashore seemed to be

a twin-sister of the one that put us aboard. But we reached the quay in safety, after running a gantlet of foul smells. Then another singular incident befell us. Custom-house officers were on the watch at our landing-place. They might have seen us when we left the steamship out there. They must have known that we had passed the night on board, for they asked questions of the boatman, which he answered, all doubtless to that effect. And yet our baggage was taken to the custom-house, not far off, for an inspection. The head-man spoke a little French, and I explained to him the facts of the case. But this did not prevent him from performing the solemn ceremony of examining the contents of the trunks, the valise, the bundle of shawls, and the hand-bag, just as if we had arrived from the coast of Africa. I thought, from the expression on the faces of the inspectors, that a couple of francs would have saved me this detention. But I was really amused at the farce, and allowed it to proceed unchecked.

Returning to the Hôtel de Gênes, greatly to the surprise of the worthy head-porter, we stopped there long enough to take a solid breakfast. A visit soon after made to the office of the steamship company was successful in getting back the passage-money, with apologies for the mishaps which had occurred. I could not quite make out whether the fault was with the young man who sold me the tickets, or with somebody on board ship who did not heed the wishes of his employers on shore, and I did not care to settle the question so long as I was not obliged to be imprisoned on that craft during the uncertain period of her voyage from Genoa to Naples.

I wonder if she has started yet? Perhaps she is still taking in cargo. I only know that, for weeks afterward, every time I saw a Naples newspaper, I looked among the marine arrivals for the name of that boat, and did not find it.

CHAPTER IV.

ROME—GOOD-FRIDAY AND EASTER.

I CAN imagine no drearier ride than that by rail from Pisa to Rome. The road skirts the sea most of the way. For many miles it traverses the Roman Campagna. The dreaded miasma which rises at night from this vast plain has left it tenantless, except by the station-masters and hands, and the herdsmen needed to watch over the droves of horses and oxen and flocks of sheep which browse on the abundant herbage. These herdsmen look wild and brigandish in their peaked hats and slashed jackets. Whether they take quinine freely, or are naturally proof against malaria, I know not. But it is a fact that most of them—as also of the railway servants—do not have the haggard and palsied look I had expected to note among them. Even they, however, have fears of the consequences of their exposure; for I noticed at every station, where there were several buildings, large young groves of the eucalyptus or blue-gum tree.

Its balsamic odor was perceptible from the car-windows. The Italian Government encourages the setting out of this tree as a preventive of malaria.

The success of the experiment is still a matter of dispute. In point of fact, the shepherds and others who live in miserable huts, hundreds of feet from the railway-track and have no such protection, seem as strong and hearty as those who dwell continually in the shade of the blue-gum tree.

We attended the special services at St. Peter's on Good-Friday. Driving through the streets we found the banks and shops of all kinds open as usual. The only indication of the solemnity of the day was the increased attendance at all the churches. And this may be, in part, explained by the extraordinary musical attractions. At St. Peter's many thousand persons must have been present between 4.30 and 6.30 P. M., when the *Tenebræ* and *Miserere* were chanted or sung by a great concourse of priests and a select choir. The music was impressive, but its proper effects were lost on all hearers who could not squeeze into the little side-chapel where it was performed. Every effort had been made to render St. Peter's gloomy, but without avail. The brilliant mosaics and frescoes were all shrouded. The eighty-nine lamps which burn about the crypt of St. Peter's tomb were extinguished. But glorious sunshine flooded the whole interior. It streamed in mighty beams through the colorless windows facing the west, and set at naught all puny attempts to make the most splendid church in the world look dark and dull. About six o'clock the throng was the greatest. For two hours people 'had been pouring in, but only a small part of the vast floor was occupied. Among the worshipers or spectators were friars of every known order, richly attired officers of every grade in the Italian army, common soldiers of all branches of the service, men and women representing every nation of Europe, and a great many Americans, besides countless numbers of the highest as well as the lowest classes of Roman society. The spectacle was one of deep interest, aside from the somber devotional exercises which had convoked this immense multitude.

On Easter-Sunday hundreds of shops were still open in the narrower and poorer streets of Rome. The day was perfect. The sun shone from a cloudless sky—just warm enough to be pleasant. We drove to St. Peter's at 9.30 A. M., and found everybody going in the same direction. But, although people had been streaming into the church for an hour before we arrived, the number on the floor was hardly noticeable. The magnificent pictures were again revealed in all the undimmed freshness of their original tints. The lights which circle St. Peter's tomb were once more burning. Red cloths had been hung over some of the marble pillars. The church was thus made as bright and beautiful as possible, but to me it seemed scarcely more so than on Good-Friday. On this joyous occasion the English cardinal, Howard—a thickset man, with a large head and a deep, sonorous voice—conducted the services. These took place almost directly beneath the dome, and were heard and witnessed by a great congregation. The singing by the choir was very fine—the boys' and men's voices mingling with exquisite effect. The chanting of the priests was less pleasing to the musical ear. While these exercises were progressing under the dome, priests were celebrating masses in many of the side-chapels, which were also partly filled with worshipers. At the boxes, which serve as confessionals, were fathers, who touched the kneeling faithful with long wands. As for the bronze image of St. Peter, there was a constant succession of persons, of all ages and stations in life, who kissed his foot in passing, carefully wiping the well-worn spot before applying their lips to the cold metal.

Interesting as was the occasion, it was tame

compared with the ceremonies observed by the Popes before the patrimony of Peter passed under the control of the King of Italy. In the old days the Holy Father read the mass in St. Peter's on Easter-Sunday, and was borne from the church in grand procession. At a later hour he appeared on the *loggia*, and gave his benediction "to the city and the world." After dark there was a wonderful illumination of the dome. All these striking rites and customs are now things of the past. Pope Leo XIII was nowhere publicly visible during the joyous festival of 1886. He was seen only by a few of the strangers in Rome—themselves devout Catholics—who had previously obtained cards of admission to the private chapel where the Pope himself officiated, and they took the sacrament from his hands.

The most popular man in Italy is the King. No statesman shares with him the confidence and affection of the people. One day I noticed a stir in and about the great doorway of the Hôtel de Londres, where I was stopping. Heads were bared on all sides. Everybody in sight was bowing profoundly. In front of the hotel stood a common open carriage with two horses, simply caparisoned, and a driver in dark livery. A tall, handsome officer of high rank, splendidly attired, sat on the left side of the vehicle. The rest of the seat was occupied by a stout, middle-aged man in citizen's clothes. His cheek-bones were high, his lower jaw was massive, his mustache iron-gray, and, as he kept up a constant motion of doffing and replacing his hat, I remarked a broad forehead crowned with hair thick and bristling. He looked just enough like the portraits of Humbert the First to convince me that he was the King of Italy. And so it proved. He had called at the Hôtel de Londres to visit the Prussian Princess Marie, who had a suite of rooms at the house. This lady is the widow of the "Red Prince" Frederick Charles. She happened to be out at the time, and so the King did not alight, but drove away in his modest turn-out, receiving from all persons on the Piazza di Spagna the most respectful salutation. Drivers of carriages on hire, and even beggars at the street corners, were greeted by him as courteously as the Roman nobles who dashed past him in equipages far more showy than his own. The day previous to this visit he had made a return-call on Prince Fushimy of Japan at the same hotel. Though politeness costs nothing, it goes far to make King Humbert a great favorite with crowned heads as well as with the Italian people. That policy of Italy, which has made friends of every nation in Europe, is dictated by the King, and represents his considerate politeness and native shrewdness. The courage which he showed at Naples during the last cholera epidemic was only one of numerous instances proving his devotion to the welfare of his constitutional subjects. His queen—the "Pearl of Savoy"—is not less successful in winning hearts. She is a fine-looking blonde, an accomplished whip, the patroness of unnumbered charities, and as courteous as her lord.

Visiting the Pantheon, I saw, just as I did three years before, many people standing in front of the tomb of the late Victor Emanuel. They were mostly Italians, by whom the memory of the man who made their country one is almost worshiped. Hundreds of wreaths of immortelles and other flowers are hung around and above the tomb. These come from all the secular universities, academies, and public institutions of Italy, and also from private hands. They are renewed from time to time, and look beautifully fresh. Long streamers of silk or satin attached to the floral offerings bear inscriptions eulogistic of *Il Rè Galantuomo*. In a large book which lies open, visitors voluntarily enter their names. Hundreds of thousands have thus been registered since the mortal remains of Victor Emanuel were here inshrined. There could be no grander mausoleum than the Pantheon.

It is the best preserved of all the great edifices of ancient Rome—identified with the mightiest power of the old world, and with the rise and progress of Christianity. No longer a pagan temple, but a Christian church, it is the proper resting-place of the unifier of Italy. Although the relations between the Quirinal and the Vatican have been much strained ever since the Pope lost his temporal sovereignty, it is not impossible that, some day, the Roman Catholic Church will be proud that she holds within her consecrated Pantheon the ashes of the king who was still her son. At the Pantheon, as at St. Peter's, I am always struck with the magnificent effect of the admission of pure sunlight, free from the intervention of stained glass. The sole illumination of the Pantheon, you know, comes from a great circular hole in the dome. It admits the rain, which leaves a round wet place on the stone floor beneath. But there is still ample room for the free movement of the crowds that come and go, without dampening their feet. Majestic as is the dome that rises in its perfect curve to a height of 140 feet above the floor, it impresses the beholder even less than the sight of the distant blue concave which he sees through that immense opening. As for the details of the interior, they appear in the flood of daylight in all their richness and variety of color. It by no means follows that a "religious light" should be "dim." St. Peter's and the Pantheon triumphantly refute that too prevalent notion.

None of my guide-books—even the most recent in date—give any description of some remarkable and interesting statues and pedestals which have been brought to light within a year. The images are life-sized sculptures of what might be called "lady superiors" of the Vestal Virgins. No one of whom I inquired could tell me where they were; but I found them for myself in an open excavated space not far from the Forum Romanum. Two or three of the statues are almost perfect. They are marble, exquisitely chiseled, and are doubtless good resemblances of the distinguished originals. Though vestal virgins, they have a matronly look. They were evidently women of intellectual ability, as also of high social rank. They seem born to command. Their main attire was the full, graceful robe universally worn in their day. Five or six thick fillets bound about their foreheads, covering also part of their hair, reminded me of a badge almost similar, worn by nuns of various orders in the Roman Catholic Church. But, though their dress was all simplicity and modesty, their bearing was anything but humble. The whole expression of face and form was one of intense self-satisfaction and pride. The pedestals to which these statues once belonged have been mostly recovered in fine condition. They bear warm tributes to the many virtues of the illustrious ladies whom they commemorate. And yet history tells us that the vestal virgins had seats of honor near the Cæsars in the Colosseum, and without pity saw Christians devoured in the arena by wild beasts, and that no spectators were more heartless than they when the fallen gladiators looked up to their boxes for the signal of mercy which should have saved them from the victor's sword!

At least once a year that dreadful old ruin—the Colosseum—is the scene of a ghastly and weird illumination. The exhibition came off on the night of the 24th of April, between ten o'clock and midnight. The interior of the stupendous structure was packed with human beings who waited for a long time with much impatience for the show to begin. Suddenly brilliant lights—many electric and others calcium—flashed out from the lofty tiers of the amphitheatre, while a belt of fire girded the top wall. The effect was startling. Every stone and brick in the huge pile was instantaneously revealed, photographing itself in imperishable lines on the brain of the beholder. The feeling excited was akin to terror. The faces of all those men and women looked pale, as they were upturned to the heights where thousands of brutal Romans had so often sat and feasted on scenes of torture and butchery. To behold the Colosseum by moonlight is something never to be forgotten, as the partial shadows lend themselves to the conjuration of specters from the dark passage-ways which one sees all around him. But the illumination of which I write is still more impressive, when red and green lights are alternately used. These are somehow infernal in their suggestiveness. When to their peculiar effects you add the hoarse cries of great companies of rooks aroused from their repose in the crevices of the topmost tiers—and circling wildly through the air overhead—you have something very much like a pandemonium, which is repeated in a nightmare when you return home to sleep.

CHAPTER V.

CUTTING A KING—MARGHERITA, QUEEN OF HEARTS.

ONE does not often have the chance of being uncivil to a king. But it was my misfortune on one occasion to be, or to seem, downright rude to Humbert the First.

We were taking a carriage-ride in the Villa Borghese. The sun glared intensely. The broad drives in the grounds had not been sprinkled, and the dust rose in clouds under the few wheels that stirred it up. My eyes were sheltered with blue glasses, and a light umbrella held against the sun cut into the view very seriously. The coachman, after the manner of his race, had been pointing out objects of interest with which we were already perfectly familiar, clothing his superfluous information in a Tuscan *patois*. We paid no attention to the numerous remarks delivered at us over his left shoulder, as our exhaustive study of the Villa Borghese on previous visits had qualified us as first-class guides to the place. Therefore, when he said something that sounded like "Eel R-ray" (*Il Rè*), I did not associate the words with the instant approach of the King of Italy.

A moment later a two-horse carriage dashed past us. The horses were black and beautiful, throwing out their fore-legs with a free and splendid action. A gentleman (whom I should not have failed to recognize, but for my blue glasses and the whirl of dust) sat bolt upright on the front seat, guiding his spirited team with a firm hand. The seat behind was occupied by a servant in quiet livery. The equipage came and went like a flash; but, quick as it was, the accomplished driver had time to take off his hat at us, moving it through an arc of about two feet, and replace it. Before I could answer this remarkably courteous salute from an entire stranger, he was off. Meantime coachee had, in his humble way, atoned for my short-coming. He had lifted his hat and bowed profoundly. When all was over, he turned clear round and said again (this time almost reproachfully), "Eel R-ray, signor." Then I knew that I had cut a king, and that our driver, who had observed my discourtesy with a side eye, was, in effect, chiding me for it.

The good fellow saw that I was flustered by this unpleasant incident; for I really burned with shame to think that I should be guilty of rudeness to the politest of kings in his own capital. So he hastened to explain to me, as nearly as I could make out from his provincial Italian, that the King would be sure to pass us again in a few minutes. For you see the Villa Borghese is not very large, and carriages keep circling about and returning on their tracks. Well, this time I determined to be ahead of the King, and doff my hat first, through as ample a curve as my arm would allow. I shut up the umbrella and pocketed the blue glasses, that nothing might impede the grace of the atoning action. Sure enough, just as we turned the end of a long oval, there was the King bearing down on us again.

Looking at him over my box-seat, I identified him easily by the front view. In all Italy there is no second pair of mustaches like his; they curl like rams' horns, and are almost as thick. His horses were trotting a two-and-a-half-minute gait, and his piercing black eyes sparkled with pleasure as he watched them. A second more, and he was on our port-bow, as sailors would say. Then was my time. Having the brim of my Derby well in hand, I made a tremendous flourish with it at His Majesty. If gestures convey ideas, then he must have seen that I meant to pay the utmost respect to him as the democratic King of Italy. The monarch instinctively raised his hand to his hat as if to take it off; then, catching a clear sight of my face, he evidently remembered me as the ill-bred person whom he had met in his rounds five minutes before. His eyes were instantly averted. He did not remove his hat. This time the King of Italy had cut me, and had served me just right.

The most affable of coachmen then managed to explain that we should probably intersect the orbit of the King for the third time, if we kept on driving around the grounds. For my own part I had had about enough of it. The King and I were even. So, to avoid the embarrassment of a third meeting, I ordered the man to leave the Villa and go over to the Pincian Hill. He turned the horses for the purpose, but had not proceeded far before the well-known stiff figure and the flaring mustaches intercepted our retreat by dashing down a side-road out of a little piece of woods. I would have given something to avoid the encounter. But there was no escaping it. As the King drew into the main road, the salute I felt bound to make was an awkward one, and I was conscious of a slight tingling in the tips of my ears. His Majesty must have noticed my confusion, for there was an amused look in his eyes, and his mustaches were not thick enough to mask the slight upward curves at the corners of his mouth. And then, in the offhand way which has made him so genuinely popular, he doffed his hat and returned my bow with accrued interest. So happily ended my first exchange of civilities with a king.

A short ride transferred us from the Villa Borghese to the Pincian Hill. We reached the crest in time to hear the four-o'clock concert, performed before an attentive audience of a hundred persons in carriages and a thousand on foot. The selections were all from Italian composers, and probably known by heart by most of the people present, who stood or sat like statues as if entranced by the music. The band, which belongs to the finest regiment of the Roman garrison, played divinely. But all the charm of their performance could not keep my eyes and thoughts from the Eternal City basking in the warm sunshine below—a wide expanse of churches, palaces and ruins. Almost every church is crowned with a dome, and each of these huge bulbs, whose slates reflect the sun with a dull glow, looks like a feeble imitation of Michael Angelo's great work. But not one of them detracts from the grandeur of St. Peter's, which, from whatever point of view it is seen, dwarfs all the rest into insignificance. St. Angelo Castle—in shape a snuff-box—the uplifted swell of the Pantheon, the Capitol, the Quirinal Palace, are easily identified through the haze which envelopes all. The blue Campagna is dimly seen in the distance. Through the foreground the yellow Tiber makes its serpentine curves, flashing like gold under the westering sun.

The next day we had the good fortune to meet the Queen while driving in the Villa Doria Pamphilj. That time royalty had no cause to complain. The most loyal of her subjects could not have outdone my obeisance, though it was rendered more to the beautiful woman than to the Queen. She did not descend upon us unawares, like the King the day before. We knew of her coming afar off, for she advertised her approach by the scarlet magnificence of her box-cloth and the blazing uniforms of her coachman and foot-guards. I saw this brilliant turn-out a quarter of a mile away, and, having kings on my mind just then, supposed that His Majesty was taking the air in state. I was relieved and pleased when our driver, pointing his whip at the flaming red spots in the distance, said, "*La Regina!*" Just at that point in the road stood a line of carriages drawn up in waiting to see the Queen pass. Some of them had been standing there a long time in expectation of the event, for it had become known that she would make the circuit of the Villa Doria Pamphilj that afternoon; and the best place of all to see her was that wide opening in the road, where our victoria had joined the many other carriages. The Queen passed us all at the slowest of paces. Each person in the long line received an individual nod from her, given with exceeding dignity and grace. She is every inch a queen; and that is saying a great deal, for she is of the Junonian order, and her uncommon height is made symmetrical by a generous breadth of shoulders and a satisfying plenitude of bust. Her arms, as guessed at by the outlines of her tight sleeves, are strong and shapely. Her eyes are a deep blue, her hair is a light chestnut, her complexion her own pink and white. People who think of Italians only as swarthy in face, with hair and eyes of jet, do not know of what delicate beauty the race is capable when it strays into the blonde type. Queen Margherita is at the head of the fair branch of the great Italian family. She is the "Pearl of Savoy." She was dressed with the severest simplicity. There was not a jewel visible, and one did not remember the colors she wore. Her own flower, the daisy, is not less ostentatious. But her native loveliness needs no ornamental setting. She reigns over men's hearts by her birthright of beauty; and I can think of no better phrase to couple with this than the homely one that she is "just as good as she looks."

CHAPTER VI.

NAPLES—SORRENTO—CAPRI—PÆSTUM.

My sanitary inspection of Naples was hasty, and did not prepare me to give the city a clean bill of health. The streets through which I passed were less dirty than those of New York. Except for certain foul smells on the water-fronts, there was nothing in Naples to alarm the stranger, ever sensitive on the subject of fever and cholera. The light-hearted Neapolitans laugh at the fears of Englishmen and Americans. They are now claiming great things for their city on the strength of their new and copious water-supply. Visitors, however, refuse to believe in its excellence as a beverage, and persist in drinking Apollinaris, Victoria, St. Galmier, Source Badoit, and some other natural or doctored water. It is not for the interest of hotel-keepers to decry those bottled waters, from the sale of which they make large profits. But the landlord of the "Nobile" assured me that none of them can possibly be purer and healthier than the fluid which sparkles untouched in the *caraffes* on his tables. The water is freely used for sprinkling the streets and sluicing the gutters. The fountains of New York are dried up and mute; but those of Naples play at certain hours of the day, if not from morning to night. They remind us of the abundant jets and cascades which we had, with so much regret, left behind us at Rome. Though the weather in early May is extremely pleasant, and the heat just right for out-of-door exercise, the sun glares at times with Italian fierceness. Then it is refreshing to see the fountains glittering aloft, and to hear the musical splash of their waters in deep marble basins.

The radical improvements which are expected to render Naples one of the healthiest cities of Europe have yet to be made. But they are all planned, and the work has begun on some of them. They include a complete system of sewerage and the construction of long, wide streets through those populous quarters where the sun and fresh air never come now. It was in this swarming, dark, and unventilated district that the cholera did its worst. Toward these great works the Italian Government has contributed ten million dollars, and the city (and province) of Naples eight million more. It is by showing such interest in the fortunes of all her component parts, especially the large cities, that unified Italy deepens her hold upon the affections of her people all over the peninsula.

Snow on Vesuvius in May! The weather at Sorrento flies in the face of all the authorities. We have been warned a hundred times not to visit Southern Italy during the "hot month" of May. At the Hôtel Tramontano we burned little sticks of wood at the rate of a quarter of a cord a day in the vain effort to keep our sitting-room comfortable. Our English friends have misled us in the kindest manner possible. They call the weather warm at 60° Fahr., and hot at 70°. Americans, accustomed to broiling summers at home, find this climate barely genial at the very time when Englishmen are roasted out of it. Therefore, I say, put no faith in their statements where temperature is concerned. Men who never wear overcoats, and who walk twenty miles before breakfast, are no guides for people less hardened. With the exception of one day (strangely enough) in London, and another in Naples, we have not stopped at a hotel where a fire at night was not a necessity as well as an expensive luxury. Of course, the thickness of the walls is responsible for some of the coldness. At Naples I looked down from the balcony of my hotel and watched some masons at work just across the narrow street. They were laying outside walls three feet thick, and walls of two feet between the rooms. The rising structure seemed to be a jail or a bank. I inquired, and found it was designed for an elegant private residence. Yet, for the exclusion of heat, it might as well be a prison, and would look like one, if the walls were not papered and frescoed.

Vesuvius is an ever-fascinating subject of study. I observe it fifty times a day with undiminished interest. The changed position of the sun and every passing cloud, and especially the shifting directions and forms of the "smoke," make a new picture of the mountain every time. The natives for twenty miles around look upon Vesuvius at once as a barometer and a weather-vane. When the vapor—for such it is for the most part—drifts, they know from what quarter the wind is blowing. The capricious shapes it suddenly assumes at times foretell them of coming storms or calms. I am not yet deep in this lore. But, all the same, it is a pleasure to note the protean changes of the escaping steam. Sometimes it goes straight up to the sky in a long, slender shaft, and at the extreme height opens out like a palm-tree. Then, again, it looks like a mushroom, with a thick stem and a "chunky" top. Often it streams out horizontally at great length, like the smoke of a steamer at sea. When the wind is out of the north or east, accompanied by a slight rain, then I notice that the vapor rolls down the mountain like its own lava. At other times Vesuvius makes a huge white cap or turban for itself—the vapor settling down on the peak and remaining stationary. Frequently this enlarges into a shroud and gradually covers the volcano from head to foot. At night, when the sky is clear, there is only one thing to be seen on Vesuvius—that is the dull-red light which crowns its dark outlines. While under my observation it was in a state of unusual activity. It "worked," as the phrase is.

One morning "Old Vesuve" (for so one finds himself calling the volcano after a short acquaintance) indicated a change of wind from the northeast to the southwest. This favored an expedition to the famous Blue Grotto of Capri, which can not be entered when the wind is driving the water against and into the narrow opening through which the little boats must pass. I made the trip from Sorrento to Capri by steamer, and was then transferred to a frail-looking but stanch canoe, most skillfully handled. The waves were pretty high— the effect of a storm which had lasted two days. As we neared the portal of the grotto, it seemed impossible to shoot through it, for it is not more than three feet high and three wide, and the water was constantly rushing in and out of it with a deafening roar and showers of spray. At times more than half of the opening was filled with the current, which threatened to dash the fragile bark into splinters and drown the passengers. The boatman himself hesitated. The conditions were much worse than those he usually overcame with ease. But he watched his chances, and, seizing a moment when the current was setting outward, he caught hold of a jutting point of rock, and, by a sudden jerk, swung us in. I had been lying flat in the boat, drenched with spray. Responding to his call, I sat up and looked around.

My first feeling was of disappointment. The grotto is not blue. The wonderful color, of which one hears so much, is in the water. The vault rises to a graceful arch in the center and covers a space —irregular in shape—equal, perhaps, to 125 feet square. Its point of greatest height is thirty or forty feet above the water. The stone is of a dirty white, and the faint reflection of light from its concave surface doubtless has something to do with the production of the phenomenon which gives the grotto its name. The water of the Mediterranean is beautiful under all conditions. One need not penetrate grottoes in order to admire its tints, ever varying on a background of blue. But here the relations of the water to the light of day are unique. I tried to study the thing in cold blood, and these are my conclusions about it: Some of the diffused daylight enters the cave through the only opening above the water-line. This light irradiates the water to a certain depth, and causes the white roof to be reflected in it. A great deal of light also enters beneath the surface of the water, through the opening which descends to the floor of the grotto. This floor also seems to be white (as observed by me) at its depth of (say) fifty feet. It therefore sends back the reflection which the water has already received from the limestone roof. This double effect gives a brilliant silver tone to the inclosed mass of blue water. One hunts in vain for some comparison to convey a clear idea of the unearthly beauty of the spectacle. Sky-blue satin with the sun shining on it would resemble the surface of the water as I saw it. But that simile fails to describe the extraordinary effects of the Blue Grotto. These are mainly derived from the depths, and are best compared to the sheen of silver and blue which are noticed in the heart of a sapphire held up against the sunlight.

I was rudely aroused from these cogitations by a boat bumping against mine. A man in it apologized, and thrust a card into my hand. Inspecting it by the faint light, I saw that it was the *menu* of a *déjeûner* which would be held hot in waiting for all comers on the arrival of the steamer at the *Marina Grande*, or chief landing-place of the island, farther on. Feeling hungry, I ordered my boatman to return to the ship. The exit was easily made. As soon as all the visitors to the grotto were safely on board, we proceeded to our other destination. The business energy of the man who chose so strange a place to advertise his *table d'hôte* breakfast was not without reward. I patronized his hotel. His quail was nice, as it ought to have been, for the island is celebrated for the abundance and succulence of that bird. But that which he served as the wine of Capri would in New York be called water with a dash of vinegar. There are some ruins of a villa of Tiberius, which may be seen, per donkey, at the top of a high hill. But one ruin more or less is nothing in this land of wrecked greatness. So I contented myself with my Blue Grotto, and, when the steamer whistled for her truant passengers, bade a good-by to Capri.

It is interesting to watch the fishermen at work just underneath my windows. The Hôtel Tramontano stands 150 feet above the sea, on a rock that is lapped by its waves. The nets have been set the night before, and at daybreak the racket begins. Men in boats go out to regulate matters and take the fish from the meshes. There is a crowd of people on shore hauling at the ropes and slowly dragging the nets and their prey out of the depths. They are mostly women, with bare legs and arms, as strong-looking as the men. They pull in unison, slowly and carefully. Presently they cease, in compliance with orders screamed to them from the captains of the boats. Then, from my height, I see one net raised to the surface with extreme caution. The harvest is about to be gathered in. The men out there tug at the seine as if it were heavy. They soon have it well in hand. Their joyous shouts tell the anxious women on shore that the catch is a good one. They lift the net now with the greatest possible care, and I begin to see its silvery contents. The fish, which almost cover its exposed surface, shine like new standard dollars. The men shake and strip them off, and they fall a glittering heap into the bottom of the boat. I should say there were bushels of them, and rejoice that the brave fishermen and their wives will have something to eat and much to spare for the market. In size and taste these smelts are exactly like those we eat in America. I shall relish them a little more at the table to-night after having "assisted," as a Frenchman would say, in the operation of catching them.

I wonder how much of the sub-Treasury building in Wall Street will still be standing in the year 4372? This question occurred to me very forcibly as I gazed on the majestic ruins of the Greek temples at Pæstum. These are supposed to date back to about 600 B. C. They are all in the same general state of decay as the Parthenon at Athens, which they much resemble. The largest and best preserved is the Temple of Neptune, which vividly recalls, by its dimensions and form, the Wall Street temple of quite another kind. The original thirty-six Doric columns, each about eight feet in diameter, are yet proudly erect, and, at a little distance, seem in perfect condition. Only when one comes near to them does he discover how the tooth of Time has gnawed into and marred their exquisite shape. The outline of the eastern front is yet so complete that it could be "restored" by the addition of a few great stones. Long rows of other fluted columns, not far off, are the remains of a structure to which the name Basilica is given for want of a better. A third ruin still farther away is called the Temple of Ceres, or of Vesta, just as one pleases. Thus uncertain is the most accurate knowledge we now possess about Poseidonia, which the Greeks dedicated to Neptune, on a lovely site near the Mediterranean, twenty-five centuries ago. It must have been a large and important settlement in their day. But, in the present year of grace, not a single stone or trace of any edifice (of the old Greek town) can be found, except of the three I have named, the massive construction of which has alone saved any part of them to astonish and delight the modern world with their noble and beautiful proportions. Bits of Roman antiquities lie around, but these are so very new in comparison with the glorious Greek fragments that one regards them without interest. Formerly a trip to Pæstum was attended with danger from brigands. Now your sole risk is malaria of the worst type. I am happy to inform any Americans who may desire to see the treasures of Pæstum that they may now be spared a long and fatiguing ride through a flat and monotonous country. A railway has been completed from Battipaglia to Pæstum, linking it directly and easily with Naples, Salerno, and La Cava. We made our journey from the latter point, starting about 10 A. M., spending two hours among the ruins, and getting back a little after six—a great improvement on any possible way of "doing" Pæstum before the rails were laid. But quinine is still as indispensable to the cautious visitor now as a pistol was thirty years ago.

CHAPTER VII.

FRESH DIGGINGS AT POMPEII—VESUVIUS "WORKING"—THE TELL-TALE SEISMOGRAPH—SOLFATARA.

It seems odd to speak of a dead city as a growing one. But that is exactly the case with Pompeii. There are many cities in Italy that do not grow half as fast as the one buried by the ashes of Vesuvius eighteen hundred years ago. A person visiting it at intervals of a year notices a marked enlargement of its boundaries. The Italians are the champion diggers. They make the shovel fly when they attack the grave of Pompeii. We saw a gang of them at work there. A government overseer watched them like a hawk. He wanted to be sure that they pocketed no jewelry, coins, or objects of art or utility yielded by the excavations. The only produce of their toil in that line, as we stood by, was a bit of iron, which the guide called a hinge, and the fragment of a small marble column. The spades, busily plied, were gradually bringing to light a beautiful house. The floors were mosaic, with simple but graceful designs in scroll-pattern—nearly as fresh of color as if laid yesterday. The walls bore frescoes of fainter tints—grinning masks, fauns, Cupids, birds, fish, and fruit. It had evidently been the home of a well-to-do citizen of Pompeii. The nervous movements of the workmen betrayed their anxiety. They were hoping at every moment to make a valuable "find." Perhaps they might hit upon a great iron chest—studded with round knobs like a boiler—and full of gold, money, or ornaments; or they might strike another wonder in marble or bronze; or they might be startled by coming suddenly upon a skull or other human remains. In the latter event the work is suspended till a careful inspection is made. The responsible and intelligent person in charge proceeds to ascertain if the dead Pompeiian has left a mold of himself or herself in the plastic ashes. If so, he prepares a mixture of plaster-of-Paris, breaks a hole in the crust and slowly pours in the liquid till the mold is full. When it has hardened, the casting is tenderly removed. Lo! there is a rough image, showing some poor creature in the agonies of death, prone on the floor, face downward.

Thus, most usually, were the inhabitants of the doomed city caught by the destroying angel. The skull, or leg, or arm, or whatever other part of the skeleton has not relapsed into its original dust, may attach itself to the plaster cast in the proper place, or may require to be joined on by a pardonable "restoration." In either case the effect is thrilling in its horrible reality. Nothing in painting or sculpture can shock the beholder more than these self-produced and truthful statues exhibited in the museum, which is the first and most interesting thing shown to visitors. But, though neither gold nor silver, nor the minutest scrap of a skeleton, nor anything else of importance was unearthed for my benefit, I quitted the new excavations with reluctance to examine those parts of Pompeii with which the world is already familiar through the medium of books and pictures. I found myself quite at home in the bakery, the wine-shop, at the oil-merchant's, at the houses of Pansa, of Sallust, of the "tragic poet," and the rest. The high stepping-stones across the streets looked familiar, as if I had trodden them before. The deep ruts cut by the carts as they groaned up the hill, coming from ancient Stabia, were like friendly landmarks. So fully have literature and art made us acquainted with this disinterred city.

The guide tells me that only about one third of Pompeii has yet been uncovered. I take his word for it. He is also of the opinion that the best parts of the city have already been dug out. He evidently wishes that the work would stop. He is very human in this, for he finds it tiresome to show people about the present Pompeii. Treble its size, and his labor would be threefold. And he is forbidden to accept money. But I imagine that this very stern prohibition does not prevent some persons from offering him quantities, quite privately, or him from accepting them. It may be true, as our guide insists, that the temples, forums, baths, theatres, and fine houses now above-ground surpass anything of the kind that may hereafter be discovered at Pompeii. But the Italian Government is not disposed to take that for granted. Liberal sums are yearly appropriated to push on the work. It bears fruits. A new temple or amphitheatre may not be struck every year, but something is constantly being turned up to instruct the world in the manners and customs of the old Romans, so well reflected in the representative city of Pompeii. Of bronze or stone statues, household implements, and tools of trades, the yield is immense and steady. These may be counted by the thousand in the splendid museum at Naples. One can see so many articles of luxury and use exactly similar to those he buys nowadays, that he is fain to pause and try to remember what besides the steam-engine, the photograph, and the electric telegraph, we moderns have invented. There being no more room at Naples to store these treasures, the excess of them is huddled together in the courtyards and houses of Pompeii herself. It is estimated that, at the present rate, this mine of antiquities will not be worked out in fifty years.

Vesuvius is the most deceptive of mountains. We know how treacherous and cruel he is. But as we see him gently smoking, in the haze of this soft, enervating atmosphere, we think him very much maligned. The chimney of a well-regulated house could not be steadier of behavior. His sides look sleek in the distance. One would never suspect that all that brown softness is lava, fifty feet deep, and covering thousands of acres. When I ascended the volcano, I realized how illusory are impressions when formed afar off. After traversing Portici and Resina (old Herculaneum), the carriage climbed a steep slope between country villas with "plenty of fruit and shade," as the advertisement of a country-house to let would say. Presently a sharp turn in the road brought me face to face with the head of a lava-stream which had been mercifully stayed at that point years ago. The road had been cut through it, showing its depth, and that was enough to have buried in its path any of the villas I had seen below. From this point on to the station of the Funicular Railway the road for the most part passes between gray-black walls of lava, the tops of which are curled like waves or twisted into capricious spiral forms, and then forever stilled. Not a flower or blade of grass grows there, except in crevices where dust may have fallen and the wind has scattered seeds.

The desolation, mile after mile, is oppressive to behold. One seeks relief by looking back over the blue Mediterranean and the reddish-white cities of the plain. Or else he looks ahead and up to Vesuvius, whose terrible majesty now begins to appear. I now see that where the sea of lava ends the ashes begin. The vapor, which seemed to curl so peacefully and thinly, from the standpoint of Naples, is mounting to the sky in a great volume, and whirling as if in a cyclone. One imagines a roar as that hot steam rushes from the crater. He sees specks tossed into the air. These are stones flung aloft two hundred to three hundred feet, and dropped back into the yawning pit to be presently ejected again. He has been told that Vesuvius is a little more active than usual. He can now readily understand of what frightful deeds the volcano is capable when in the maddest humor. Not only all the little cities near his base, which have been rebuilt in the childlike faith that they will never again be destroyed, but proud Naples, which has so far been spared, are at his mercy.

After I had ascended by railway to a nearer

view of the monster, and completed my acquaintance with him as far as it was safe, familiarity did not lessen my respect for his power. It seemed impudently inquisitive for a party of tiny mortals to be throwing stones into his enormous mouth, poking canes into his ribs and stirring up the red fire there, and laughing as the dense, sulphurous fumes rose in our faces. The guides roasted eggs for us, and we ate them with a pinch of salt, chucking the shells into the crater, which answered back with a shower of red-hot stones. These luckily missed their mark. I incline to think that some of the fun made by our company of visitors was like whistling to keep up one's courage; for I noticed that the noisiest of them clung hard to the guides and gave a wide berth to the crater's edge, and looked most pleased when the signal was given to return. Just as we started on the downward path, Vesuvius made a noise between a sob and a shriek, and belched forth a farewell volley of stones, which might have spoiled some hats, and even heads, if they had been shot accurately.

For the information of those who have never ascended Vesuvius but hope to do so some day, I add that the trip by carriage from Naples is three and one-half hours long to the foot of the Funicular Railway. Thence to the upper station is a ride of twelve minutes, by a line much resembling that of Mount Washington or the Righi, in ease and safety. From there to the top of the crater is a steep climb of fifteen or twenty-five minutes, according to the age and wind of the climber. Persons with weak lungs or shaky legs, or in any respect infirm, should not attempt the latter feat. For them is provided the *chaise-porte*. Two strong young fellows carry this like a bier—their customer sitting composedly (unless he or she is badly scared) in the chair which is swung in the middle of two long poles. The bearers are like goats in sure-footedness, strength, and agility. It is wonderful to see them pick their way among the huge, jagged pieces of smoking lava and up the steep slope of hot ashes, ankle-deep, without slipping. In an hour one may do reasonable justice to the cone and crater, and in two hours and a half more be back in Naples.

On my way down the mountain I profited by a little spare time to do what most tourists omit: I visited the observatory. This building is securely placed on a spur of Vesuvius where the lava-wave parts in its destructive course. Here dwell day and night, all the year round, an accomplished scientist and an able staff, whose duty it is to note all the phenomena of eruptions and earthquakes. In reality most of the work is done for them by instruments of almost inconceivable delicacy and precision, and they have only to keep these in perfect order. This exquisite automatic apparatus reports everything the world wants to know about earthquakes except their cause. They give the direction of the movement, its speed and intensity and duration. Though the man who climbs to the crater does not observe the faintest throb beneath his feet when the volcano is most active, there is a little tell-tale machine down in the observatory which vibrates passionately at that precise moment. It is not at rest five minutes together during the whole day. If the motion of the trembling is horizontal, then a hollow brass ball swings toward the north, south, east, and west, as the case may be. This indicates unerringly the direction of the earthquake-wave. If the motion is vertical, then a spiral coil of fine wire visibly shortens and springs back again. Every discharge of stones from the crater above causes an extraordinary agitation of the wire. You see the shower and the sympathetic action of this sensitive coil at the same instant. The director invites you to dance a jig on the floor, within a foot of the wire, to show that its movements correspond only to actual tremblings of old Mother Earth. You do so, jumping as high as you can. But the apparatus makes no sign. The heavy rumbling of a wagon in the road outside does not disturb it.

The "seismograph," as it is called, does only the work for which it was designed. The director, however, was good enough to switch off its connection from the bowels of the earth to my pulse. No doctor with hand on wrist could have counted the beats more accurately. They were more regular than those of Vesuvius, if not quite as fierce. Out of the millions of observations taken here in the course of years, it is hoped that some time an exact science of earthquakes may be constructed, with possible usefulness to mankind. For three or four days before the appalling calamity in Ischia (just off this coast) in 1883, all the apparatus of the observatory was greatly excited. Something frightful was brewing. That was evident to the watchers up there. The world knows the result. If it could have been foretold in time to save hundreds of lives on that unhappy island, that would indeed have been a triumph of science.

At the center of the old volcanic district west of Naples is the great crater of Solfatara, not yet quite extinct. Eight centuries ago it was active and destructive; now it is full of stunted bushes and tall grass. The sulphurous vapor rising from a hole about three feet in diameter, on one side of the vast bowl, shows that a fire still burns in its bosom. One can not see the red-hot lava in the crevices, as on Vesuvius. But if the hand is held in the ascending steam for a moment, a scalding heat is felt. The guide who conducted me about the crater actually crawled into this hole at a point where it could be entered horizontally. To escape suffocation he covered his mouth with his hand and kept close to the ground. After about a minute of anxiety on my part, he returned with fine specimens of sulphuric deposits exactly like those I had seen fringing some of the chinks in the burning flank of Vesuvius. The offensive smell and acrid taste of the vapor which poured forth incessantly from this subterranean passage were the same that make an ascent of the Vesuvian cone so trying to many persons. The guide assured me that the connection between Solfatara and the great volcano on the Bay of Naples was intimate and instant. Whenever Vesuvius is inactive, Solfatara " works " quite fiercely. Whenever Vesuvius is very active, Solfatara is disappointing. It would seem from this statement that, though the mountains are miles apart, they both communicate with a common reservoir of molten matter.

There is no certainty that Solfatara will not break out again. There have been periods of centuries between the eruptions of Vesuvius; and it is a recorded fact that at times its crater has been lined inside with foliage, so reduced was its capacity for mischief. As there is no present prospect that tourists can descend in safety to the floor of its crater and study minutely the phenomena which can not be fairly seen from the rim, they should not fail to visit Solfatara. They will not burn the soles of their boots, and yet they can, if they please, roast eggs by digging down about a foot in places indicated by the guide. They can realize the thinness of the crust over which they walk by raising a large stone and throwing it down violently. The ground gives back a hollow sound. It is true that Solfatara does not eject red-hot stones, even the smallest. But that is a point in its favor, enabling the visitor to look on with a sense of perfect safety. There is but one Vesuvius. No other volcano is as accessible, or offers as many advantages for all kinds of observations. But if one is at Naples, and does not care to incur the fatigue or other discomforts of an ascent of Vesuvius, Solfatara is a good substitute excursion and is hereby recommended; and, as something supplementary to the greater event, it is also of much interest.

CHAPTER VIII.

ITALIAN BEGGARS — A NEGLECTED GRAVE — THE BLUE-GUM TREE AND MALARIA — PERUGIA — ETRUSCAN TOMBS.

If, by a stroke of this pen, I could banish every beggar from Italy, I should hesitate to do so. They may deserve the punishment. But they are amusing rascals. Life here would be duller without them. The other day when a span of tired horses were dragging me up Vesuvius, three men sprang out of the ground in front of the carriage. I do not know how else to explain their sudden appearance. They were beggars of the musical variety. One carried a fiddle, the second a mandolin, the third a guitar. Bowing to me, they formed a line on my right and marched up the mountain, Indian file, playing as they went. I was just then trying to realize in imagination the terrible splendor of the eruption that had caused the flow of lava fifty feet deep, through which the carriage-road was cut. These three fellows with their lively Neapolitan airs disturbed me greatly. But the absurdity of the situation soon overcame my resentment. I laughed heartily and permitted them to escort me about a mile before dismissing them with a few soldi. We parted friends, and they proceeded to levy tribute on the carriage behind me. It takes philosophy to extract amusement out of these seeming pests. But happy is the man who can do it, for Southern Italy swarms with them.

At Baiæ where we were taking a bad lunch at a wretched little inn, four women entered the room, and, without asking our leave, began to dance the tarantella. They were probably the wife of the landlord and three servants. Their dancing was a fitting accompaniment to the lunch they had provided for us. One of the women strummed a tambourine as big as an old-fashioned kitchen sieve. This supplied the only music, except that the other three kept time with castanets. They made a horrible din, and, being ill-favored and shabbily dressed, were anything but pleasant companions, as they flirted their skirts almost in our faces. But after a few minutes we found them with all their faults more interesting than the lunch, and made them a present altogether too large for their deserts. This was a serious mistake, for they all rushed off and speedily returned, with bouquets, coral jewelry, and antiquities that must have been at least forty-eight hours old. All these they wanted us to buy at exorbitant prices. Our refusal to do so angered the whole party. This, of course, put an end to the fun. So I settled the tavern score hastily and we returned to Naples. But the incident, unsatisfactorily as it terminated, remains to-day the pleasantest memory of a visit to ruins that were not worth seeing.

On my visit to the Blue Grotto at Capri, it required the utmost obstinancy to refuse the demand of my boatman for a two-franc piece. He wanted me to throw it into the water, and see him dive and bring it up from the bottom. If I had accepted his offer, he would have whisked off his coat and shirt (if he had one), and gone down fifty feet for the piece, and recovered it for himself without fail. But I was anxious to get back to the steamer which was waiting for us, and resolutely declined to be amused at that price. At Sorrento, the hotel guests standing out on the balconies overlooking the sea were constantly importuned for "pennies" by boys in the boats below. When the money was thrown down, the little fellows would watch its course through the air, and, the moment it struck the water, they would dive into the pellucid depths and in a flash reappear with it, holding it aloft between thumb and finger. These are but a few out of the hundred methods in which money is extracted from you, under the pretense of some service rendered or amusement supplied. And still I say that it pays to humor all these people to a moderate extent. And, furthermore, I would not refuse a very modest coin to the ragged but picturesque creature who stands at every church-door and lies in wait for me at every bit of rising ground. He does not pretend to give any equivalent for the money received. He is a beggar pure and simple. He has been begging for thirty, forty, or fifty years. In all that time he imagines that he has acquired "rights," and I confess I almost feel ashamed of myself when I drop my insignificant alms into his dirty hand.

"Shelley?" asked the man in charge of the Protestant Cemetery at Rome, when we appeared at the gate, one beautiful afternoon in May. It is the only English word except "Keats" that he can pronounce correctly. Three years before the same man put the same question to us. We again answered "Yes." For, with many others of the English-speaking race, we took a sad pleasure in visiting the graves of those two most gifted and unhappy beings. Shelley's heart alone rests in the cypress-shaded inclosure, which is now full of graves. The rest of his body, we remember, was reduced to ashes on a funeral-pyre, in the presence of Byron and some others, at that spot on the shore of Spezzia Bay where the drowned poet had been cast up by the waves. As this is an age of monuments to neglected genius, I was curious to see if anything had been done for Shelley by his ardent admirers since 1883. No! there is the old small stone flat on the earth, looking moldier than ever. The inscription "*Cor Cordium*" is filled in with dirt. A weed, looking like burdock, grows rankly about the grave. There is not a flower near it, unless one should count in a withered and blackened rose which some pitying soul had thrown down on the center of the dingy marble slab. This may have been lying there for two or three months. I dare say fragments of it will be found there a year hence, unless the wind blows them away. For it is evident that Shelley's tombstone is never swept and cleaned except by the elements. Trelawney, the life-long friend and stanch defender of the poet, rests beside him. He died at the age of eighty-eight, and Shelley at thirty. In standing beside these two graves, equally destitute of human care, one pays a tribute to friendship as well as to genius.

Another old man—Severn—sleeps alongside of young Keats. Their graves, situated in a free and wind-swept place, outside of the stuffed cemetery, are well cared for. The same good people who put up the exquisite portrait of Keats in *alto-rilievo* against the wall of the portal and erected the tombstone in memory of Severn, doubtless provided for proper attention to the graves. The wall near by is thick with climbing roses. Daisies, buttercups, and some flowers not so familiar to us, star the lush grass on every side. A trim hedge incloses the two who, in death, as in life, were not divided. Keats sleeps under the shadow of a laurel-tree, which has grown much in the last three years, and still supplies leaves in abundance to be plucked and pressed as souvenirs. As we stood there and watched the sharp shadow of the venerable pyramid of Cestius slowly creeping toward us, the spell was broken by the harsh voice of a man at my elbow. "What a shame," he said, "that such an epitaph should be allowed to stand above a grave!" I turned and saw an Englishman. He referred, of course, to the bitterness of the inscription, alluding to the savage criticisms which, doubtless, hastened the death of the consumptive, broken-hearted Keats. The Englishman thought it was high time to erase this memorial of a by-gone literary feud. "True," I replied, "the epitaph does seem out of place now, when the position of Keats among the English immortals is assured. But, after all, should it not be kept there as a warning to future critics? It should teach them to be more tolerant of young authors, with their new and daring styles." The other man could not accept that view of the case. I did not care to discuss it. So we touched hats and parted.

It is not easy to find out the exact sanitary value of the eucalyptus, or blue-gum tree. Americans who inhabit malarial districts, and are waiting for Italy to test the tree thoroughly before planting it in their own grounds, will be sorry to learn that a blight has fallen on a great many promising groves of the eucalyptus in this country. At most of the railway-stations in South Italy the trees are withered, if not yet dead. Their leaves are yellow and curled up, and have only a faint resinous smell. Many of the trees, whose leaves are still green and balmy, are stunted. They do not grow here with the rapidity and vigor of the eucalyptus in Australia. The trouble is less with the climate than the soil, for I observed at some stations every sign of health in some trees. A specimen would show robustness in every leaf, and fill the air with its peculiar odor, while another one not two hundred feet away would be drooping and scentless. In those few places where the tree has done justice to itself, as one may say, men speak well of it. They regard it as a preventive, to some extent, of malarial fever; they ought to know. The good fathers at the Abbey of Tre Fontaine, near Rome, have the highest opinion of the eucalyptus. It is an undoubted fact that the very free planting of the tree in and about the abbey-grounds has made them habitable. It takes kindly to that particular locality. The monks have mastered the art of raising it to perfection. They have a vast nursery where it is grown by the hundreds of thousands, and sold cheaply. The trees which I had noticed at so many railway-stations all came from Tre Fontaine. The monks make a handsome revenue out of this product. It would not be quite fair to say that their interests prejudice them in its favor, though one could hardly expect them to underrate something the cultivation of which is so gainful for them. To sum up the matter, according to my present light, I should say that where the eucalyptus can be made to thrive it is a check on malaria.

The old town, Perugia, is well worth visiting on many accounts. Traveling by rail from Rome to Florence, one sees large clusters of houses perched high on the hill-side. They are crowned with campaniles and domes, surrounded by high walls, and provoke one's curiosity to make their closer acquaintance. But on consulting his guide-book, the tourist finds that these elevated settlements contain few objects of interest, better examples of which can be found elsewhere. He also learns, which is as much to the purpose, that they have no good hotels. Now, Perugia is very old, very quaint, full of venerable historical associations, a center of Etruscan tombs, and other antiquities, seventeen hundred feet above the sea, and has a first-class hotel. This modern structure, the "Grand," occupies the highest ground of the town, and commands a magnificent view of the Umbrian Valley. East, south, and west I survey all the details of a landscape of variety and beauty unsurpassed. It is intersected by the Tiber and some smaller rivers, which flash in the morning sun. Many villages are visible as brown patches, among them Assisi, famous as the birthplace of St. Francis. Mountains bound the view on all sides. Some of them are still tipped with snow, and their summits would easily be mistaken for clouds if these were not scurrying past in the south wind. As I write a haze is beginning to blot out the more distant villages. A heated term is threatening. But Americans are not to be frightened by that. Only I wish the roads were not so white and dusty.

This country is a vast cemetery. No one can say how many races were buried here before the Etruscans passed away in their turn and left the ground honey-combed with their tombs. When one sinks a well or digs a cellar for a house, he is apt to strike his spade against a rock, which gives back a hollow sound. It is the roof of an Etruscan burial-vault. From this subterranean chamber the air has been excluded for more than two thousand years. I am told that strange things are sometimes seen in the tombs at the moment when they are opened, and then vanish forever. They say that glimpses are caught of old Etruscan lords and ladies sitting at banquets, and that these disappear the instant the outer air touches them. When the finder proceeds to open and examine the tomb, he discovers nothing but a heap of dust in place of the vision that had startled him. These are obviously fables, for the most part. Though I believe it is true that an Etruscan knight, in full armor, collapsed to dusty nothingness in precisely this way when his tomb was invaded a few years ago. We have been to see the Sepulchre of the Volumnii, about five miles below Perugia, and found it and its contents very strange and interesting. It is supposed to date back to the third century B. C. A descent of some thirty steps leads down to it from the road-side. First, a chamber, about twenty-five feet square, is entered, and from this smaller apartments branch to right and left. The sepulchre is hewn out of the tufa-rock. It is very damp and cold. Heads of Medusa, dolphins, and serpents are carved with much skill on the top and sides of this tomb. All around stand small stone urns, each one bearing in *alto-rilievo* the representation of a fight. One man is always killing another, unless the scene is varied by the sacrifice of a bound and helpless woman or child on an altar. The covers of these urns are higher works of art. They are surmounted with recumbent figures of men and women. These are dressed in the costume of their age and sex, and each has in his or her hand a bowl for tears. Lifting off a cover, I find inside the urn about a hatful of ashes. I run my fingers through this mass and feel fragments of burned bones. But I am rudely stirring up all that remains of some gallant warrior or some haughty beauty, and withdraw my hand with a sense of remorse. A great many personal ornaments of exceeding richness and grace have been taken from these receptacles, and are separately exhibited by the custodian. But if one wishes to realize the full extent of the arts and sciences familiar to the old Etruscans, he should inspect the splendid collection in the University Museum at Perugia.

CHAPTER IX.

FLORENCE—BOLOGNA—COMO.

SUNDAY, May 23d, being at Florence, we went to the Duomo. Advancing from the door to the center of that magnificent cathedral, we noticed a crowd of persons standing there, and heard a musical voice sounding above their heads. The edifice is so vast that the thousand or more people who composed the throng occupied comparatively only a small space on the floor. The voice, the source of which we could not trace at first in the dim light of the place, proved to come from a pulpit in mid-air. The speaker was a fine-looking man about fifty years old. His face was highly intellectual, and at moments intensely spiritual in its expression. He spoke Italian with a sweetness and a rhythmic swing delightful to the ear. One might not know a word of what he said —as at the Italian opera—and still enjoy hearing him. But it was not necessary to understand more than a few words—here and there—of the beautiful language that rolled so fluently from his lips in order to catch the full purport of his remarks. His theme was the consolations of religion in earthly sorrows. He spoke without manuscript or notes. The man's heart was full of his message, and he delivered it with an eloquence that held his audience spell-bound. Officers and privates of the army, gray-headed civilians, rich men and beggars, women and children, all stood there with parted lips gazing upon his face and drinking in his words of faith and cheer. His gestures were few and natural. They seemed freighted with meaning. At times he would point up to the glorious dome, as if apostrophizing the angels and saints who make that great concave seem a glimpse of heaven. Then he would press his hand fervently upon his heart, as if to testify a sincerity for which no such gesture was needed, as truth and zeal shone before all men in every line of his face. Suddenly, while the attention of his hearers was rapt and almost painful in its intensity, he stopped, gave the congregation his blessing with a quick motion of his right hand (a sign of the cross), and abruptly left the pulpit. A moment later I saw him glide rapidly through the throng with a thick cloak wrapped about him, and a shawl tied around his neck. His impassioned sermon had heated him up, and he was very wisely taking care of himself.

His name is unknown to me, and I may never see him again. But his eloquent discourse, which would have interpreted itself had it been spoken in Chinese, will ever remain one of my pleasantest recollections of the grand old Cathedral of Florence.

On the way back to my hotel I passed the Palazzo Vecchio. As I stopped to inspect its venerable front, a small boy handed me a printed slip of paper. Looking at it, I found it to be a recommendation of somebody with a long name for the office of delegate in the National Assembly. It was signed by numerous citizens of Florence, all highly respectable, probably, but strangers to me. Just before me I observed one man button-holing another, and whispering something in his ear. Groups of people were conferring mysteriously on every side. Then, for the first time, I noticed that the Palazzo Vecchio itself was plastered over with enormous placards of assorted colors—red, green, blue, white, and yellow. Letters a foot long proclaimed all these show-bills to be election posters, quite in the American style. They were all dated the night before the eventful day—namely, Sunday—which had been assigned for the great struggle between the friends and foes of the present Italian ministry. Politicians are the same in all countries. The cunning fellows in Italy understand as well as their American kind the art of issuing "last cards" and "final appeals" at an hour too late for refutation by their opponents.

Desiring to compare the Italian with the American process of balloting, I climbed to a large upper room in the palace where voting was then in progress. Admission was impossible without a *permesso*, which it was not worth while to procure, as I saw at a glance through the doorway how the business was done. A number of officials sat at a long table; upon it were glass globes for the ballots, and books for identifying and checking off the voters. The formalities were in substance the same as those which so effectually deter very busy men from voting in New York except in presidential years. With a population of 150,000, Florence is entitled to cast about 15,000 votes; and out of these the proportion of stay-at-homes is as large as in our own city. Very little interest was actually taken in the election, although the political journals had been trying for a week to "get up steam" with pictorial caricatures and big head-lines. The contest was evidently one between the ins and the outs, and the great majority of voters had no real concern in the issue. But the lesson was no less instructive to an American. All that I saw on that election Sunday in Florence convinced me that political tricks and "dodges" are by no means confined to our beloved country.

The tourist's purse should be well stuffed if he wants to buy Florentine mosaics at the shops of the most famous manufacturers. The prices of some of their products would be called high even in New York. Extra fine pieces are ticketed at five thousand francs and upward. Some of the makers of mosaics have grown rich on American patronage. It is not at their shops that you get bargains. There is no shade of color, I believe, which the artist can not find among the stones, shells, or corals with which he produces his wonderful effects. As all great works of art require a master for their accomplishment, it stands to reason that the finest original landscapes, portraits, and flower and fruit pieces can never be very cheap, as most people estimate cheapness. But it is possible to pick up fairly good mosaics in Florence at reasonable rates, though these are not the rates asked by the seller. He does not expect you to give more than a half or two thirds his nominal price. I have visited a number of factories of fancy goods in Italy, and observed that nearly all the labor is performed by mere children. They toil many hours in the day, and are poorly paid. Under the pretense that they are being educated to a trade, they continue for years to do a journeyman's work, and it is to their cunning hands that we owe some of the most marvelous imitations of masterpieces in wood-carving, filigree, and mosaic. When, therefore, the manufacturer takes off a half or a third of his asking price, he is still making a large profit on his goods. No American need think that he can ever get the better of an art-dealer in Europe. That is impossible.

One of the most interesting sights in the environs of Florence is the Carthusian Monastery. I had the pleasure of visiting it with a party of American ladies. The monastery is an immense structure, covering acres of land, and contains ten or a dozen chapels of different sizes. This is enough to give each monk a chapel all to himself —the inmates not exceeding that number. For reasons best known to the Italian Government, it has been decided to wind up certain spiritual retreats, and this Carthusian Monastery among them. But the work is done gradually, and the buildings and grounds will not revert to the Government until the last of the few remaining monks is dead. They do not seem likely to die in a hurry. Some of them would take the prizes in any human exhibition for fatness and sleekness. Their loose and flowing robes of some cream-colored stuff, perhaps, impart an unreal fullness to their figures. One wonders if their lives are quite as austere as represented. The monk who piloted our party about is magnificent in physique. He stands about six feet two inches, as straight as an arrow, weighs fully two hundred pounds, has a winning, slightly sunburned Italian face, and is in manner a perfect gentleman. To the ladies he is at once dignified and courteous. Somewhere in some other days he must have mingled with refined society, and I catch myself in a state of keen surprise when I contrast his presumably monastic life here with the gay times that he may have had elsewhere. He is very fluent in Italian and French, as if he were making up (poor fellow!) for the enforced silence of his vows. For we are told that this ready talker is allowed to converse with his brethren no more than one hour in a week. We are shown his suite of small, miserable, cheerless rooms where he receives and eats his frugal meals, which are shoved to him through a hole in the wall by a hand attached to an unseen person. We see the wretched straw pallet on which he stretches his giant frame, and the bare table where he makes his solitary repast. Then we look again at his healthy face, and still wonder by what alchemy he can transmute his solitude and privation into apparent contentment and even happiness. The ladies all think that our handsome guide must "have a history." They imagine that somewhere among his antecedents is the inevitable "woman." They speculate fondly on the probabilities of some love-affair which drove our friend from a luxurious court to this penitential abode. They unanimously agree that it is "too bad" to keep such a fine-looking gentleman confined in a monastery, when society outside is pining for precisely that kind of material. But our monk makes no revelation of his own thoughts. After he has patiently taken us all over the monastery, and picked flowers for the ladies as mementos of their visit, he bids them good-by with the one unchanging expression of contentment on his face. May his ample shadow never be less, nor his beard of raven blackness be shorn of its luxuriant proportions!

Entering the ancient and famous city of Bologna May 24th, I could think only of the sausage that bears her name. The ideas of Bologna and sausage were one and inseparable. Could anything be more ridiculous? There was a large, rich, enterprising city, with her fine picture-galleries, churches, and important university, two remarkable leaning towers, and many branches of industry in which she excels. And yet I found myself looking out of the carriage-windows, right and left, for nothing but sausages! Not a single specimen of them could be seen between the station and the hotel. You may believe I was much disappointed. But at dinner, among a great variety of French dishes, the waiters bore around plates covered with the thinnest possible slices of the celebrated sausage. For a moment I hovered over it with a fork, and then gave myself the benefit of the doubt. All the Italians present scrambled for it, but the English people and at least two Americans at table let it alone. Such is prejudice. After dinner, walking about the shops near our hotel, I saw plenty of sausages. Indeed, these were the most beautiful ornaments of the shop-windows. Some were a foot in diameter, and their finely-cut surfaces looked like Roman mosaic. Aside from her sausages, Bologna is well worth a visit, and even those persons who are squeamish about eating them can not help admiring their decorative effect when exposed for sale in the busy parts of the city. Their artistic combinations of tint lighten up the shop-fronts like so many chromos or colored photographs.

Next day we examined the two leaning towers. One of them is particularly interesting, because it is claimed by some authorities to be the only tower in all Italy which leans "on purpose." The taller of the pair deflects only about three and a half feet in a height of two hundred and seventy-two feet; while the other, with a height of only one hundred and thirty-eight feet, is eight and a half feet out of plumb. According to tradition, if not history, this obliquity is the work of design. One may suppose that the original intention was to carry the short tower to the same height as the tall one, and that the architect and the workmen became frightened as they proceeded. One feels like "standing from under" as he looks up and sees that massive chimney-like pile apparently on the point of toppling over with its own weight. I can understand, too, that the masons may have struck for higher wages or fewer hours as the tower began to lean more and more. It should have needed no trade-union or Knights of Labor to impel them to make a demand on their employers. To them as to us it must have seemed very absurd to build a tower at enormous expense for the express object of showing how much it could be made to lean without falling. After one has looked at these eccentric structures a short time he becomes the prey of a singular optical illusion. Every other campanile or steeple or chimney appears to be leaning more or less. The fronts of tall buildings do not seem to be exactly up and down.

The spectator insensibly compares one upright object with another, and discovers, as he imagines, a variance of a yard, or a foot, or an inch, from the true perpendicular. He becomes painfully skeptical about the stability of all things, and does not get rid of this disagreeable impression until he leaves Bologna, and ceases to see the pair of leaning towers looming always above the horizon.

Taking one's lunch on the upper deck of a Rhine steamer is very pleasant. The same operation is highly agreeable on a Danube boat. The picturesque scenery of both rivers is enjoyed all the more while the inner man is duly refreshed. But a lunch eaten in full air on the smart little craft that plies on the most beautiful of Italian lakes between Como and Bellagio is an experience no less delightful. The food and the wine are good, to begin with. If one comes up from Milan on a hot and dusty day, he revels in the coolness as he sits under an awning and is fanned by breezes that have swept over yonder snow-fields of the Alps. The hotter he has found Rome and Florence—and the more wearisome the great valley or prairie of the Po has seemed to him as he traversed it—the more he feasts on the prospect of mountains now all around him, and the promise of lower temperature which they do not hold out in vain. The hills which form the immediate frame of this exquisite lake are clothed to their tops in green—not barren on the summit like those of Southern Italy. This green is reflected in the clear, deep water, and perhaps of itself explains the fine aquamarine tint for which Como is as famous as Lake Leman for its matchless blue.

Perhaps no person who ever heard or read Claude Melnotte's description of Como, as poured by him into the too credulous ear of the Lady of Lyons, can look on this lake without recalling some or all of that delicious bit of poetry. This is unfortunate. Because the shores of lovely Como do not abound in orange-groves as he has been led to expect. Neither does he see anywhere fountains gushing forth in the midst of roses. Besides, the environments of the lake are far from soft and sensuous. The entire effect partakes of the grand and rugged. It is only of the water itself and the villas on the banks that the epithet beautiful is spontaneously used. But we know that Claude Melnotte was only romancing when he painted Como to the love-lorn Pauline. Bulwer must not be held responsible if travelers do not find here exactly those charms which they had been prepared for. But none the less is the Lake of Como peerless in Italy. If it has a rival anywhere it is in America. Those who have seen Lake George may with some show of justice assert its equality with Como in the chief elements of beauty. I have heard the comparison made more than once by Americans here — to the disparagement of Como. But why compare them at all? They are different in certain respects; and I should say that in those variations, and those only, each is more charming than the other.

In a world's competition of roses the Lake of Como would stand a good chance of carrying off the highest honors, for the profusion, size, variety, and fragrance of those flowers. The villas here recall Byron's flowing line about "the gardens of Gul in their bloom." And then the nightingales! They are singing all night long in the forest on the hill-side. There is an accompaniment of sweet woodland music to odors almost oppressive in their richness. The old fable of the nightingale loving the rose seems to be possible in this Eden of Como.

CHAPTER X.

PEASANT-GIRLS—NIGHTINGALES—ISOLA BELLA—
SAN CARLO BORROMEO IN COPPER.

A LUCKY accident enabled us to get an inside view of some little Swiss and Italian villages rarely seen by tourists. We missed a boat through the fault of a servant, and were obliged to take a carriage from Lugano, on the lake of that name, to Luino, on Lago Maggiore. The day was beautiful, the team fresh, and the route not described in the guide-books. The old post-road which we traveled is still kept in good condition for local use. We did not pass a single carriage all the way. The villages of Northern Italy are almost uniformly neat and clean. The inhabitants are honest, industrious, and self-respecting. We have not seen a beggar within the boundaries of the Italian lakes. The scarcity of men in these out-of-the-way places is very noticeable. All the young and strong fellows are at work in the larger towns along the lakes, where there is plenty to do for willing hands in the "season." We saw no natives except old men, children, and women. The latter do everything inside and outside of the houses, the shops, and the taverns. They were gathering in a crop of hay from all the fields along both sides of the road. The fragrance of the new-mown grass filled the air. Except for the women with their rakes and forks the scene in early June very closely resembled that of a New England meadow in a later month. There are the same stone walls dividing the fields, only a little better built than those in America. Daisies and butter-cups are the wild flowers in greatest abundance, though there are many others peculiar to this part of the world. The one object in the landscape which, above every other, makes a difference, is the high square tower of the Campanile. The traveler is never out of sight of that substitute for the American steeple, and there is hardly an hour of the day when he does not hear its sweet accord of bells ringing in the distance. And the people of these little hamlets are never so busy that some of them can not steal a few minutes from their day's work to enter their church and kneel in silent prayer. As we walk on tip-toe down the cold stone aisles to look at some bit of painting or sculpture of surprising excellence, we feel ashamed of disturbing the poor women at their devotions. But they do not seem to mind it, showing far less curiosity about strangers than the average congregation of a church in any small American village would exhibit.

In this memorable ride we frequently met girls with large wicker baskets strapped to their shoulders. The bearers were healthy and strong, and did not appear to need the aid of the thick stick which served as a cane. There are no tramps hereabout. But if one should spring from the road-side and insult that muscular young creature, I imagine that he would be sorry for it; for her stout staff is gripped in a large hand and her arm is sinewy. She is just such an athlete as the girl who rowed us all about the Bay of Lugano. That rower, by-the-way, handled the oars more neatly than any boatman we have seen on these lakes. Her stroke was faultless. And all the time that she was cleaving the water with a powerful sweep she was talking with feminine facility, divining by instinct the questions we were about to ask, and giving us the very information we would have sought. If such a girl—instead of a stupid boy— had been the driver of our carriage, I might have learned more worth the mention between Lugano and Luino.

Returning to the lasses on the road, I would add that the monstrous baskets were filled to the top with something that seemed heavy. The girls may have been trudging home from market with goods obtained in exchange for their own handywork. For they are dexterous at spinning, weaving, and lace-making, as well as in the manufacture of butter and cheese. It is no wonder that the men confidingly leave all the interests of home in their charge. Seeing how true and brave they are, we can not help regretting that those straight, handsome forms should so soon be bowed down by the excessive burdens thrust upon them. But they would be the first to reject the traveler's commiseration. Those who are barefoot would tell him that they enjoy treading the earth with their naked soles. Most of the girls whom we met, however, wear bandages of white linen or other material wrapped around the feet and wooden sandals lightly strapped to them. This arrangement gives more play to the feet than the stockings and shoes of other countries. The wearers would spurn with contempt the tight fits and high heels which no fashionable woman of the period could do without.

The Lakes Lugano and Maggiore are less picturesque and interesting than Como. The tourist ought, if convenient, to reverse the circuit we made. Como should be kept for the last if possible, since all the rest pale in comparison with it. But each of the other lakes has its separate fascination, either of tint or of surrounding mountains, or something else. For example, we saw on Lake Lugano no less than four cascades of great height and fullness. They looked like fresh and foaming milk as they streamed from precipices a thousand feet high. Any one of them would make the fortune of a hotel-keeper in Switzerland, where such objects are greatly in favor; but here they are too common to excite much interest. As for Lake Maggiore, it enjoys the distinction of being larger than any other of the group. This gives space for longer steamboat trips, which some persons enjoy greatly, and I can certify to the pleasure of them. But the same lake surpasses the rest in the glory of the snow mountains, which, though miles away, seem to spring out of its depths. These are the Simplon and its spotless associates. They raise their sharp crests far above the snow-line, and show great masses of gleaming white on which the sun has yet made little impression. As we entered the Bay of Pallanza, the haze prevented our seeing the lofty range. But next morning, when I flung open the shutters, there stood the Simplon, cleaving the sky with its wedge. The rays from the east struck it full in the breast and made it sparkle. One could see without a glass all the divisions of rock and snow and ice that compose its towering bulk. Somewhere beyond are the far sublimer Matterhorn, Weisshorn, Monte Rosa, and others. But they are not needed to enhance the picturesqueness of this part of Maggiore. Simplon and his companions answer the purpose just as well.

That man must be very sleepy who would complain of being kept awake by nightingales. These birds inhabit the thickets around my hotel. About eleven o'clock, the first night of our arrival, one of them awoke me from a sound sleep. A window stood ajar, and music flooded the chamber. The singer was a soloist. Not a sound of any kind interrupted his performance. Even the crickets stopped to listen. Somebody has taken the trouble to jot down every note and trill of the nightingale's song. It may be reproduced, I believe, on the upper octaves of the piano. But it can never be made to sound as ravishing as the "wood-notes wild" of that bird in those bushes. Perhaps imagination has something to do with the effect. Memory quickly recalls fugitive scraps of poetry about nightingales, and one listens to them the more greedily. Suddenly the music, which was so enchanting, woke echoes far and near. Other nightingales, as if accepting a challenge, responded to the soloist. It was too much of a good thing. The sweet sounds ran together and became confused. What had been perfect as an air was discord as a chorus. In the midst of it the chief singer ceased. A few minutes later, and all was quiet.

"Napoleon the Great slept there," said the guide, pointing to an alcove-bed in the huge château on Isola Bella. There was room enough in it for six little corporals. Fancy the conqueror curling himself up into a ball and trying to hush to sleep the ambitious schemes that seethed in his brain! Not long after his visit at Isola Bella he fought the battle of Marengo. After one has wandered through the labyrinth of rooms, he is turned over to the gardener. This man takes you to a little gully hard by, and stops before an enormous laurel-tree. "There," says he, "Napoleon cut the word *battaglia* with his own hand." Still fresh from the inspection of Napoleon's bed, one gazes almost with awe on a tree which he actually gashed in a moment of abstraction. But nothing can be seen. The liveliest fancy can make out nothing more than worm-holes in the bark. The gardener is then good enough to explain that the highly prized inscription rotted away years ago. This is too bad. He tries to make up for the loss by showing us what wonderful things the beautiful island, as it is truly called, is capable of producing.

It is not for an American to be astonished at anything in the gardening line. So I suppressed any surprise I might have felt when the cork-tree, the camphor-tree, the tea-plant, and bamboo in every variety, growing comfortably side by side, were shown to me. It was a happy family, whose members had been brought together from every zone but the Arctic. Perhaps the gardener may have easily guessed our nationality; for it is a fact that he spoke with the greatest pride of all the different American trees in the collection. To resist such delicate flattery was impossible. I hope I sustained the reputation of our country by the size of the *pour boire* which he received as we left. The Borromean Islands, of which Isola Bella is the queen, would well repay one for a visit to Lago Maggiore if there were no other attractions.

The most illustrious member of the Borromean family in all its eventful history—St. Charles—has been made the subject of a colossal statue. It was erected about two hundred years ago at Arona. Its material is copper, except the head, hands, and feet, which are bronze. Having seen Bartholdi's statue of Liberty in Paris, in 1883, I was impelled to compare it with this old giant. Some people say that Bartholdi's masterpiece will easily become the prey of wind and weather—that the thin copper sheets of which it is made will not last long, and that the first stiff gale will blow it down. But San Carlo Borromeo is perpetuated in just such copper for the most part. That metal does not show the least trace of age, save that it has become of a darker and richer tint with time. As for the wind, there could be no worse site for a large statue than the high hill north of Arona, where the gusts are frightful at times. I beg to cite this towering image—sixty-six feet high and surmounting a pedestal of forty feet—as hopeful evidence that the greater achievement of Bartholdi will be seen and admired in its perfection centuries hence.

Art-critics, in their off-hand, dogmatic way, call the statue of San Carlo "worthless." They say that the hands—one of which holds a book, while the other gives a blessing—are badly managed, that the pose of the figure is ungraceful, and that the ears are too big. As to the ears, I admit that they possibly do the saint much injustice. They seem about the shape and size of meat-platters. But if one's attention were not called to them, they would not look so bad. This defect, if such it is, might perhaps be remedied by turning the unfortunate ears upside down or back side front. All the rest strikes me as dignified and effective enough.

CHAPTER XI.

THE SIMPLON IN JUNE—VISPACH TO ZERMATT—THE MATTERHORN—A FINE VIEW FROM THE SNOWS OF GORNER-GRAT.

CROSSING from Italy to Switzerland by the Simplon Pass early in June, we found the remains of a great snow-drift near the summit. The crest of the heap rose above the top of our carriage. On the Italian, or south, side of the Alps the weather had been quite warm and even enervating. Although the sky was overcast and rain fell at intervals, I became unpleasantly heated whenever I walked, to ease the horses and pick flowers. But the moment we began to descend from the extreme height of about 6,500 feet, a cold wind struck us in front and flank. Rugs and shawls which had been carefully strapped up were unbound and put to use. The road was as good as when Napoleon made it, and the horses were fresh from a night's rest at the half-way inn of Isella. The carriage rattled down the steep grade, the driver cracking his whip merrily, and making echoes in the deep and narrow gorges. We knew that a few hours of this pace would bring us to Brieg and warmth. I never before realized the full difference between a northern and a southern aspect. As we made the gradual ascent from Domo d'Ossola, snow had been occasionally seen, but always far above us. It filled crevices at the height of 7,000 feet, or crowned the very peaks. But when we had passed the little village of Simplon and neared the Hospice, there was snow in patches far below us. And from the road upward it still covered large tracts, and at times threatened avalanches. These, however, are of rare occurrence on the Simplon in the first half of June Rude crosses mark the spots where travelers had been swept into the profound gulf which yawned on our left. At one place, the driver said, four men had been carried to that awful but immediate death. An enduring crucifix of bronze had been firmly set in a stone socket, just where they were overtaken. This is the part of the road where so many "refuges" have been provided. Those places of shelter, as well as the more comfortable Hospice, have saved the lives of many persons crossing the pass in the fall, winter, and spring. The *tourmente*, or whirlwind of snow, is a cause of more deaths than avalanches in the high Alps.

It is bitterly cold and blinding, and in a few minutes raises mounds of snow through which horses and men can hardly make their way. We were glad to know that the icy plague was out of season at the time of our crossing.

The waterfalls—among the greatest charms of the Simplon Pass—were at their best. The rains had been heavy for some days, and the sun was melting the snow in all but its highest lodgments. The white peaks of mountains, ranging from 9,000 to 11,000 feet above the sea, were sublime and beautiful. One never tires of gazing at them and using some more familiar mountain at home as a sort of measuring-scale in order to form a better idea of their height. Americans are in the habit of recalling their impressions of Washington, Mansfield, Graylock, or the Catskills for this purpose. In the Alps, however, this plan does not help us much. For some of the most majestic of the range have their bases at a height of 5,000 feet to begin with, and never seem to be as high by several thousand feet as they really are. A mountain of much less stature would look just as lofty springing from a foundation nearer the sea-level. I soon gave up Washington, Moosilauke, and the rest, and began employing Trinity Church steeple and the Produce Exchange tower as wands of memory in trying to measure Monte Leone and the Aletschhorn. The system was amusing if not satisfactory.

But when no lofty mountains are in sight then one's spirit is refreshed by the waterfalls. I never before conceived of the widely different forms which falling water could assume. We passed hundreds of cascades between Domo d'Ossola and Brieg, and no two were alike. They resembled each other as little in shape as in size. Some were simple mill-streams. They came rushing down the mountains in great volume to turn wheels. But they found no corn to grind or logs to saw. They were only conducted off through culverts beneath the road-bed, where they could do neither harm nor good. What might be called lace-patterns were innumerable. They were flat waterfalls, thin and very wide, slipping gently over smooth rocks of easy slopes. Wavy bands of lines made the breadth of these falls look in the distance exactly like snow-white lace. Bridal veils of the most exquisite texture were common. Some kept their symmetry in leaps of at least five hundred feet. There were falls which reminded one of the dropping of brilliants from fireworks high in the air. Each flashing wavelet seemed to preserve its unity as it fell over the precipice, and to come down slowly till broken up by some jutting rock below. A fall that always pleased us dissipated itself in a transparent vapor, and sparkled in the sunshine like a cascade of diamonds. This is the sort of fall that Swiss innkeepers are said to manufacture in the dry season. It only needs a small boy with a few pails of water. He is out of sight on the heights, and turns on the fall when he sees a carriage coming through the pass. There were too many falls of this kind to make us question their genuineness. Another style that never tired came down in numerous short leaps. The effect was that of stairs made of silver. Sometimes they were solid—as one might say—and made so little spray that they seemed to be shining steps leading from the gloomy depths of the ravine to the white and serene land above.

We used up the best part of two days traveling from Pallanza (on the Lago Maggiore), Italy, to Brieg, Switzerland, which is the upper end of the Simplon road, and would not have abridged the journey by a single hour. It is delightful and exhilarating to every lover of Nature—in fine weather. Few persons who seek the Alps for health and pleasure will be sorry to learn that the proposed tunnel of the Simplon is likely to remain a dream many years longer. In a shed of the little *auberge* at Isella may be seen a boring-machine which has been tried on the Italian side and laid up for want of funds. The tunnel would be about twelve miles long, and nobody knows how much it would cost. And nobody in Italy, at least, seems to care. The scheme is of French origin, though the Swiss are very friendly to it, and its projectors have hoped that Switzerland would subscribe liberally toward its execution. But, at present, there is little prospect that help will come from that quarter or any other. Admirers of the picturesque who do not want to see the noble Simplon road discarded will not, however, object to the construction of a narrow-gauge railway between Domo d'Ossola and the Italian lakes. This would save them the delay and expense of a carriage-ride of four or five hours through a somewhat monotonous country. I can testify to the solidity of the road-bed as far as built. The bridges are particularly strong. Work is now suspended on this enterprise, also for lack of money, and the natives told me that they did not expect to see it in operation under four years — if ever.

At Brieg we took carriage for Vispach, though the railway from the former place connects the two villages and continues on to Geneva. Vispach is the only point of departure for the Zermatt country, where the Matterhorn reigns supreme. Thousands of persons — mostly Alpine climbers — visit Zermatt in July and August. It is strange, therefore, that for half the way there is no carriage-road where one could be made at moderate cost merely by widening the present bridle-path. As a walk, the distance is a good nine hours, and is readily taken by many English men and women. But people like ourselves, not used to such performances, are glad to mount horses, or, if timid or not strong, prefer to be borne on the chair with poles (which one sees everywhere in these mountains) by the strong hands of two young Swiss giants, with two others to "spell" them and carry the "traps." Light-weight ladies are greatly in favor with these porters. They trot off with their little burden at a rate which soon distances my horse. It is fun to notice that sometimes they pretend to find the load heavy and slacken their gait, as if fatigued. The object of this artifice is to justify the employment of the second pair of giants, one of whom has a bundle of umbrellas and the other a small black hand-bag, which is popularly supposed to be full of money, but in fact contains only bottles. The horse is led by a fifth man, not, I flatter myself, because the rider does not know how to ride, but in order to make number five seem indispensable. This man carries a small package of shawls. It is the poor horse that does most of the real work and receives no *pour boire*. For, besides the person on his back, he bears the only piece of baggage worth mentioning. This is a leather valise of modest dimensions. Wise people who go to Zermatt get themselves up in light marching order, leaving their trunks behind to be picked up on their return. For you are obliged to come out of the Visp Valley the same way you go in, unless you cross into Italy on foot over a glacier about two miles high, which we do not propose to do.

If one were not looking so sharply after his horse and his scattered property, and keeping the little procession on the go in order to lose no time, he would enjoy the scenery between Vispach and St. Niklaus more than he does. It is always wild and in places is magnificent. On both sides of the valley are crags of great height and occasionally a snow-tipped peak. Sometimes we rise far above the river Visp, and then again descend to its level. We are always within hearing distance of its deep gurgle. On the whole, it was a relief to change off for a rough mountain-wagon at St. Niklaus and do the rest of the way with no attendant but the driver. Rain came on about that time, and we lost some of the finest views to be had before reaching Zermatt. But we did see the enormous blocks of stone which were shaken down by the earthquake of 1885 and rolled to the middle of the valley. The force required to detach these masses from their everlasting foundations is comprehensible.

But it is not so easy to believe that an immense section of the Bies glacier which overhangs the village of Randa, slipped with such initial velocity as to clear that hamlet completely and fall on the other side. The story goes that, although this monstrous ice-cake missed the village, the wind of it blew down all the houses! But we prefer to accept all the astonishing statements about glaciers, and thereby heighten our enjoyment of those remarkable objects.

At half-past five the next morning, I obtained my first and best view of the sublime Matterhorn from a chamber of the Hôtel du Mont Rose. It was like an instantaneous photograph. Perhaps not a second elapsed before a drifting cloud covered the summit. But in that fleeting moment the view was complete. In the pure air of Zermatt (itself 5,300 feet high) the stars shine with an intensity unknown to lower regions, and mountains which are miles away seem to overhang the village. The height of the Matterhorn is about 14,700 feet. This, great as it is, would not count for so much but for the peculiar shape of the peak. As seen from Zermatt it presents two sides of a pyramid of solid rock. These rise at very sharp angles from a slender base and terminate in the form of a tusk, which actually curves at the top. It recalls to mind a walrus-tooth or the horn of a rhinoceros. A slight coating of snow mantles only a part of this rockiest of mountains. Nothing could seem more difficult than the ascent of the Matterhorn. As one looks at it the wonder grows that the little churchyard of the hamlet, which holds the bodies of the three who paid with their lives for the honor of "conquering" it twenty years ago, is not filled with victims of the same ambition. In the precious moment of my observation I mark the route by which those daring men made their ascent. There is the "shoulder" which they passed triumphantly. There is the steepest of slopes up which they were the pioneers. There is the precipice of 4,000 feet down which four of the party slipped as they were returning from their victory. And, somewhere down there among the eternal snow, perhaps in the fathomless crevasse of a glacier, is still buried the body of Lord Douglas, one of the most intrepid members of the expedition. But, while I am making out these points of interest, a cloud eclipses all. I had seen just enough of the obstacles of the Matterhorn to increase my amazement at the well-known fact that it is often ascended with safety now-a-days. It should be remembered that ropes have been securely fastened to the sides of the mountain in the worst places, and render the task less difficult than formerly. There are guides standing in the street in front of the Hôtel du Mont Rose who would conduct you to the top of the Matterhorn and bring you back alive for a moderate sum. But they would not start to-day or to-morrow. They would wait until July, when the snow had melted and left the lower part of the mountain bare. Even now, however, an offer large enough will procure the attempt— and probably a successful one—to accomplish this greatest of Alpine feats.

One day I happened to meet in a shop a veteran guide who had retired from the business on his fees and laurels. The old fellow had just dined freely, and was feeling well. Knowing who he was, I playfully asked him if he would take me up the Matterhorn and plant the American flag on the top for 1,000 francs? My manner should have showed that I was joking. The aged guide, entering into the humor of the thing, as I supposed, said he would think about it and let me know. Sure enough, that very night he hunted me up and said he was ready to start the next day, if required, on the terms mentioned. He seemed very much disappointed when I told him I was only "in fun." Since then I am aware that all the guides in the street are watching me anxiously. They hope that I may prove the first candidate for their services on the Matterhorn this season. Last year they assisted more than twenty persons up and down that terrible rock without a single accident. August is the best month for the ascents.

Taking advantage of a fine morning, I started off with a trusty guide, and in about five hours gained a height of nearly 10,000 feet. Our route was by a bridle-path up to the Riffelberg, where there is a summer hotel 8,430 feet above the sea. This establishment was tenantless at the time of our visit. It is not usually open before July. Leaving the horse there, the guide and myself proceeded on foot. At first snow-patches alternated with naked rocks, but presently we struck a continuous deposit of snow, which gradually increased in depth from three to six and eight feet. Fortunately for us, Mr. Seiler, the energetic proprietor of all the hotels in and about Zermatt—five in number—had that very day directed his men to break a path through this immense snow-field. We reaped the benefit of their work, and in fact followed on their heels. At noon we had reached a point on the Gorner Grat which commanded all the mountains and glaciers I desired to see; and, as the sun was fast softening the snow and making our task more arduous, we rested. At that elevation we had fine views of the Weisshorn, the Rothhorn, Monte Rosa (15,217 feet, and next in height to Mont Blanc), the Lyskamm, Castor and Pollux, the Dent Blanc, and nearly all the Alpine monsters of this region except the Matterhorn—coyest of the family. Five or six glaciers could be distinctly seen for the greater part of their length and breadth. While feasting on this incomparable scene of icy magnificence drops of rain began to fall, the majestic outlines of Monte Rosa vanished in a cloud, the whole prospect became blurred, and, most reluctantly, I decided to return to Zermatt. But, that nothing might be wanting to make the excursion prosperous, we were, on the way, favored with a view of the Matterhorn only a shade less admirable than the one I have already described.

CHAPTER XII.

EARLY ALPINE FLOWERS—A WEDDING-FEAST—THE RHÔNE VALLEY AND GLACIER—FURCA PASS.

WHAT do you say to meadows so thickly set with forget-me-nots that they are unbroken stretches of blue? If pieces of the sky had dropped on the grass, the effect would have been about the same as that which we saw often repeated in the valley of the Rhône. The shade was the faintest of the many blue tints that one sees in Alpine fields. The corn-flower grows rank in June, but is not coupled with the flaming poppy as often as in some other countries of Europe. In the upper pastures are two species of flowers—each as blue as a perfect sapphire. Both grow close to the ground. One is small and star-like. The other is bell-shaped and slender. I have picked it at a height of 7,000 feet. The yellows are in great force. Dandelions and buttercups everywhere remind the American tourist of home. There is a large, graceful anemone of a yellow so delicate as to be almost white. If it does not thrust its exquisite head through the snow, it follows hard upon the disappearance of the icy mantle. A flower of the kind we call "ladies' delight"—of a pure lemon-color—is profusely distributed. In some parts of Switzerland one comes upon fields all ablaze with buttons of gold. I give the English equivalent of the French and German names by which this showy flower is commonly known here. And the reds of various depths are only less abundant than the yellows. Of these the Alpine rose—as it is just breaking into blossom this month—is most captivating. The bud, as it begins to open, looks like a cutting of coral. Daisies supply the white to this wonderful enameling of Nature. Or, shall I say that it is a carpet so deftly woven as to defy the imitation of its combined hues in any piece of mortal handiwork? "You could not see the grass for flowers." This extravagance of the poet does not overstate the floral wealth of some of the fields that border the Rhône between Brieg and Viesch. Stay! I must not omit to mention some wild violets of extraordinary size and beauty. These I found in only one place—far above the Rhône glacier—and earned their possession by a hot scramble up a very steep hill while the carriage was taking its long and zigzag way round.

At Viesch we came upon a scene that is interesting everywhere—a wedding-feast. As the carriage rolled through the narrow street of the little village, the driver fired a volley of shots from the end of his whip. He was a fine fellow, and wore, as a badge of his calling, a dashing green hat with a blackcock's feather stuck in the band. There were three spirited horses, their necks encircled with bells which jingled musically. We were conscious of producing an effect as we rattled up to the door of the only inn, but were hardly prepared for the reception which seemed to await us. There stood not only the landlord and his staff of attendants, but a large number of men and women, evidently dressed in "their best." They all stepped forward as if to welcome us, and at the same time a brass band inside of the house struck up a joyous air. The situation was really embarrassing; and we were relieved when we discovered that this effusive reception was intended not for ourselves, but for some other people who were very much expected. The faces of the bystanders lengthened when they saw that we were not the persons so anxiously looked for. All but the landlord and his immediate aids went back into the house, and our reception became not more marked than that of all other travelers alighting at these hospitable shelters for man and beast.

Then we learned that we had innocently interrupted the tranquil flow of a wedding-breakfast—having been mistaken for some belated guests of great importance. The bridegroom was the landlord himself. He looked radiant with happiness. The bride, whom we saw later on, was a buxom lass, attired not in the high-colored and fanciful Swiss costume of which one reads in books. Her dress, if not a creation of the great Worth himself, was irreproachable in its Frenchiness. And there was not a single sign of Swiss nationality in the garb of any man or woman present. This was disappointing. But then the wedding-party was composed of the richer and "upper" classes of Viesch and the neighborhood—of twenty miles round.

The landlord, in the fullness of his heart, had spared no expense. In the dining-room were two long tables, from which a hundred guests were just rising as I peeped into it. Long rows of bottles, conscientiously drained to the last drop, were the principal objects in sight, save some Cupids in sugar which the knives of the banqueters had spared. As fast as the guests vacated the room they began dancing in couples. Up and down the hallways they went, waltzing furiously, while the band of twelve brass pieces played selections from Strauss. Every player had before him a bottle, which was replenished by an attentive waiter as fast as emptied. I never before realized the enormous cubic capacity of a brass band! While we were gazing on this mirthful scene, loud cracks of a whip were heard, and up came the delayed guests for whom we had been mistaken. There was another rush to the door, followed by a storm of shouts and kisses. The new-comers entered the house in a whirlwind of excitement. Without even stopping to doff their overcoats and cloaks, they plunged into the mazes of the waltz. A few minutes later the dining-room had been cleared of all obstructions, and the dancing then set in with an earnestness that would shame the languid beaux and belles of a New York ball. We reluctantly left the festivities at their height, and resumed the journey to Münster, where we purposed spending the night.

At the little inn of Münster we were received by a woman who had a handkerchief tied about her face, and looked tired out. She did not seem to care whether we stopped there or not. The house was in a state of fresh paint and repair, and the prospect for the night was not inviting. We were shown into a chamber which had neither carpet nor rug upon the floor. But that floor was scrupulously clean. The sheets on the beds were coarse, but they smelled of lavender. Everything was cheap but reassuringly neat. When the dinner was served — at the exact minute ordered — we could easily have criticised the crockery. But the plates were hot, as well as the soup, the fillet of beef and chicken tender and cooked to a turn, the pudding and cake nice, and the Swiss Muscat as delicate of flavor as it should be. After dinner a roaring fire in a wide-throated chimney and an Argand lamp burning on the table of this same room made the place far more comfortable and home-like than are many of the "Grand Hotels" of which Europe is full. A good night's rest and a capital breakfast completed the recommendations of this humble inn to the traveler's confidence and patronage. Its substance is in inverse ratio to its show. Besides all else, its windows on the west command in clear weather perfect views of the Weisshorn. This is about 14,800 feet high, and is the greatest object of interest in the Rhône Valley. As one toils up the ascent, he keeps the splendid white peak in sight mile after mile. He admires it from several view-points, but it never shows up to better advantage than when seen on a fine day from the elevation of Münster.

When you have been following up a river for two days, and seen it dwindle as you rise above the junction of one tributary brook after another, it is a great satisfaction to trace that river to its source. In its narrowest part the Rhône is a powerful stream. Its turbid waters rush along with a noise of thunder. They have cut in places a deep gorge, the bottom of which is far out of sight of the road. They have polished all the stones in their path into a general condition of smoothness. Nowhere is the erosive action of water more strikingly shown. When you stand at the foot of a stupendous glacier and see the beginning of this boisterous river, you no longer wonder at its youthful vigor. There is a great, dark cavern in the side of the glacier. It is now of a triangular shape. From this opening the Rhône issues with a fierce bound, as if straining to be free. Looking into the hole, you can see nothing beyond a distance of twenty feet. But you can hear the young torrent, as it tears its way down to the light, far back in the bowels of the ice-mountains.

Scientific observers have placed rows of stones painted black, in the valley just below the glacier, to show how much it is receding year by year. It is also shrinking in breadth, as you find out for yourself when you notice the old lateral moraines, or deposits of earth and stones, on the two sides of the slowly moving mass. These are many feet higher on the flanks of the channel than the mounds of the same kind which are now accumulating. Nevertheless, as you look up at an angle of about 45° and see this glacier rise for a mile or so until its tooth-like *scracs* stand out against the blue sky, you feel that the Rhône will not dry up at its fountain-head for many a year to come. This conviction is deepened as your horses struggle up the scientifically perfect road which takes you across the Furca. You keep the glacier under observation for more than an hour as you rise to the height where it bends and is lost in the recesses of the parent snow-field. You understand how frightful a thing is a crevasse, when you look down into one and discover that what seemed from below only a little rift, is a yawning gulf in which your coach and horses might sink to perdition without touching its sides. Individual *scracs* loom up from thirty to fifty feet high. And behind this awful fringe of ice you see a snow-slope (*névé*) of thousands of acres stretching far back to the base of a mountain which is itself crowned with a hoary burden. And then, if not before, you discover that the mighty Rhône glacier is but the protruding tongue (which it resembles in outline) of a body of snow and ice whose duration will outlast the arithmetic of puny men.

On the Furca Pass the snow is not deeper than on the Simplon, but there is more of it. Snow-banks higher than the driver's head line one side of the road at intervals for distances of a thousand feet. On the other side they had been in part pitched down the slope by the laborers who are always on hand. The summit is nearly 8,000 feet above the sea. As we climbed to it the horizon widened to the west and opened up a glorious view of Monte Rosa. As seen from the Furca Pass, this nearest rival of Mont Blanc looks like a pyramid —showing but a single peak in place of the two or three crests which I had made out as I looked across the long level of untrodden snow on the Gorner Grat. Thus it is that mountains, like everything else, look differently when viewed from different standpoints. The Matterhorn could barely be distinguished by reason of a haze in its vicinity. The Weisshorn and other nearer mountains had been so long in sight that we were glutted with them. It was the unseen which we longed to see. And when, as our team pulled up at the door of the Furca Inn, and we found that the great Finsteraarhorn of the Bernese group was not visible from that point, nothing we had seen before made up for the disappointment. I fear that this is only base ingratitude; for the day was an uncommonly good one for June 15th, and unmixed thankfulness should have been the only sentiment.

The Furca Inn enjoys the distinction of having been the home of Queen Victoria for three days in August, 1868. As Americans would say, she "ran the concern." The house was hired for her exclusive use. The royal bed, cooking-utensils, and all the domestic belongings were brought on from England. So were the doctor, the cook, the gillie, and even the humblest but still useful members of the Queen's household. In the dining-room hangs a framed list of the names of the whole party, save the Queen, whose photograph surmounts it. Among the autographs is that of John Brown. The proprietor exhibits with pride the little room in which Her Majesty slept. Whether the charges are higher in consequence, the present writer can not say, as he came and went with a rapidity quite unpleasing to the landlord.

From the summit of the Furca Pass down to Andermatt the ride would be prodigiously interesting if one were not satiated with the sights on the western ascent.

After a night at Andermatt the journey was resumed by carriage to Fluelen and then by boat to Lucerne. Of the scenery along that part of the route—savage and tame, gloomy and bright, by turns—one could write more enthusiastically if his impressions of the Furca were not still fresh.

CHAPTER XIII.

AVALANCHES ON THE JUNGFRAU—THE GUIDES OF GRINDELWALD.

THE avalanche about to be described started just below the peak of the Silberhorn, a few minutes before midday. At that hour the sun was beginning to make his rays felt in the frozen bosom of the Jungfrau. The Silberhorn is the showiest ornament of that most bewitching of mountains. It is an acute pyramid, and has a surface like frosted silver. It seems so dead and cold that one does not suspect its latent capacity for motion and sound. Yet it is from this statuesque spur that some of the most terrible avalanches of the Jungfrau are let loose. The sides are so steep that the ice and snow are always about to slide off, and, when the afternoon sun shines straight and hot upon them, the watcher for avalanches is never disappointed. I had been staring at the dazzling Jungfrau through smoke-colored glasses for some time, and waiting for the show to begin.

My point of observation was on a knoll or excrescence of the Wengern Alp—itself no mean mountain—from which the peerless Jungfrau can be seen at the shortest range. The day was perfect, the sky cloudless and the wind hushed. The only signs of life around me were the fluttering of butterflies and the humming of bees. The silence was awful. Far off, down in the Lauterbrunnen Valley, I could see the Staubbach Fall sparkling in the sunshine. From my exalted station its course could be tracked for a long distance before it flung itself into the abyss and kept its horsetail form complete for nearly a thousand feet. It looked so near, through the transparent air, that sometimes I fancied I could hear its roar. But this was an illusion. The only sound that breaks the stillness of the solitary height is that of the avalanche for which I was so patiently waiting.

Suddenly there was a gleam as of particles in motion on a part of the Silberhorn at which I had often looked with keen expectations. For just there could be discerned, without a glass, a series of long, parallel scratches such as avalanches always make. These are the grooves in which, like many human institutions, they may be said to run from year to year by force of habit. The rate of the motion was so slow and indeterminate—for a reason which I afterward found out—that one might, for a moment, question if the shining atoms were not stationary, after all. But no! though the pace seemed to be that of a snail, it was real and downward, and was soon too accelerated to be mistaken. The whole breadth of one side of the Silberhorn was moving, beyond a doubt. I was witnessing the sublime spectacle of a great avalanche. More swiftly it descended, and yet it seemed to crawl. In this way it slid along for a short distance—about 2,000 feet, as I afterward learned—when the mass fell over a jutting piece of ice or rock. Then it looked something like a waterfall. Below was another steep slope scored with the furrows of old avalanches. Here the motion was more rapid, but still surprisingly slow. Then, and not before, I heard a sound as of thunder. If the sky had not been one unspotted blue, I should have supposed a storm to be bursting somewhere among the mountains. It was the noise of the avalanche, at that moment reaching my ears from a distance, which was so deceptive. Later on, studying the phenomena of avalanches more deliberately, I ascertained that the scene of action —apparently not more than half a mile off—was often seven miles and never less than three. By noting the avalanche at the instant of its birth and counting the seconds of time till the first boom reported itself, one can calculate the distance with sufficient accuracy.

The Silberhorn being many miles from my standpoint in an air-line, it follows that the terms "small" and "slow," used in connection with its avalanches, are irrelevant. The breadth of the falling mass should be expressed in rods and not in feet. Its movement was exceedingly swift. What seemed to start as snow was, in fact, a great ice-cake, acres in extent, and perhaps fifty feet thick. This, striking against rocks in its course, broke into fragments which were indistinguishable in the distance. The apparent waterfall was composed chiefly of large lumps of ice. These were destined to be pulverized in good earnest as they continued their descent. Then I heard a sound as of hissing mingled with the deeper reverberations. A short distance—more than a thousand feet, probably—was thus traversed when the avalanche entered upon another stage of its career. It tumbled over another ridge—this time looking more like a waterfall than before. Here its volume was much contracted, and I could clearly see that this fact was due to the depth of the rock-bound channels through which it ran. Then it sprawled quite freely over a great open space or plateau, where it rested and formed a perceptible heap, thick at the center, and flattening out gradually toward the edges. Judging of its dimensions by my revised standards, I should say that it covered many acres, and was deep enough to bury an Alpine village of the average size.

Between noon and two o'clock, when I left the fascinating scene to seek for luncheon at the Hôtel des Avalanches, about three hundred feet below my mound of solitary observation, the Silberhorn had contributed nothing further to the pile at its base. But, at other points of the imposing range visible from the Wengern Alp, and especially on the main body of the Jungfrau, on a shoulder of the Monch, and on the steepest part of the Eiger, some avalanche was always in sight of the attentive observer. They usually resembled cascades from beginning to end. Rarely could one see the popular idea of an avalanche realized. Most people, I find, think of avalanches as broad tracts of snow which are transferred from the upper part of a mountain into a valley at its foot, keeping their general shape all the way. The Silberhorn specimen corresponded to this ideal for a short distance, as I have said. But all the others trickled down in a water-like way from top to bottom. The behavior of the falling ice and snow was so much like that of water that one could be convinced that he was beholding an avalanche only when he saw what took place at its terminus.

For, in five cases out of six, the icy torrent ended in a white heap, which still remained far up the mountain-sides, though below the true snow-line. Except that they lacked the well-known green tint, the tracts of snow and ice thus deposited looked like glaciers. Brooks ran from the lower end of them into the valleys far beneath.

The grooves—or deeply worn passage-ways—through which these avalanches descend, seem as if made by human hands. Some of them run as straight as bowling-alleys. Others have easy and graceful curves, as if laid out for a railway. But, almost without an exception, the transit of the avalanche from peak to base is interrupted by narrow rock-gorges. Against these it dashes itself with a fury expressed to my ear by a sound like that of a small cannon, which is heard far above the rest of the racket. The latter generally reminds one of the irregular firing of infantry, and appears to be caused by large fragments of ice and stones which are brought down with the lighter material. It is only an avalanche of the broadest pattern that imitates the deep roll of thunder. And this reminds me to mention that some of the most deafening sounds that one hears in the Alps are not easily explained. As he is gazing intently upon the Jungfrau, he is startled by an ear-splitting report as of a 500-pounder. He expects, as a matter of course, to see some enormous cornice of ice tumbling down. But all is motionless up there. He asks his guide what has happened. The man tells him that probably a big rock has fallen on the other side of the Jungfrau, or in some ravine on the spectator's side, but out of his sight. I have observed that, wherever there is a glacier, this loudest and most striking of all the mountain sounds is most often heard. At our hotel (de l'Ours), in Grindelwald, from which two glaciers can be seen, these extraordinary noises called the guests to the doors and windows many times on sunny afternoons. But not once did they see anything which served to explain the mystery. In defiance of the guides, I attribute the sounds to the cracking of ice in the glaciers under the influence of heat. There is something strangely uncanny in the occurrence of such appalling noises without any visible cause.

The guides of Grindelwald, and of all the Bernese Oberland, are an aristocracy. I am referring to those who pilot you safely among the real dangers of the Jungfrau, the Wetterhorn, the Schreckhorn, the Finsteraarhorn, and the other first-class peaks. The most distinguished of them are named in all the hand-books. They pose as objects of admiration in the streets. And they are well worth looking at. They are lithe and sinewy, with frank, resolute faces. They mostly dress in corduroy velveteen, with slouch hats of the same. Their yellow beards sweep their breasts. A provokingly slow gait also identifies them. They walk—unless under the spur of necessity—about half as fast as the ordinary American or Englishman. A friend of mine, in tow of a guide, consumed six hours in the ascent of the Wengern Alp from Grindelwald. The usual time is only three hours. But he arrived at the top perfectly unblown, and then appreciated the wisdom of going slowly. These men are very taciturn. They give opinions about the weather with great reluctance, if at all, and will not converse about anything while in the act of climbing. Thus they save their wind, the want of which is so trying to inexperienced Alpine tourists. But, what they lack in affability they make up in essential service. They will stand by their employer in every tight place, and will rescue his remains and bear them back to the valley, if he persists in despising the guide's advice and perishes in consequence.

These trusty fellows make great friends of members of the Alpine Club, and are sometimes well paid for leaving their beloved Switzerland and aiding in the conquest of high mountains in the antipodes. One of the corps has visited both India and New Zealand for this purpose. He showed as much sagacity in attacking the redoubtable giants of those distant countries as if he had known all about their weakest points from his infancy. In every case he took his patron successfully to the top, by a route which he instinctively chose as the easiest and the best. This guide returned home through London, and, while there, his employer made him the subject of an interesting experiment to test his "bump" of locality. One evening the man was asked to take a ride across London in a cab. He was driven a distance of many miles, and the route was purposely made as tangled and intricate as possible. Arriving at their destination—the house of an Apine celebrity—the cab was dismissed. After a short detention, the guide was told to return with his employer through the same streets which they had traversed in their roundabout journey. And he did it without making a single mistake, although an entire stranger in the great city. The man had not the faintest suspicion that he would be asked to do this difficult thing. He had almost unconsciously marked down the whole labyrinthine route. He did in London exactly what he would have done without the least effort among the mountains of his native land. His observation and memory of trifles supplied the unerring clews by which he retraced his way through the maze of the metropolis.

CHAPTER XIV.

EXCELSIOR AND THE MAIDEN.

THE hero of Longfellow's poem, "Excelsior," has long been a favorite subject with artists. Among the many full-length fancy portraits of that rash young man, is one which represents him in a loose sack-coat with knee-breeches, a rolling shirt-collar displaying his open throat, and the long ends of a necktie streaming in the winds. The costume was charming, but too airy for the higher Alps, to which he was bound. He had a little kit, presumably of clothes, slung across his shoulder. He held aloft a stick to which was tied a white flag or banner inscribed "Excelsior." The artist had caught the spirit of Longfellow's verse, and had stamped enthusiasm and high resolve on the pleasant face of this young fellow.

I had been sitting for some time over an outdoor luncheon in front of the Hôtel des Avalanches, with lines of "Excelsior" running in my head. Before me was the Queen of Mountains.

The landlord had assured me that the top of the symmetrical peak was fifteen good miles away. It did not seem more than a mile off in the transparent atmosphere of that perfect June morning. It was equally impossible to realize that you could not see, with the naked eye, the figures—showing black against the spotless snow—of persons climbing the Jungfrau by paths directly opposite the house. There was no one so occupied that day, as the season for ascents does not begin till July. So I was obliged to take the landlord's word for it that the largest parties attacking the mountain were invisible from his hotel, except through the fine telescope which stood there on its tripod with joints greased and ready for use. Then I fell to meditating on the sad fate of the willful young hero of the poem. I amused myself imagining him as he toiled up those awful heights, after dark, floundering through the snow waist-deep, just missing the crevasses by an inch, starting little avalanches of loose rocks and ice (the larger, more overwhelming and dangerous snow-slides occurring only in the hours of full sunshine), and finally succumbing to fatigue and exhaustion and cold, and dying up there, far from human aid, with his banner still gripped in his hand. How much better, I thought, if he had taken a fancy to the maiden of the valley, and remained comfortable and happy down below!

And there was the identical maiden at my elbow! She had just poured out a cup of smoking, fragrant coffee for me, and stood waiting meekly to take another order. A prettier girl never 'tended on travelers. I addressed her in English, and found she spoke it well; and when she added—noticing that I was an American—that she had relatives in the United States, and had spent two years there on a visit, I felt that here was a sort of country-woman in this out-of-the-way place. Surely I had seen few American girls of twenty or thereabout comelier than this true daughter of the Alps. She was a niece of the landlord, she said, and she had the manners of a lady. As the season had but recently opened, and the tide of tourists not yet set in, there was a scarcity of hired help at the inn. She was assisting in the humblest ways to make everybody contented. She served me without any sense of humiliation, such as possibly I might have observed in her had she passed a few more years in America before returning to her dear old Swiss home.

Her pretty face and innocent, winning ways had divided my attention with the avalanches. I am not sure but that I missed some little ones while chatting with her. As I sipped the delicious coffee, my imagination paired her off with that headstrong youth in "Excelsior." I could not help thinking what a fool he was not to rest his weary head on that breast, as per invitation, instead of climbing the terrible mountain after dark.

Perhaps it was the mountain air—perhaps it was the coffee. Anyhow, my imagination became so excited that I thought I saw that same young man right before me, coming up the steep road from Lauterbrunnen. He was not two hundred feet away. There was no mistaking him. He had on the knee-breeches, the bob-tailed jacket, the cutaway collar and flowing necktie of the picture, and a small knapsack of the roll-pattern was strapped to his back. There, too, was the attractive face stamped with fierce resolution. But the most striking mark of identity was a white flag attached to a walking-stick which he carried over his shoulder like a musket. The wind was brisk and blew the flag out straight behind him. It did not, so far as I could see, bear the inscription "Excelsior," and this was the first shock to the illusion. As I looked wonderingly at him, he turned on his heels and shook his flag, which I could now see was only a pocket-handkerchief, high in the air, as if signaling some distant person.

This dumb show lasted about half a minute. Then he lowered his flag and strode up to the hotel. As he drew near enough, I saw that his eyes were deep blue, like those of the hero of the poem. So, for all these reasons, I at once christened him "Excelsior."

Excelsior, though a young man, was not a green traveler. He knew a good thing when he saw it. There was a pretty girl, and there was a little table covered with a clean white cloth, all set out with plates, glasses, knives, forks, and napkins, under an awning that screened it from the sun, with the peerless Jungfrau in full view. So, when he took his seat at the spare table near me, I was not surprised. He looked at the maiden, and she looked at him. Everybody would have said they were made for each other, so far as good looks are reasons for mating. She was not a full-blooded brunette, but her deep-brown hair and eyes and swarthy ruddiness of cheeks differentiated her from the blonde school of beauty. He was fair-haired, with a skin which the sun had reddened but not freckled, and just such a forehead (now that he had cast his slouched hat aside) as you see in Shelley's portraits. As he sat there, with his strong, shapely arm flung over the back of his chair, he looked the embodiment of youthful vigor and careless grace. The misleading outlines of modern clothes could not conceal the symmetry of his figure. How the sculptors must have wanted him for a model, if he ever came under their eyes, in Rome or Florence And they would have been equally glad, I am sure, to secure a like favor from the Swiss maiden.

Suddenly he glanced at his watch, and then accosted me in the language I expected to hear, for I knew him to be an American at first sight.

"Not a bad job, that—only four hours and ten minutes from Interlaken, and the muddiest road I ever saw, up the Wengern Alp."

"Well done," I replied. "The guide-books give six hours for it. But aren't you tired?"

"Not the slightest," he said, laughing pleasantly, and showing his fine white teeth. "Lucky for me, as I must do Grindelwald and the lower glacier before night."

This astonished me. I had found the ascent from Grindelwald over thousands of rude stone steps and through seas of mud, hard enough on horseback, and was dreading the descent as still more trying. And here was Excelsior talking about it as if it were only a little promenade on Broadway, not to mention the visit to the lower glacier, a good two hours' stretch (going and returning) from Grindelwald and more mud from three to six inches deep all the way, except for the stepping-stones.

"Well, you are plucky—young America all over!" I at length remarked, with a pride in the gameness of my countryman.

"I'm from Illinois," said he.

"And I from New York."

"Then we're sure not to quarrel," he rejoined, "for I've noticed that New-Yorkers and Westerners get along better together in Europe than Americans from any other parts of the country."

I said that I had often noticed the same thing, without being able to explain it. There was a singular instinctive aversion between New-Yorkers themselves and also between them and Bostonians and Philadelphians. But, whenever New York and Chicago met in any foreign country, the fraternization was spontaneous. Then I took the liberty of asking my young friend why he waved his handkerchief on the end of a stick just before pulling up at the hotel.

"Oh! only to signal a fellow over there on the Murren. We had walked together up the Lauterbrunnen Valley, and he turned off to climb the Murren while I kept on for the Wengern Alp. We agreed to exchange signals from the tops of the two mountains, or foot-hills, or whatever else they should be called. But he hasn't got up there yet, for I don't see a flutter of his handkerchief."

"Possibly because it is at least eight miles from here to Murren in an air-line," I said, smiling.

The maiden, who had been listening with great interest to this dialogue, her tender eyes fixed on the younger of the two speakers all the time, here broke in to say:

"Perhaps you would like to look through the glass down there. That will show you everything on the Murren plain enough." She spoke English with a foreign accent so delicate that types can not reproduce it.

"Thank you, miss," said Excelsior, sweetly, "I shall be very glad. But let me order the lunch first."

The young girl seemed happy to serve him. She handed him a bill of fare, and waited by his side while he looked it over. It was as good as a play to watch the two thus thrown together by Fate.

Excelsior examined the bill with great apparent interest. Every item in it seemed to raise a question which he asked in a voice so low that I could not hear him. I never saw a man so particular about his luncheon, and so long ordering it. But at last he got through, and the maiden hastened into the house.

"Fine girl, or rather, young lady, that," said I to Excelsior. "The niece of the landlord, and has been in America two years."

"I thought she was superior," replied Excelsior, "and wondered where she picked up her good English. What a musical voice and lovely—"

But while he was speaking the fair object of our comments reappeared upon the scene. I may have been mistaken, but it seemed to me that a cherry-colored ribbon, over which rolled a plain, broad white collar, had been retied in her absence. And this reminded me that Excelsior had, while speaking to me, been smoothing out the rumpled ends of his blue neckerchief. To my eye it looked more pleasing before, but I dare say he was not thinking of my taste in dress.

What I had told Excelsior about this young girl had caused a perceptible change in his manner toward her. He had been civil enough before, but now he was quite polite, as one who recognizes the difference between a landlord's niece and a common house-servant. But it was plain that her two years' residence in America had impressed him most deeply. To him she was in some sense an American girl. It was with a bow almost deferential that he said, if she pleased, he would now try the telescope, and perhaps be able to get a sight of his friend on the Murren. The maiden acted very much as if she expected and wanted this, for she smiled and tripped down the little slope before the house to the spot where the glass rested on its three spindle legs. Excelsior followed. What was said down there I do not know, for I did not think it my business to join them, and from the place where I still sat, watching for avalanches, I could not catch a word. I only repeat what I saw.

It seemed to take a great while to get that telescope into working trim. Nothing was the matter with it when I used it twenty minutes before; but now they had the greatest trouble in lengthening or shortening the focus and elevating or depressing the object-glass. For me one hand was enough to adjust the instrument, but now it took four hands, and they were for a long time unsuccessful. As far as I could make out things clearly, these hands appeared to be getting in each other's way occasionally; and, besides, there was one head too many. It sometimes seemed as if they were both trying to look through the telescope at once, and this was obviously impossible. And, finally, when they had the telescope all right, as I supposed, and Excelsior was about to pick up his Murren friend in good earnest, they would stop and lean on the long brass tube and fall to conversing with each other, as if they had clean forgotten the business in hand. Then, looking up, they saw me gazing down at them, and resumed their absurd manipulations of the glass with increased energy.

I felt just mischievous enough to shout to them: "Anything the matter? Can I help you?"

"No, thanks," he cried. "We are just catching the range now; something the matter with the swivel. Oh, there he is, swinging his handkerchief on the piazza of the Murren Hotel! And now he is looking through a telescope, too. He sees us!" Excelsior thereupon fluttered his own signal for about one minute with great enthusiasm. By means of the two glasses the friends had exchanged salutes across an interval of eight miles.

This ceremony over, Excelsior apparently transferred his interest to the Jungfrau, the Monch, the Eiger, and lesser peaks, as well he might have done, for there is no single view in the Bernese Oberland more sublime and satisfactory in all its details than that of the mountain-chain seen from the Wengern Alp. Here, too, the telescope was continually getting out of gear and defying the joint efforts of Excelsior and the maiden to make it work right. I do not know if they would ever have quitted the task which occupied them so intently had not a horseman and a lady in a *chaise-porte*, swinging between two stalwart peasants, arrived on the scene. The new-comers, of course, required immediate attention, and the maiden was too good a niece of the landlord to neglect his interests. So, with this single remark, made so loud that all of us could hear it, "I think you understand how to do it now, sir," she bounded up the slope like a chamois to look after the new guests. Excelsior followed a moment later, and sat down at the little table where his hot luncheon was about due.

I felt that a pretty comedy of real life had been interrupted by these arrivals. I hoped to see a second act of it when the maiden served Excelsior with his repast, but in this I was disappointed. She soon brought out the dishes and the half-bottle of Yvorne he had ordered, and put them before him. But she was silent and demure now, for there were new eyes upon her. Excelsior himself had an attack of gravity, for he ate and drank without saying a word to the maiden, who came and went. If it was not a case of love at first sight on his part, then I am no judge of the symptoms of that passion. As for the maiden, who can tell?

I am sorry not to gratify the legitimate curiosity of my readers further on this point; but I could not tarry longer on the Wengern Alp, even to report the progress of a genuine love-affair. An appointment at Grindelwald compelled me to hasten my departure. I bade good-by to Excelsior, with a hope that I should meet him at the Hôtel de l'Ours that night or next morning. He replied, in a confused manner, that he did not know. Perhaps he would spend just one night on the Wengern Alp; the house there seemed so snug and comfortable. "It would not be a bad idea, you know, to visit the glacier over there in the morning, while the snow is still hard and the footing good."

I did not feel familiar enough with Excelsior to joke him about another attraction—a second Jungfrau—so I only smiled. When I said good-by to the maiden, I could not help adding that I hoped she would see America again some day, and perhaps stay there; and, by a natural association of ideas, I glanced at the same time at Excelsior. For, far-fetched as the thought may seem, the mountain air was so stimulating that I persisted in imagining that the chance meeting of these two emotional young persons on the Wengern Alp was the beginning of a romance destined to end in a happy marriage. What a good-looking couple they would make!

I have never seen him or her from that day to this. But we all find out for ourselves the truth of the old saying that the world is small. I should not be much astonished to meet Mr. and Mrs. Excelsior some day; and then I shall tell him how much more sensible I think him to be than the young man in the poem, who had no taste for pretty Swiss girls.

CHAPTER XV.

AN ENGLISH ADMIRER OF THE "AMERICAN LANGUAGE."

At the Hôtel de l'Ours (the Bear Hotel of Englishmen and Americans who do not care to expose their French) I added another to the list of my pleasant English acquaintances. One morning, while sauntering in front of the hotel before breakfast, I noticed a young man with bright-yellow hair, whiskers, and mustache, calm gray eyes, and that perfect freshness of complexion which one rarely sees in men's faces outside of England. He was habited in corduroy from his jockey-cap down to his knee-breeches, and wore stout walking-shoes of the Alpine Club pattern. In his right hand he sported a sharp-pointed Alpenstock, which looked stained and worn with use, but was unscarred by branding-irons. His well-knit figure and his good face were a recommendation to all beholders. We exchanged glances, and would probably have spoken to each other then, if one of the long-bearded guides had not appeared and taken off Corduroy in the direction of the lower glacier. Corduroy was the name which, in absence of the authentic one, I conferred upon him. I regretted his hasty departure, for he seemed just the man to draw into an interesting conversation.

The next morning, at about the same hour, I found Corduroy standing alone, in the same place as before. He was again dressed for an outing, and had his Alpenstock still in hand. He was looking fixedly in the direction of the mighty Wetterhorn, whose snowy summit was now visible and now concealed, as the lazy clouds or mist-wreaths drifted back and forth. He puffed at a brierwood pipe calmly, and seemed engrossed in that occupation and the study of Wetterhorn's top, until he saw me looking at him. Then he pulled the pipe from his mouth, as one who expects to speak and be spoken to, at the same time walking toward me with a look of friendly recognition.

Being the older, I was the first to break silence, and I did so with a commonplace remark upon the weather, which was a little uncertain, but promising to be fine. And I could not resist the temptation to add that it reminded me of the day I ascended the Gorner Grat, 10,000 feet above the sea, only two weeks before. That being my only really hard climb in the Alps, I was as proud of it as a boy of his first trousers.

Corduroy's face expressed great interest. He asked me a number of questions about the state of the weather at Zermatt, and whether the hotels were crowded, and as to the condition of the road from Vispach to St. Niklaus, a bad bit generally. I answered him very fully, only too happy to show off my familiarity with the most wonderful mountain district of Switzerland. And I said patronizingly, I must confess: "Really, now, you ought to see the Matterhorn. It's worth the trouble, I assure you. I was the second man on the Gorner G,at this year, and as the snow was then about eight feet deep, and only a foot-path broken through it part of the way, the climbing was no joke. You would find it easier next—"

"But I have already seen the Matterhorn," said Corduroy, who had been quietly smoking his pipe during my remarks.

"From what point?" I asked.

"From the top. I made my second ascent last year. And hope to get round there in July for my third."

I have seen, in my day, many undemonstrative Englishmen. But this one beat them all. Who could have thought he would have listened so patiently to all my brag about that ant-hill of a

Gorner Grat when he had done the awful Matterhorn twice? I was astonished, and at first doubtful of Corduroy's entire veracity, though truth seemed to ooze out of every feature of his prepossessing face. I inadvertently glanced at the Alpenstock and saw no record of any performances written there.

Corduroy read my thoughts. He cast an eye on the smooth old Alpenstock and smiled as he said: "Oh! we never do that, you know."

Then I remembered to have heard that the people who do the least climbing generally have the most names of conquered peaks on their Alpenstocks; so that, in fact, the absence of the dreadful Matterhorn from Corduroy's staff became a sort of proof that he was not lying to me. I blushed at my unworthy suspicion. It was now my turn to become deeply interested. I asked him many questions about his ascents of the most difficult mountain in all Europe. He answered briefly and modestly, and I also learned from him by the corkscrew process (for I never saw a man with less vanity) that he had ascended Mont Blanc, the Jungfrau, the Weisshorn, Shreckhorn, and Finsteraarhorn once each, and that he was now on the point of attacking the Wetterhorn, toward which he had been gazing, but feared that the impending change of weather might compel him to give it up.

I asked him where he had been the day before, with the long-bearded guide.

"Oh, only up to the Eismeer there," he said, jerking his thumb toward a white and heavenly sea of ice, which shone at that moment, through a rift in the clouds, forming a horizon line of 12,000 feet above the ocean-level. It almost gave me a crick in the neck to look at it.

"Of course no guide was needed for a thing like that," he added. "But the old fellow wanted a job; so I took him along to carry the lunch-basket. Aren't you going to do the Eismeer?"

"Well," said I, laughing, "I might perhaps get as far as the foot of the glacier. But I guess I should have to discount the rest."

Corduroy broke out laughing. "Excuse me," said he, "but you Americans are so amusing. Ha! ha! Discount! what a capital word! So expressive, you know. It means, if I understand it, that you would go to the foot of the glacier, and say that you had been to the top. Ha! ha! No offense meant."

"Not quite as bad as that," I replied, laughing in turn. "To discount it, in my sense of the word, is to imagine the rest of the glacier and the Eismeer at the top, from the sample seen below. Have you never discounted anything that way?"

"Ha! ha! No! no! we are never allowed to

do that. Discounting would be dead against our rules."

I noticed that, for the second time, he employed the pronoun "we," from which I inferred that he was a member of some association of mountain-climbers. As he seemed so much amused by the slang use of the word "discount," I thought I would favor him with a few more of our latest and choicest inventions in that line, which happened to have lodged in my memory:

"You tumble to my exact meaning now, I hope."

"Ha! ha! Tumble to, signifying to understand, of course. That's better than discount, if possible. I do so admire the American language. So rich, you know. Ha! ha!"

I never saw a man so easily tickled. In the ecstasy of his mirth he capered about like a dancing bear, while his laughter rang out till it woke the echoes in old Mettenberg which frowned above us. The noise drew a number of the hotel guests to the door, and others peered through the windows at him.

"They'll think it's a circus," said I, innocently.

"A circus. Ha! ha! how forcible, and so funny—just like you Americans! And perhaps you'll next say I'm the performing clown." And that idea started Corduroy off in another fit of laughter.

"That's about the size of it."

"The size of it! How good! So humorous, you know. Ha! ha!"

"You seem to catch on to American slang like a native," said I.

"Catch on. Ha! ha! Well, that's the best yet. A sort of figure of speech meaning to seize something as it flies, I suppose."

"You have got it down fine."

Corduroy laughed gently in an accommodating spirit; but I do not think he caught the precise meaning of this last expression. He made no comment on it, and I was glad he did not ask me to explain it, for I could not have done so.

"By-the-way," said Corduroy, "as you are an American, perhaps you can tell me why an old story or joke is called a chestnut in your country. It may be very funny—in fact, it must be, as it is American. But I don't tumble to it, as yet. Ha! ha!"

For the honor of my country, I would have liked to clear up the great chestnut mystery to this delightful young Englishman. I had heard some accounts of the origin of the word in its application to threadbare anecdotes and moldy conundrums, but they were all unsatisfactory. "I am sorry I can not answer your question," said I, at length; "but I can give you points on the chestnut-bell."

Corduroy was all ears while I explained to him the construction of the little instrument which had already worked so useful a reform in the clubs of my country.

"Well, well," he cried, "American inventions are truly wonderful. And this chestnut-bell beats them all. Ha! ha! I'm so glad I met you this morning! I'll have a chestnut-bell made according to your description of it down at Interlaken by a metal-worker I know there. It's just what we have long wanted. You see, some of our fellows don't climb any new mountains. They keep telling all about the old mountains they climbed years ago. Now, I just want to shut 'em up. And the chestnut-bell is the thing to do it. Ha! ha!" And Corduroy roared with delight.

"All right," said I; "but as the chestnut-bell is the latest thing out in my country, let me offer you a piece of advice."

"What is it?" asked Corduroy, eagerly.

"It is this: Don't give it away."

"I see—I see. You mean I must keep this idea of a chestnut-bell to myself, so as to get the start of all the other fellows. How very expressive! Give away. Ha! ha!"

I was about to make some other valuable suggestion on the subject, when I saw among the group which then filled the open doorway a slight figure beckoning to me quite earnestly. When that small hand is gesticulated in that peculiar way, I do not pretend not to see it. Experience has taught me that it is much easier to answer the summons in person at once than to explain later on why I did not do so. I said "Ta! ta!" to Corduroy, and moved toward the house.

As I hurried away, he called out to me, "There is no getting ahead of you Americans, you know."

"It will be a cold day when we get left, and don't you forget it!" was my answer shouted back at him, exhausting my small stock of slang in that supreme effort.

"Just so," he cried. "Ha! ha! Cold day! Get left! What a world of meaning! Be sure I won't forget it! Ha! ha!"

I never saw Corduroy again. We had a little unambitious excursion of our own to make that day, and did not get back to the Bear before dinner-time. Then I inquired after the gentleman in corduroy, and learned that he had given up the Wetterhorn on account of the thick weather, and had started off for a walk over the Grimsel to the Rhône glacier. He was well known at the hotel, being one of its regular visitors. This steadiness of patronage might naturally be expected of him, for he proved to be one of the most distinguished members of the Alpine Club, famous for his devotion to mountain-climbing in Switzerland, and a terror even to the hardiest guides, by reason of his courage and perseverance against all obstacles. He had, it seems, a passion for new routes and short cuts, which I hope will not some day end the merry life of Corduroy. After this explanation, I understood his occasional allusions to "we" and "us" and "our fellows" and "our rules," which forbade this and that. And sometimes now, at two o'clock in the morning, while I am lying awake and thinking over many things, I catch myself wondering if Corduroy has ever introduced the chestnut-bell to the Alpine Club, and, if so, how the retired climbers like it.

CHAPTER XVI.

PREHISTORIC LAKE-DWELLERS—AN ISLAND INN AND ITS MEMORIES.

If one cares to inquire about that mysterious prehistoric race known as the lake-dwellers of Switzerland, he can do so to his heart's content at and about Zürich. If he wants to dig up their remains for himself—and has plenty of money and time to spare—there is nothing to hinder him from doing so. He has only to run a deep plow through places along the shore of Lake Zürich where there are indications of peat, and it is almost certain that sooner or later he will come on traces of a primeval village. The first sign of it would be the badly decayed fragments of a thick stake or pile. Sometimes well-preserved specimens of these piles are found in great numbers, though more often they are rotted out of all recognition. They are the props which held up the lake-villages high and dry. They were driven into the chalky soil of the lake-bottom, where they stuck fast. In the unknown centuries which have flown since then, those parts of the lake have filled up, peat has formed to the depth of five or six feet, and on top of this are two or three feet of mold and loam. Having struck a pile, our investigator must go straight down through the deep peat-bed which surrounds and underlies it. He will soon come to a half-earthy stratum, in which, if lucky, he will find numerous queer things. For this particular layer may contain many kinds of objects —useful and ornamental—once highly prized by, if not indispensable to, the comfort and happiness of the simple lake-dwellers. It may readily be imagined that such articles would accidentally fall from the house into the water beneath, there be buried in the mud, and never be recovered by the owners. Doubtless some of them, when broken or worn out in use, were thrown down there with a "good-riddance."

It is believed, from many indubitable signs, that these lake-houses (built of wicker-work) were destroyed by fire to an extent that would appall any insurance company of our day that took risks on such property. You see, these people, like some savage tribes now existing, had much difficulty in starting and keeping fire. They obtained it only by the rapid twirling of a pointed piece of wood on a flat piece. The friction ignited some tinder-like substance. As they had no stoves, hearths, or chimneys, this precious fire was kept — so far as modern conjecture goes — upon a stone in the middle of the hut. There it was watched night and day to preserve it and see that it did no harm. But occasionally the watchers slept, or went off fishing or courting, and then the fire, as is its mischievous habit, caught upon the nearest combustible stuff. And so in five minutes poor Mr. Lake-Dweller was houseless and homeless, and all his earthly possessions were at the bottom of the lake. It was a great piece of good fortune if the entire village did not disappear at the same time. Think of such a catastrophe occurring, and no newspaper to do justice to it!

We left our enthusiastic explorer with his boots ankle-deep in the boggy soil beneath the peat-bed. It has cost him a great deal of money to lay open the treasure-bearing stratum. But he feels amply rewarded even if he has lighted on nothing better than the stone age of the lake-dwellers, for there he will find most interesting proofs of the identity of human nature in different ages and climes. The earliest period in their shadowy history is called "stone," to distinguish it from the "bronze" age that followed. In point of fact, the former overlapped the latter, but for convenience the two designations are employed as best expressing the chief characteristic of the two ages. In the first, stone was the material out of which hammers, adzes, and arrow-heads were made. The patterns of these closely resemble those adopted by our North American Indians. In weight as in shape there is no recognizable difference; and the same good judgment was shown in the choice of stones best adapted for every purpose. The most skillful lapidaries of our day could not produce finer work in porphyry, flint, and crystal than may be found among the relics of the lake-dwellers. Though a very practical people, they were not without æsthetic tastes. Otherwise, in making their rude pottery by hand they would not have introduced decorative lines and dots. Nothing could be more severely simple than the designs which appear on their water-jars, cooking-vessels, and drinking-cups. The lines are crossed like a hedge-fence. The dots are arranged in rows, several of these forming a band. You there see the art of pottery in its infancy. Utility was the chief end sought, and, doubtless, the unsymmetrical and clumsy pots, bowls, pitchers, and goblets of the lake-dwellers answered their purpose admirably.

As to the fishing-nets of their day, no improvement could be desired. The specimens recovered are made of the strongest hemp lines, of large size, with "bobs and sinkers." Lake Zürich supplied the table with excellent fish in that far-off time, as now. And the lake-dwellers were mighty hunters also. Bones of the bear and deer and all the wild animals of the present Switzerland, with those of creatures now extinct, are mingled with the other remains. They were a pastoral race, besides They raised millet and other cereals, and ground these into a coarse flour, as appears from samples of their baked bread. Instead of the horse they had the reindeer as a servant, and, with training, he proved a useful one. For aught I know, he carried his master into battle—in which case his speed would have enabled him to make a quick retreat when the enemy's fire of arrows became too hot. For, alas! the lake-dwellers were either a persecuted race or an aggressive one at some stage of their history. Implements of war are the most common of finds, and the site and structure of the villages—so far as we understand the subject—indicate extreme precautions for defense. It is evident that the settlements were situated at some distance from the old shore of the lake and approachable only by boats, or possibly by a bridge, which could be raised or turned on a pivot at pleasure.

It might be the fortune of our patient friend the digger to strike a mine of bronze implements. Then he would realize the inventive capacity of the lake-dwellers. The discovery or adoption of the art of combining copper and tin as bronze stimulated their native ingenuity wonderfully. It is supposed that they obtained the two metals (rare, if found at all, in Switzerland) from England, Wales, or some other country, in the course of trade. Be this as it may, the quantity of bronze in use was large. It was employed for every purpose of war and peace. Spear-heads, knives, and daggers or swords of the "Roman" pattern, lie in the stratum by the side of coarse needles, hair-pins, bracelets, and other articles of toilet use and ornament. The composition of the bronze is about ninety per cent of copper and ten of tin. This is slightly varied at times. The objects distinctively ornamental have a brighter red or even a golden color, and are really beautiful.

But all the trouble and expense of attaining this knowledge about the lake-dwellers of Switzerland may be saved by the diligent searcher for truth. He need only visit the magnificent collection of antiquities at Zürich as I did, and learn all these things much better at second-hand. But he will be baffled if he expects to discover from any evidence before him how many centuries ago the lake-dwellers lived, and suffered, and passed away. Speculation is rife on this subject. Antiquaries hold to views widely different. Where they disagree, it is not for the humble learner to decide. It is much wiser for him to enjoy unquestioningly the inspection of these remarkable relics of a prehistoric age than to rack his brains in futile efforts to fix the precise period of the lake-dwellers in the eras of man.

When we were shown into a chamber of the Insel Hotel at Constance, my curiosity was at once excited by the singular appearance of a room which opens out of that apartment. It is not large enough for a parlor. It is too poorly lighted for a study or boudoir. It has three narrow windows which are partly overgrown with ivy. They look on Lake Constance, which then shone a deep green under the setting sun. The wall of the chamber at the place where the two rooms join is about two and a half feet thick. Putting my hand upon the showy paper that covers the walls, I know by the touch that these are stone. Then, as I observe that the little room is round in shape, the thought flashes upon me that it is part of a tower, and perhaps in by-gone times may have been a cell in which somebody was confined.

The servant, who had been watching me in an amused manner, then made his dramatic stroke. " This was the dungeon of John Huss," was all he said. And it was enough. His words recalled the fact that Huss, at some time previous to his execution by order of the Council of Constance, was imprisoned in a Dominican monastery of that city. Now the "Insel" is that identical retreat, transformed into one of the most picturesque and interesting hotels of Europe. The venerable cloisters have been preserved intact. The great refectory of the monks is now a restaurant full of good cheer in meat and drink. It witnessed scenes of revelry in the old monastic days, as one may gather from the jovial inscriptions still preserved on the walls. The church of the fraternity is now the immense dining-room of the hotel, modernized and made secular of aspect. This building was a stronghold four centuries ago. Then, as now, it was surrounded by water. For this reason it was selected as one of the successive prisons of John Huss. There he was beyond the hope of rescue by his friends and partisans.

Visiting the Guildhall of Constance next day, I saw additional evidences of the precautions taken for his safe-keeping. There is the massive door of oak, with iron bands and enormous locks, which was rarely if ever opened during his confinement. For a little wicket in this door served for the inspection of the prisoner by his jailers and also to pass in food to him. There is the great stone in the dungeon-floor to which he was chained. The windows of the cell as they now appear are small; but much larger than the old apertures. One of these openings for air and light is exhibited at the Guildhall. It is only a slit of three or four inches wide, cut through the thick stone. Among the other objects relating to the martyrdom of Huss, in the same collection, are the van in which he was borne to the place of execution and the brocaded chairs occupied by the Emperor Sigismund and the Pope at the council. In the plain of Brühl, just outside the city of Constance, one may see a rude memorial which marks the place where Huss and later on Jerome of Prague were burned at the stake. It is a great rock, quite rough, covered with ivy and bearing appropriate inscriptions. A tall iron railing prevents a near approach to the spot.

CHAPTER XVII.

CARLSBAD—PRAGUE—DRESDEN.

IF people would take only half the pains to keep their health that they do to recover it when lost they would be spared a great deal of trouble. At Carlsbad—the fashionable spa of Austria—we found everybody getting up at five or six o'clock to drink doses of scalding brine. A light leather strap slung across the shoulder of each person supported a porcelain mug. The wearer took his place in a long queue, and the procession moved slowly on to the fountain. Carefully surveying the patients as they stood in line, one could see that they were mostly a "damaged lot," as the auctioneers say. Their dress and bearing indicated that they belong to what is called "good society." Their ailments are the probable results of indolence and high living. If overfeeding is the matter with them, then Carlsbad is the very place for their cure. For I have never known a town where, at the hotels, the minimum of portion and the maximum of price are so scientifically adjusted in the interest of the landlords. It is bad manners to lick the platter clean; but if the guests of the Carlsbad hotels refrain from this, they miss an important part of their meals. It may be all very well for the landlords to collude with the doctors for the benefit of patients; but on behalf of those who are not invalids, and are suffering sharply from hunger, I protest against the universal adoption of the system.

It is the prescribed rule at Carlsbad to take as much hot water as possible on an empty stomach. Everybody knows that there is more available room in the human frame for such a purpose in the early morning hours than at any other time of day. And so we find all Carlsbad up with the sun. This rule is rather hard on the brass bands of Carlsbad. For the municipal ordinances require them to play lively tunes at the principal fountains while the melancholy processions are filing on. With what contempt those mighty drinkers of beer and wine over there in the orchestra must regard all the people who think so highly of hot water! It seemed to me as I looked upon the ruddy faces of the musical performers that the continual pounding of drums and wrestling with trombones must be as promotive of health as any other known form of manual labor. But of course it would be hard on the well people if every patient should join a brass band to recover his "tone."

When a member of the procession reaches the spring which is his goal, he unslings his porcelain mug and hands it to a boy in waiting. The water at most of the springs—they are many—issues with some force amid a cloud of steam, from a small pipe. The mug is filled in a trice and handed back to its owner. If he likes it very hot, he gulps it rapidly. If he prefers it lukewarm, he lets it cool a little. Many persons suck up the water through a glass tube, as if to prolong the enjoyment. The Carlsbad waters taste differently, and perhaps no two people find exactly the same flavor in the outcome of the same spring. With regard to the stronger waters of the group, one often hears it said, "Why, it tastes like chicken-broth, with too much salt in it!" If this is true, then I can only say that some of the salt ought to be extracted and the water put on the bill of fare of the Carlsbad hotels, where the article called "chicken-broth" does not resemble the real thing at all. Because of this pleasing flavor — reminiscence of the full meals of happier days—the drinkers seem really to like the waters.

As each person can have only one mugful at a time, he must go back again to the tail end of the line as often as he wants more. This gives him plenty of exercise, if he happens to want two or three quarts the same morning. Meantime, those who have dutifully taken their doses—as ordered by some medical tyrant—saunter up and down the pleasant walks of Carlsbad and chat with their friends, and make themselves as cheerful and agreeable as it is in the nature of things possible for a human being to be an hour or two before breakfast. No time of day could seem more unfavorable for flirtations. But, unless all the usual signs mislead at Carlsbad, I should say that, as in the familiar song, " the old, old story is told again at five o'clock in the morning," often, in and about the peopled colonnades of that place.

The Sprudel Spring, which spouts the highest and sends out the most water, is also the hottest. It is said that eggs may be boiled in it; and I am prepared to believe the assertion, after observing the timid way in which the most confirmed drinkers put the water to their lips. The spring is irregular in its action. At intervals varying from five to ten minutes it shoots with a force which makes the bystanders step back to avoid the scalding spray. People who claim to be wiser than the rest of us, say that the Sprudel and all the other springs result from the following operations in Mother Earth: The water of some river or lake in the vicinity of Carlsbad filters through the ground and between the rocks to a depth of two or three miles or any distance you like. On the way this water becomes saturated with salts of various disagreeable kinds. At a certain point in its downward journey it encounters the "internal fires," or, at all events, a heat sufficient to decompose some of the salts in the water and produce an explosive gas. This gas, in its turn, projects the heated water through some convenient hole clear to the surface of the earth, like shot out of a gun. As nobody knows anything about what takes place away down there, this explanation is, perhaps, as good as any that may be offered. It is an interesting fact, by-the-way, that at the time of the great earthquake which destroyed Lisbon and shook up so many other places, the Sprudel stopped flowing for three days!

Sign-painters ought to make a good living in Prague. For its population is about equally divided between Germans and Bohemians, and each race prefers its own language to that of the other. As a result, the enterprising merchant is obliged to hang out signs which may be read by both races. In order to catch the custom of those who can not read at all, he also calls the pictorial art into play. Everybody can understand the picture of a sack of flour standing on end, or of loaves of bread, or of bundles of hay or wood, or a pile of coal, or a man pulling a tooth. But these embellishments are reserved for the poorer quarters. In the really handsome, newer parts of Prague the double sign suffices to meet the demands of all intelligent purchasers among the two peoples. As every cashier and clerk is expected to understand both German and Bohemian well enough to sell goods to either race, you will readily see that accomplished linguists are a necessity in the business circles of Prague, especially when French and English and American visitors to that city are not uncommon.

Though differing widely in race and language, the people of Prague are one in the matter of dress. Their costume is that of the rest of the world, as affected by that great equalizer, the railway. The Graben is full of precisely the same persons, externally considered, that one sees on the boulevards of Paris, in Oxford Street, or Broadway. During my drives and walks about Prague I did not note a single item of attire which might not be found in the most conventional of New England villages. Jews abound in Prague, but not one of them could be identified by that peculiar and very gloomy apparel which is worn by their brethren in some other parts of Austria —say, in Carlsbad. There the Jew is known afar off by his long, flowing black robe, matched by a cap which he pulls down on the back of his head. This robe lends to the wearer a gravity and dignity in full accord with his serious face. The Carlsbad Jews are good-looking, and the human parade at and about the springs would lose much of its interest if they were left out. The tiresome uniformity of dress which we find in all the cities of Central Europe is fast robbing Continental travel of a charm once potent. It is bad enough to have the hotel bills-of-fare everywhere just alike, though one can put up with lack of variety if the food is well cooked and wholesome; but, when one sees, on all sides, the same dresses, even to the cut of a collar, and the nice adjustment of a neck-tie, he feels cheated out of his just and reasonable expectations. This is one of the worst respects in which pictorial geographies and cyclopædias too often lead their readers astray.

You would hardly expect ever to be called on to complain that people were too courteous. Yet, when it involves you in the necessity of taking off your hat and describing a semicircle with it every minute or two, you get just a little tired of the extreme politeness that greets you all through Bavaria and Austria. I do not now allude to the profound bows of your hotel landlord, your porter, your "boots," and your cabman. I do not speak of the man who sells you something—if it is nothing more than a cake of soap—and bends almost to the floor when you leave his shop. These men have relations with you which make their courtesies a matter of course. You do as you please about bowing back to them. As a rule, you do it if you are not stiff-necked and hard-hearted. I now refer to the army officer or other gentleman who doffs his cap to you most politely every time he enters or leaves a railway-carriage in which you are sitting. But I have chiefly in mind the pedestrians of high and low degree whom you meet 'n great numbers along the country roads of Austria and Bavaria. These men, if natives, never fail to bare their heads to you. And you must do the same to them, or lose that good opinion of your own manners which every man naturally wishes to preserve. Perhaps we Americans need those lessons in politeness which are forced upon us in some parts of Europe. But it is nevertheless a little trying to be continually required to exchange the most respectful salutes with perfect strangers. I don't think there is any danger that our fellow-countrymen will ever catch the habit very badly.

The superintendent or chief inspector of the great Picture-Gallery of Dresden was quite indignant when I asked him if the Saxon Government intended to refuse to American artists and students access to that treasure-house, as had been reported. For his answer he sent at once for a promising young American, who was then copying one of the masterpieces of the gallery. Placing his hands affectionately on this young man's shoulders, he simply said, "No! no! impossible!" Then he fled from the scene, as if my question had stung him. It is true, as I have since learned, that Saxony, while feeling affronted by the American thirty per cent duty on the paintings and statuary of her subjects, does not propose to retaliate by excluding our compatriots from her world-famous collections of art. On the contrary, American artists are very popular there, and will continue to be welcome visitors at all the galleries. The Saxon Government hopes that the American art-tariff will be abolished or reduced some day, in response to the demand of the best artists of our own country, and without the pressure of any reprisal. If one would know how valuable are the privileges enjoyed by American artists and students abroad, let him enter the famous gallery of paintings, which is the chief glory of Dresden, and look around him. He will see in almost every corner some person sitting before a renowned picture and copying it at leisure. Sometimes the picture still hangs on the wall, in which case the body and the easel of the artist half conceal it from view. Several masterpieces which I wanted to inspect closely were partly eclipsed in this way. Sometimes the gem is taken down and put at the artist's exclusive disposal. You find its wooden back confronting you in some nook of the gallery, and, if you try to peep round for a look at it, the person at work copying it is apt to make you feel that you are an intruder. I say that it is a great thing to enjoy these advantages over the general public, and be able to derive a profit from them by selling copies to American customers, who can take them home duty free. One may not like the thirty per cent tariff, and still may feel most kindly disposed toward every American artist and art-student in Europe, and earnestly hope that their privileges will not be curtailed in the least.

There is one room in this picture-gallery where I have not yet seen an easel set up with a man or woman toiling behind it. That is the apartment solely occupied by the immortal Sistine Madonna of Raphael. Such a presence there would seem almost a profanation. For that greatest work of the greatest of artists is a shrine before which men of all religions and of no religion pay the same unaffected homage. You remove your hat instinctively as you enter the little room. You cross the floor on tip-toe. You gaze upon the wonderful canvas in silence. If you exchange words of admiration about it with your companion or neighbor, you do it in a whisper. As you reluctantly quit the place to go directly to your hotel—for nothing in the gallery interests you much after you have seen the Sistine Madonna—you realize better than before what is the highest and truest mission of art in the world.

CHAPTER XVIII.

BERLIN—ITS MILITARY ATMOSPHERE.

Two men sit on their horses like statues in front of the Brandenburg Gate of Berlin. They wear spiked helmets. The numerous buttons on their tight-fitting coats gleam in the sun Their weapons are swords. When you ask to what crack regiment they belong, you are told that they are policemen. You find hundreds more of the same grave, martial persons, mostly on foot, in the Berlin streets. You soon come to distinguish them from the regular troops whom they so much resemble. But it is hard to tell where the policeman ends and the soldier begins. If the moral effect of this grim constabulary is as great on the citizens of Berlin as on the stranger within her gates, then there are few breaches of the peace committed here. At the railway-stations you see other men who are soldierly in their dress and bearing. They wear the well-known fatigue-caps with broad colored bands and a little circle embroidered just above the visor. Their breasts are decorated with metal badges, of which the crown emblem is a part. You naturally suppose them to belong to the army, and to be ornamented with some kind of "order," until you go near enough to read the word " Portier," with which they are labeled. Thus it is that a strong military air is imparted to Berlin, over and above that which comes from the corps in garrison here. This corps comprises all arms of the service. The various uniforms—sometimes simply neat, but often very showy—exhibited in Unter den Linden during the evening promenade, form one of the chief attractions of that most beautiful of Berlin streets. Such, at least, is the verdict of visitors—especially Americans with whom army accoutrements are happily things of the past.

It must be confessed that the most peaceful-minded person may catch the military fever here. The people of Berlin, like all other Germans, protest to you that they hate war and desire peace above all things. No men can look more pacific as they smoke their pipes and drink their beer, and listen to the best music in the "Gartens." Still, it is the truth that they impress the impartial tourist as the most warlike race in Europe. No capital that I have seen compares with Berlin in the predominance of military ideas and suggestions. The officers and privates everywhere on view are but a small part of this total. The aged and heroic Emperor, the Crown Prince, Bismarck, Moltke, Roon, and other heroes of the Franco-German War, are served up in every possible way in the shop-windows of every street. Statues, busts, oil-paintings, photographs of these distinguished men in full "regimentals," are as thick in Berlin as crucifixes and other religious symbols in the most devout city of Southern Italy. It is a patriotism which runs to idolatry. In the Königsplatz stands a splendid monument, designed to commemorate the victorious issues of the recent wars with Denmark, Austria, and France. On each of the four sides of the pedestal are bronze reliefs of the Kaiser and all the rest of the gallant company. If one is not tired of these repetitions of figures and faces, he may climb an interior staircase of the column and come out on a balcony, where he can regale himself with the sight of a noble work in mosaic, in which the identical celebrities reappear in new combinations and with still more brilliant effects. Visiting the modern picture-galleries about town, he can not enter a nook or recess so obscure that it does not hold at least one first-rate picture, or marble or bronze bust of the Emperor or his heir, or his great Chancellor, or his incomparable Field-Marshal and strategist.

It is but natural that the Germans should love to honor the illustrious sovereign, the statesman, and the general who have made their country united and powerful. They know perfectly well that what they have won by the sword can be kept only by the sword in that terrible struggle for national supremacy, and even for existence, of which Europe is the theatre. As long as the profession of the soldier is thus exalted above every other by force of circumstances, what wonder that the Germans should indulge their passion for hero-worship to an extent unknown in all modern history?

The American who passes through France and Germany finds this question a very interesting one: How long will it be before these two countries will be fighting again? He takes it for granted that they will fight some time. All the signs point to that conclusion. He sees troops incessantly drilling in all parts of Germany and France. If he can read the native papers, he finds in almost every column some allusion more or less covert, but unmistakably unfriendly in tone. If he inspects the rows of yellow-covered pamphlets at the railway book-stalls, he will be sure to see " Avant la Bataille," or " Pas Encore," or the spirited replies in German, of which those and other sensational volumes have been the occasion. Works like these are multiplying on both sides of the frontier. They seem to be pilot balloons sent up to try the winds. It is true that the authors are unofficial persons. They do not speak for nations. But they do, nevertheless, succeed in straining the relations between countries which require for the preservation of peace the observance of mutual forbearance, if hearty good-will can not be expected of them.

A great many Frenchmen have made no concealment of their burning desire for revenge ever since the war of 1870-'71. But in my previous visits to Europe I have never found the Germans so outspoken on this ticklish subject as at present. Every one with whom I have conversed believes that the renewal of the struggle is not far off. No reason is given for this belief. It is one of faith, resting on portents in the skies. There does not seem to be, in Germany, the least doubt of the sequel, if France, single-handed, should attempt to recover what she has lost. But there is some anxiety to know whether she would have Russia as an ally. In that event the Germans are counting on the support of Austria and Italy. These, however, are questions of the future, and there we will leave them, with the single remark that the physical and mental health of Bismarck and Moltke, as trusted counselors of the indomitable Kaiser, constitutes the best present security against any surprise in diplomacy or war at the expense of Germany.

I never saw in any one place in France as many French cannon as are packed in the great courtyard of the arsenal of Berlin. They line the sides of the quadrangle, and point to the center. Each of these pieces bears some terrible name—"Le Vengeur," "La Terreur," "Le Destructeur," "Le Volcan," "Le Borreau," and the like—which now read strangely by the light of history. Some show ugly scars, like bull-dogs gashed in fighting. A frequent mark is the tearing away of a lip of the muzzle, the effect of German shot. Others have deep scores in the sides, where the balls struck them and glanced off. They are mostly bronze of slender, graceful shapes, and profusely ornamented with arabesque raised patterns. They have a certain Gallic look of trimness and taste, and, if they failed to frighten off the German invader, they still survive as works of art in the German capital, and fulfill the peaceful mission of amusing the Berlinese. I roved among these trophies, and patted them on the back, stopping occasionally to decipher the date of their making. The year is cast in bold figures near the mouth of the gun, and is often accompanied by the name of the sovereign in whose reign it was born. There are specimens dating as far back as Louis XIV; others are marked "Napoleon," "Louis XVIII," "Louis Philippe," and the larger number "Napoleon III." As

I saunter among these grim souvenirs of the wreck of the Second Empire and the terrible humiliation of France, I wonder how a French soldier would feel if he were present among this throng of exulting Germans, with whom the exhibition is a treat inexhaustibly popular. But then, of course, no Frenchman visiting Berlin could bear the idea of witnessing these proofs of his country's disaster.

As this thought passed through my mind, I looked up from a long, handsome gun—"Le Tourbillon"—which I had been inspecting, and noticed a martial face near me. It had piercing black eyes, a clipped, white mustache, a prominent chin, and instantly reminded me of the portrait of Marshal Pelissier, Duc de Malakoff. The lips were grimly set, and there was no mistaking the frown in those corrugated lines of the brow which the civilian's hat did not conceal. Caught unawares, this remarkable face showed shame, rage, hate, and revenge, or I am no judge of the human countenance. But the moment the stranger's eyes met mine, this expression of the passions vanished. He smiled forcedly, and whispered, "Pardon, monsieur," then moved hastily away, as if to avoid conversation or observation. The incident impressed me deeply. He was certainly a Frenchman, perhaps an officer of high rank, who, while visiting Berlin and out of his uniform, could not resist the temptation to see what use the victors were making of all the spoils of Sedan, Strasburg, and Metz, and of those venerable trophies of Waterloo which fell into Blucher's hands. He was too young for old Pelissier; and, besides, that hero of the Crimea had been dead about two years.

After glancing at the immense display of other cannon, home-made and captured, old and new, the apparatus for mining and sapping, the elaborate miniature plans of fortresses and (most curious of all) the topographical models of historic battlefields, with tin troops in position on both sides, just as they were drawn up at some crisis of the conflict—all these on the vast lower floor of the arsenal—I climbed an easy flight of stairs, and found myself in another hall of trophies. The objects here exhibited were French muskets and French standards. There were enough *chassepots* to equip a division of troops. A Frenchman himself, if he could dismiss his patriotic sensibilities, must admire the highly artistic way in which the Germans have grouped these shining weapons. Thousands of them are set in racks, and look like organ-pipes, recalling Longfellow's lines on "The Arsenal at Springfield"; others are displayed against the walls as spokes of a wheel, as triangles, as pentagons, and other geometrical forms, beautiful in their perfect regularity. A committee of

French artists could not have treated the material more effectively.

Above and all around droop the flags of conquered France. Some are old and rent by bullets. I read among their folds such names as "Jena," "Austerlitz," "Borodino," "Alma," "Inkermann," "Solferino." Others are new and untorn and unstained. Their fresh, tricolored hues make the long gallery gay as I look down its perspective. What would the French officer say (to himself) if he could gaze upon these flags of his country which now serve only to decorate the enemy's arsenal? There he is again by my side. His face is pale. His lips pinch each other. His eyes shoot fire. He is staring intently at a poor old flag in tatters—a mere rag—on which I spell out the word "Marengo." No wonder his patriotic soul is cruelly disturbed by the spectacle! How can he endure it? As I ask this question, the object of it is suddenly aware that I am looking at him. His eyes again meet mine, his face mechanically becomes smooth if not pleasant, and his lips move as if murmuring, "Pardon, monsieur!" in apology for not more successfully commanding his emotions. Then he disappears among the crowd—there is always a crowd at the arsenal—as before, and that is my last sight of this mysterious personage.

During one of our rides in the outskirts of Berlin we came upon a regimental drill. It was taking place in a large, perfectly flat and dry field or parade-ground. We sat comfortably in our carriage close by, and watched the operations. An entire regiment was present, with all its officers in command, and fine-looking men they were, from the colonel down to the sous-lieutenant. It may be largely a question of clothes. Perhaps the long frock-coat, with two rows of buttons on the breast, and the spiked helmet, should be credited with part of the effect. The bobtail, white coats of Austria, and the short, blue tunics and red breeches of France, somehow detract from the impressiveness which should adhere to the followers of Mars. And the *Pickelhaube* of the Germans is unquestionably more warlike than the French *kepi*, or the cloth cap of the Austrians awkwardly set on the back of the head, or the plumed, top-heavy, round hat of the Italian *bersaglieri*. The German officers, for one reason or another, are more soldierly of aspect than any of their European brethren in arms. The studious and impartial observer must also give the German privates the palm over all others of the rank and file, the English troops always excepted. They look healthier, larger, stronger, with more staying power, than the common soldiers of Austria, France, or Italy.

These officers and these men are machines with

souls. We are looking at some wonderful automatic exhibition. Every arm and every leg of every soldier responds to the orders as if pulled by invisible wires. When they march in company columns, the line along the waist-buckles of the men is perfectly straight. When they ground their muskets, a thousand strike the earth with one thud. To me the most remarkable part of the show is the goose-step parade, never seen outside of Germany. It is a survival of the great Frederick's iron system. The men throw out one leg after another from the hip-joint, without a bend at the knee. There is absolute uniformity in this strange combined movement. A line of puppets operated by steam could not perform it better. A Prussian officer would take that as the highest compliment, his purpose being to impart to these thinking bodies before him all the formalism of a machine complete in every part, thoroughly oiled and working faultlessly. The goose-step parade is the pride of his heart. The fierce colonel, who sits on his coal-black horse at a little distance, and watches his regiment with merciless eyes, beams his silent approval as they all stride toward him, with their thousands of stiff legs rising and falling together as one.

At Munich, on the way to Berlin, I had seen Bavarian soldiers taking their gymnastic exercise out-of-doors. The same severe physical discipline is enforced upon all the conscripts throughout the empire; but it is not often that the tourist catches them in the act of training every muscle in succession for the exigencies of a campaign. By looking over a fence which separated me from the Munich drill-ground, I could watch the performances at close quarters. There, within a rod of me, were tough young fellows playing all sorts of games. They were climbing ropes and letting themselves down head-foremost. They were jumping over bars four or five feet high without touching. They were scaling barricades fifteen or twenty feet high by mounting on the shoulders of comrades. They were crossing imaginary streams on narrow planks. Some of them, with wire masks and iron breastplates, were fiercely lunging at one another with bayonets on the ends of muskets. The sharp point was covered with a wad of stuffed leather. Hundreds of men not thus engaged were marching incessantly up and down the grounds and going through the manual of arms, under the severest of tutors. When I had looked upon these men and these games about half an hour, I understood better than before why the Germans are formidable in war.

The Emperor and Empress were at Ems in mid-July, the time of my visit. Parliament was not in session. The opera-houses were closed. The month was in no sense part of "the season." And yet the hotels and *pensions* were full and prices "way up." It is worth while to know the special reason of this. Berlin was holding a great exhibition of pictures. It purported to take in "the world," but I can not admit this claim, for America was not at all represented in the long galleries through which I paced in the vain hope of finding some scrap from the brush of a fellow-countryman. None of the official persons whom I consulted knew or cared anything about it. One or two of them had a vague impression that some American artist had sent in something after the catalogue had been printed, but could not "spot" it for me. So I patriotically hunted for myself, and after much searching gave it up. Whether our artists did not care to send coals to Newcastle, or whether the managers of this immense picture-show had forgotten to invite, or had declined to accept, offerings from the United States, I can not say. Perhaps the jealousy and feeling of resentment which the American art tariff has provoked in Germany may explain the phenomenon. Excepting for the regrettable absence of contributions from America, the Ausstellung of 1886 wanted for nothing. No better collection of modern European paintings has ever been made. It was this that packed Berlin in mid-July. There is a lesson just here which should be taken home by every city in which ambition and enterprise are not yet extinct. Great galleries of fine pictures are unfailing attractions.

Perhaps, when New York has doubled her supply of Croton, she will provide a fountain worthy of the name. Nothing seems to captivate a crowd quite as effectually as a big jet of water. It must be fired into the air straight and high. It makes little difference whether the stream is thick or thin at the nozzle. At the Interlaken Casino there is a slender fountain of this kind. Its topmost drops tremble some hundreds of feet above the ground. No one dreams of quitting the scene till the water ceases to play, and I believe the spectators would stay there all night if it were not turned off. At Dresden, behind the Zwinger, there is a jet of far less pretensions. But, while it is playing, everybody from far and near flocks around to see it. Visiting the park of Sans Souci, not far from Berlin, I found the great fountain just as irresistible as all of its kind have proved everywhere else. The by-standers never tired of watching the sparkling column as it shot aloft. They would hardly move out of the way, even when its spray drenched them as the wind swayed the flashing summit to and fro. Nature and art have combined to make the old pleasure-ground of Potsdam lovely. But there is nothing in it as beautiful as its fountain.

The linden-trees in the great street upon which I look as I write, have shed almost all their blossoms. The wind brings with it the faintest trace of a perfume which is delicious when not too strong. The renowned Unter den Linden must be the paradise of thoroughfares when its long double lines of trees are in their full flower. Its noble palaces, museums, universities, and other public buildings make it attractive at all times. But its wealth of lindens is its unique charm in the summer. Only I am a little disappointed not to find among the leafy rows a single specimen of the tree as high as that which is so common in Southern Germany. But, in years, perhaps, they will grow to be as lofty as their predecessors in the same street which were cut down in their old age and decrepitude.

CHAPTER XIX.

ST. PETERSBURG IN JULY.

THE Russians play their alphabet of thirty-six letters for all it is worth. Having plenty of letters, they string these out into long words. How our German friends, with their addiction to polysyllables, would enjoy such alphabetical resources! What tremendous jaw-breakers they would manufacture! Our first acquaintance with the beauties of the Russian language was made from the window of a sleeping-car at daybreak. We were then in Russian territory, far from the frontier. As the train jogged along without stopping, we could see the Russian names of the stations. At first, perhaps, there would be four or five regular English letters, mixed up anyhow. Then would come a Greek character. Next would occur an unmistakable figure 3. This would possibly be followed by an N or an R or an L turned upside down or otherwise distorted. And in the midst of these capital letters there would be a sprinkling of "lower case," as printers say. The whole effect was that of "pi" of the most exasperating description. I can imagine no mental exercise more debilitating than that of trying to spell out Russian signs with the misleading help of the English letters on them. Even if all the rest were smooth sailing, there are fatal snags in the shape of gridirons, double saw-horses, and other symbols of unknown import.

On the tongue of a polite Russian this language is musical and fluent. We heard its accents first at Wirballen, where the baggage inspection takes place. It is no joke for persons who have been traveling for fifteen hours from Berlin to be wakened at midnight and put through a custom-house ordeal. As I stepped off the train into the cold and damp of the Wirballen station, a pleasant voice saluted my ear with a long sentence, of which I caught only the word "passport." Looking up, I saw, by the dim light of a lantern, a Russian officer of gigantic stature. He was most becomingly dressed in a blue tunic, flowing trousers tucked into highly polished boots, an Astrakhan cap with a red top and white pompon, and a long sword trailed from his side to the floor. His large, healthy face beamed benevolence. If he had asked for my pocket-book, I believe I should have given it up to him without hesitation. I handed him

Mr. Bayard's valued certificate, with the single word "American." You should have seen the smile on his face stretch into a positive laugh of welcome! He bowed profoundly, and pointed the way to a spacious room which had been depicted to me as a torture-chamber.

We had been told that the Russian examination was most inquisitive and merciless. We had heard that all English books and newspapers were confiscated. Having read our stock of these on the way, we were ready to surrender them cheerfully to the Russian censor. But we were expecting to have great fun out of a quart-bottle half full of lemonade and tightly corked. We had painted to ourselves the disappointment and disgust of the officials when they opened that bottle in pursuit of brandy and found only water. I confess I was almost sorry when they did not smell or even look at it. As for the books and papers, these gave the worthy men no more concern than the wisp-broom and slippers. Mind you, the search was not a pure farce. Those engaged in it did not look at you all the time as if they itched to be bribed. They did not examine some trunks and "chalk" others without opening them, and then expect you to pay for their forbearance. It was a strict and honest business throughout. But there was a liberal construction in favor of travelers. I had some paper rubles in my vest-pocket for an emergency. But slight observation of the men at work convinced me that they did not look for a gratuity from me, and that possibly they might be affronted if I offered them one. We have undergone many custom-house inquisitions, but that at Wirballen is the only one in which there was not something strongly suggestive of bribes or gifts.

It was this same national politeness on the part of a Russian to Americans that first induced us to try the rail route from Berlin to St. Petersburg. At Dresden, where we took train for Berlin, the only other occupant of our carriage was a gentleman of middle age, with a finely shaped head and a shrewd, kindly face. Some trivial incident started a conversation, and he soon learned that we were Americans. It was at once evident that this fact thawed any little fragment of ice that yet clung to our intercourse. Our fellow-traveler then proclaimed himself a Russian, and spoke with feeling of the friendship that had always existed between his country and America, and hoped it would be lasting. We echoed his sentiments every time, you may be sure. These international comities having been exchanged, we proceeded to extract from our friend some much-needed information about the Russian facilities for traveling, the best hotels and shops in St. Petersburg and

Moscow, and a great deal else in respect to which our guide-books are imperfect or stale. His knowledge of all these matters was full and exact, and I took mental notes of his advice, which, during our whole stay in Russia, proved of great value. A talk which was certainly very profitable for us—and in which he manifested the utmost interest and willingness to assist—was abruptly broken by the arrival of the train at the German capital. Rising to take leave, he shook hands with us heartily, and then informed us that he was Count Paul Schouvaloff, Russian Embassador at Berlin, and said he would be happy to be of any further service if we would call at the embassy. He was received at the station by military and other *attachés* of his staff, and driven off to the palace on the Unter den Linden, which is his official residence. It was under such agreeable auspices that we began our Russian journey, and they were but a foretaste of the kindness which everywhere met us—as Americans.

The trip from Berlin to St. Petersburg takes about thirty-six hours. You start at 9 A. M. in an express train, and do not strike the "sleepers" till you reach Wirballen. The Russian conveniences for night travel are almost perfect. The compartments are large, the beds good, the ventilation is scientific, and the motion easy. The springy gait of the carriage rocks you to sleep. The attendants are all alive, and do not ask for or seem to expect fees. The train stops often and long enough after daylight to "refresh" the hungriest and thirstiest of mortals. At the tidy-looking stations—wooden, one-story, painted yellow, each with boxes of flowers in the windows—he finds glasses of delicious coffee or strong tea, "screeching" hot. The tea is served from the *samovar*, or big urn, and is on tap night and day. A slice of lemon floating on top makes this cheering drink look like brandy-punch. There also may be had the whitest bread, the most golden butter, and dainty Russian dishes, of which I am most happy to recall mutton and rice drowned in a brown sauce that would kindle an appetite under the ribs of Death. Such comforts and such luxuries made the long ride from Wirballen to St. Petersburg unfatiguing. The country is flat, with a large allowance of forest and swamp, and is sparsely settled. The little aisle of the car was a common meeting-ground for passengers, who were amiable and talkative.

And so the time did not drag badly till we rolled into the Petersburg station (they all say Petersburg here) a little before nine o'clock, P. M. It was broad daylight in effect, and, as we were driven to our hotel (d'Europe), we could see and enjoy the out-door life of this great, modern-looking, wonderful city as well as if it had been high noon. There were signs of business enterprise and prosperity on every side. The *droschkies* burned the pavement, as the French say, but the drivers held their horses well in hand. These "cabbies," by-the-way, are almost the only class here whose dress is not European. Their long wraps, like bathing-robes, buckled about the waist, and their little hats, which look like the stove-pipe pattern badly crushed, are the only marked oddities of attire in the streets. The pedestrians, although through with the business of the day, walked rapidly. The general aspect of the city, as of the people we saw, was more American than French, German, or English. But for the maddening inscriptions on the shop-fronts, and the golden domes and peculiar crosses of the Greek churches, the city of Peter the Great might pass for a compound of Chicago and Washington. The wide, straight streets—the *Prospekts*, or perspectives, as they are called—remind me of the latest type of American cities. On arriving at the hotel, I again surrendered my passport (which had been countersigned and stamped by the Russian consul-general at Berlin, and handed back to me after a brief detention at Wirballen). It was returned next day, without any additional mark upon it.

The famous St. Isaac's Church, about which so

many writers rave, does not impress us as much as we expected. Nothing could be simpler and nothing richer than its outside and inside. It is immense, but it looks small. Its great dome is a sheet of pure gold. Its interior has columns of malachite and lapis-lazuli, massive shrines made of precious metals by the hundred-weight and blazing with diamonds, sapphires, rubies, and emeralds. One knows that millions of dollars have been lavished on all these things, and yet the whole effect is not magnificent. The money is not put where it shows on casual inspection. For a repetition of visits I prefer the Kazan Cathedral, of which less ado is made in the guide-books. That is the church beloved of Petersburgers; while it is not dowered with as much malachite, lapis-lazuli, gold, silver, and gems as fall to the share of St. Isaac's, it is very rich in all these gifts, and it has one shrine of incomparable splendor. That is our Lady of Kazan. The Greek Church does not tolerate images among its symbols. Reverence for the Saviour, or the Madonna and Child, or any of the saints, is expressed by heaping up riches upon their portraits. Our Lady of Kazan appears in a gold frame about three feet square. You see only her face and hands. The rest of her is buried under solid gold and silver crusted all over with the costliest jewels. She is a special object of veneration.

Princes and generals, opulent merchants, beggars, old and young, women and children, all sorts of people, may be seen at almost any hour of the day struggling to kiss her hands. Before doing this the more devout bow and touch the cold stone floor with their foreheads and cross themselves repeatedly. They bring little votive candles which they light and stick in places provided for them. Priests and women all dressed alike, in black robes and high hats minus the brim, stand around with dishes to receive donations. I heard the service intoned by lay readers with deep-bass voices, but did not see a priest performing his sacred functions. The religion of the people seems very real, so far as outward signs reveal it. Shrines are set up at the street corners and in the fronts of shops and houses, and no Russian fails to remove his hat and cross himself and bow deeply in passing one of them.

The most remarkable curiosity in this city is the perfect skeleton of a mammoth dug out of an ice-bank in Siberia nearly one hundred years ago. It is in the Museum of the Academy of Sciences, and I lost no time in inspecting the bones of the colossal beast. He stood, in his original full dress, as high as the lamented Jumbo at least. His general appearance as to head, tail, trunk, legs, and chest was that of an elephant. But his tusks, ten or twelve feet long, curved outward and upward, as if they were trying to tie knots in themselves. Remains of mammoths have often been dug up in Russia, but this skeleton is the only one to which some of the flesh and skin and hairs still adheres. The hide is about an inch thick. The hair is half a foot long, of a whitish brown. At what remote date this monster was browsing around in Siberia, what use he made of his queer horns, and how he got frozen up in a mass of ice and mud, are questions which I leave to the lively fancy of Jules Verne.

Most smokers are proud to own a real amber mouth-piece. What would they say to a room, seventy-five or one hundred feet square, lined on all sides with amber clear to the high ceiling? That is what we saw at Tsarskoe Sélo, an imperial summer palace near St. Petersburg. The precious fossil gum was cut and dovetailed so as to make beautiful figures of Cupids, fruits, and flowers. The whole is in the highest state of polish. It reflects the light not only from its surface, but from its depths, and is lovely to look upon, even if one does not think of the treasure expended in procuring all that rare product of nature. We made the weary round of a hundred rooms, all gilded and upholstered magnificently, and full of art-objects from every part of the globe, but saw nothing that spoke so eloquently of boundless wealth and luxury as that amber-lined chamber. When a Tsar undertakes to do something really splendid in this line, he leaves all his brother sovereigns far behind.

I shall never take the least interest in the band-chariot of a circus after having seen the forty or fifty gorgeous state carriages of the Tsars. The best artists and artisans of all Europe have contributed to the production of these wonderful objects, in which expense is of no account. They are deeply gilt all over, and each panel bears a painting from some master's hand. In the midst of this brilliant collection stands the traveling-sledge of Peter the Great, made entirely by himself, and an honest and strong piece of work. It was built for service, not for coronations and weddings, like the rest. Adjoining this venerable relic is a *coupé* of the simplest style, to which our courteous guide points as he says, with emotion, "Alexander the Second." We look, and are startled to see that the rear part of the *coupé* is split open in several places and a little sunk down on one side. Then we know at once that before us is the wreck of the carriage in which the monarch sat when the first bomb exploded beneath it. Within as well as without the havoc of the missile was terrible to behold. It is a wonder that the doomed man escaped alive only to perish by the second bomb, which his murderers held in reserve for him. The memory of this martyred emancipator of the serfs is cherished with the deepest affection by the people. His portrait is one of the commonest in the shop-windows. In the Cathedral of Saints Peter and Paul (within the fortress of that name) is the tomb of the unfortunate Emperor. Like the sepulchres of his predecessors, all about him, it is of marble unadorned. But its top is heaped with fresh flowers. Above and around are hung wreaths of immortelles and other floral tributes and elaborate mourning emblems in silver and gold testifying to the love of his subjects and the admiration of men of other lands.

CHAPTER XX.

THE FIRST DROSCHKY-RIDE—SUNSET AT THE ISLANDS—EARLY MORNING VIEWS OF THE NEVSKOI PROSPEKT.

"Don't forget Firkin! I will write his name for you on the back of my card." Such were the closing words of a long conversation about Russia held between myself and a young American who had recently visited that country. The person to whom he referred was the celebrated St. Petersburg guide, with headquarters at the Hôtel d'Europe. This injunction to remember Firkin was laid upon me across the breakfast-table of the Hôtel Grande Bretagne, Naples. I thanked the young American, and placed his card thus indorsed in a select compartment of my pocket-book. About two weeks later, dining one day at "Schweizerhof," Lucerne, my neighbor on the right, an English tourist, led up a desultory talk to Russia. I have noticed that persons who have been to Russia are apt to apprise others of that fact upon no provocation at all. He also said, with great emphasis—speaking of St. Petersburg—"By all means secure Firkin as a guide"; adding, "without him you are helpless." Frequently afterward, when we were pursuing our devious journey to the great northern capital, some misgivings would arise about difficulties to be encountered there; and then these would all vanish when we recalled the magic name of Firkin.

When we arrived at the Hôtel d'Europe, my first inquiry, after securing rooms, was for this treasure of a man. The polite manager scoured the reading-room, the restaurant, the smoking-room, and all the passage-ways of the ground-floor in search of the famous guide. "He must be out now with a party," explained the manager, in French. "Did you telegraph ahead to engage him?"

Ah! I had forgotten that. I had thoughtlessly assumed that, as I was visiting St. Petersburg out of the busy season, he would be entirely at my disposal. Rash confidence!

Next morning, after a good night's rest, my first thought was of Firkin. Even before breakfast, I resumed my inquiries for him, and could have hugged him with delight when he was at last brought before me by the courteous manager himself. He was a man of middle height and age, with an ingratiating manner, and spoke English—his native tongue. He looked the model guide. He smiled and shook his head when I told him I wanted to engage his services during my stay. Then he referred to a tablet in his hand, and, after carefully inspecting a series of entries, said, "You wish to see the most remarkable sights in Petersburg, I suppose." I nodded. "Well, then," said he, "I can give you from nine to twelve day after to-morrow. That is the best I can do. But it will afford you some idea of the manners and customs of the natives. Strangers have no conception of them, I assure you."

Three hours seemed very little, and day after to-morrow was far off. But I was curious to learn something about the real native life in Russia, and jumped at the proposition. "All right," said I, "we shall be through breakfast by nine on Wednesday, and ready for you."

"Breakfast, my dear sir?" he cried. "Dinner, you mean; 9 P. M. is the hour of starting. Between that and midnight I can show you the most wonderful—"

I laughed at the mutual mistake, and explained to the accomplished guide that the sights we had in mind were those best seen by daylight -- churches, palaces, museums, picture-galleries, etc.

"Ah! I see," he said, with a smile, "there is a lady along."

Thus ended my negotiations with Firkin. I tried in vain to engage another guide at the hotel, one who spoke French a little. But he was also booked far ahead. There was nothing left but to trust to my own ingenuity and the judicious use of "tea-money," as tips are called in a land where tea is drunk even more generally than corn-brandy. I bethought myself of the tourist's best friend—the head-porter. He was a Russian giant, amiable, like all oversized men, and speaking some French. He promised me his best assistance, and, I will say at once, was very useful. Whenever I wanted to go anywhere, he would give all the directions in Russian to the droschky-driver. As the driver was usually stupid, and, I should think, deaf, from the thundering tones in which the head-porter invariably addressed him, it always took some time to get us fairly started. Woe be to the *ishvoshtnik* if I had any occasion whatever to complain of him on my return, as I sometimes had! Then the head-porter would seem to grow in stature to about eight feet. He would shake his enormous fist in pretended rage at the blundering fellow, and roar at him in the purest Russian. I could not understand a word, but I knew by the driver's looks that he was "catching it hot." It is on such occasions that the Russian alphabet of thirty-six letters comes out strong. It enables one to do justice to the subject. The man would quail before this frightful shower of expletives until I would really pity him, and touch the shoulder of my good friend the head-porter to call him off. After several repetitions of this severe but wholesome treatment, the drivers made fair substitutes for the lamented Firkin himself.

Strange as the statement may seem, my principal difficulty at first was getting back to the hotel. Not a single one of the drivers engaged for me knew the name "Hôtel d'Europe," which was painted in letters six feet long on the blank side of that immense establishment. I was obliged to say "Nevskoi Prospekt," which they all understood; and, when they had entered that broadest of avenues, I piloted them to the hotel, which fronted it. Finally, I obtained from the head-porter the Russian name of the house—something like "Europeiskaya Gostinnitza"—and made that work every time.

Most of the streets are paved with large cobble-stones, and, if the droschkies ever had springs, these have become unelastic by much bumping over them. One mounts a droschky in St. Petersburg as he steps into a gondola in Venice—with a feeling of romance. It is something that shows off beautifully in pictures. You see a miniature victoria, with thick little wheels—the front ones just the size for barrows—drawn by a horse whose back is spanned with a high ornamental arch of wood, to which bells are attached. The driver holds in the flying steed with both hands—a graceful attitude. The whole turn-out is so fairy-like and different from any other elsewhere, that the tourist looks forward to a ride in a droschky as one of the greatest treats of St. Petersburg. Among the few Russian words he picks up as indispensable are *poshoi* (go ahead) and *stoi* (stop). Armed with these, he sets forth on his first exploration of the city, careless, light-hearted, prepared to enjoy everything, and particularly the droschky.

When we proceeded to seat ourselves in this vehicle, we barely found room for two, and there was no back to it except a little rim, three inches high, to prevent our falling out. We instinctively clung to each other for support. If we were a little crowded, and there was any danger of our tumbling into the street backward, those very facts were new and interesting. The safe and comfortable carriages are always commonplace, you know. We really felt like extolling the inventive genius of Russia which had produced something totally unlike any of the equipages of Western Europe. There was fascination in the risks of it. The *ishvoshtnik* (I roll this word like a sweet morsel under my tongue) starts off quickly. This gives us a jerk, but, while holding on to each other, we have each a spare hand with which we grasp the end of our thin cushion. We are not thrown out, or likely to be, and we murmur: "What fun!" "How exhilarating!" "What novel sensations!" as we go jolting over the bowlders.

The *ishvoshtnik* has a good horse, and is proud to show him off. The animal and his master seem to understand each other well. The one bends back his ears, while the other pours a stream of unintelligible words into them. No whip is ever used. We both feel much inconvenienced by the horrible pavement, though we heroically suppress our emotions. We suppose that we will soon get used to it. To distract our attention, we try to amuse ourselves with the enigmatical signs on the shops. We study the strange faces in the streets. We note the golden domes and spires as they flash under the morning sun. We make every effort to lose ourselves in the contemplation of this interesting city. But it is of no use. The cobble-stones keep our teeth chattering, and at times threaten to dislocate every bone in our bodies.

We strike a bowlder of extra size, and the droschky bounds up a foot.

"How horrid! do stop him, do!" are the words I now hear. I yell *poshoi* at the driver. A voice at my side says, "How lucky you remembered the word!" The man hears me, and he calls out *poshoi* to his horse. Now we shall see the sagacity of the animal. But no! The brute does not understand his own language. He has broken his trot; he is galloping. I hear a shriek—"Oh, pull his what-d'ye-call it, do!" I grasp the driver's baggy and greasy robe just above the girdle and nearly jerk him off his seat. He looks around astonished, and I then signal him to check his horse. He nods, and calls out *stoi!* And the beast comes to a halt. Then the thought flashes upon me that I have got my two Russian words mixed. Such is the fact, and we have a good laugh over it in which the driver joins; and I have no doubt the mistake would have amused the intelligent horse, if he had been told of it. We were glad to get back to the hotel at a walk. This was our first and last joint experience of a droschky in the rough streets of St. Petersburg, though for little trips about town I tried it alone and became somewhat hardened to it.

Late one afternoon, the head-porter, who was always making useful suggestions, said to me,

"Have you seen the sun set?" I told him I came from the land of the setting sun. "But you must see it set here!" pursued the good fellow. And before I could object, he whistled a springy phaeton out of the court-yard of the hotel where it had been standing awaiting orders. We stepped into the carriage, and he gave directions in Russian to the driver. We were bound to a summer garden or fashionable park, situated on what is known as "the islands." We crossed the Neva for the twentieth time, perhaps, as it divides the great city in twain and lies between the Hôtel d'Europe and many places of interest; and I again admired its noble breadth, its tranquil flow, the dark steel-blue of its waters. From any of the bridges the view along the quay is striking. The most imposing public buildings face the Neva. The private edifices on the same alignment are only less stately. It is here that the visitor recalls Paris as he has seen it from the Pont de la Concorde; only the Neva is twice as wide as the Seine. And this suggestion of Paris is strengthened when his eye catches a reminder of the dome des Invalides, in the golden hemisphere of St. Isaac's. But for the frequency of the gilded bulbs and the square Greek crosses that shine above the horizon of roofs, there is nothing Russian or peculiar in the general view of St. Petersburg.

Across the river we pass through streets destitute of novel features. The fact that we are in the Tsar's capital invests all things with a certain glamour. We are far from home, and feel as if we ought to be rewarded for our trouble in getting there, by the constant exhibition of strange things. But, save for the puzzling signs and the universal custom among the poorer classes (and all the military) of tucking trousers into boots, and the low-wheeled droschkies with their drivers in badly-crushed hats and tunics like blue meal-bags loosely tied in the middle, little challenges our wonder or admiration. We leave the busy streets for the green and shady gardens. These seem in no wise different from public grounds elsewhere. The trees—spruces and firs preponderating—are the same that thrive in all parts of Northern Europe. The summer flowers are equally familiar to us. There are restaurants, with people in the latest Paris styles, sitting in the open air and drinking tea or something stronger; and bands are playing for their delight just as they do in the Bois de Boulogne or Central Park. The roads are macadamized and free from dust. Our carriage is luxurious and from the depths of its cushions we look out idly on the shaven lawns, the clipped shrubbery, the crystal ponds full of swans and wood-ducks, the birds and butterflies spreading their wings to the soft, caressing air, and shiver to think of the change that a few months will make in this summer scene. For, perhaps, as soon as mid-October, these little lakes and the Neva, of which we get frequent glimpses between the trees, will be solid ice and all the landscape Arctic.

But we are coming to the sunset. We emerge from a thick wood at a point where the glorious river widens out into the Gulf of Finland. There is nothing to interrupt the view. Accustomed to American sunsets, we can not fully share the enthusiasm which we see expressed in the eyes of other persons, sitting in carriages and looking intently at that pile of gold and rubies in the west. The driver, not hearing us utter any exclamation of delight, turns half-way round and points to the setting sun. I nod approvingly, and then we square off at it. It is indeed a splendid exhibition of cloud-forms and luminous effects. Broad bands of light shoot aloft like the pale tails of comets. There are many peaks that turn rosy as if with an Alpine glow. Among the golden clouds one traces the shapes of domes, as if another St. Petersburg were sinking into night over there in the west. This is a brilliant spectacle for the lover of Nature. But it sets us thinking of home and friends, so many thousands of miles away in the direction of sunset. I dare say the other people there looking at that wonderful sky as we do with alien eyes, feel the same tender memories come over them with a rush, for we are all silent together for a few minutes.

The driver took the liberty of breaking the spell by moving on. We rode through more woods, past more lawns with parterres of flowers, skirting more lakes looking like duplicates of those we had before seen. Finally, after about fifteen minutes of this pleasant but slightly monotonous route, we came out upon another view of the sunset. It was the same that we had seen before, but a quarter of an hour farther along. The surrounding scene also appeared identical with the one we had but just left. There was a small restaurant of fantastic design, a precise copy, even to the large gilded weather-cock, of one I had previously noticed, in front of which several carriages were drawn up, while the owners or riders sat on the stoop eating ices. And there, beyond the possibility of mistake, were a pair of bob-tail grays and the same party of four ladies finishing up their light repast. We had been taken to the same place twice to see the same sunset! It was all the more vexatious as we were getting hungry, and I peremptorily waved off the sunset with one hand and motioned with the other to go ahead. The man evidently understood me, for he said *poshoi* and off we started. As we whirled along we fell into a talk about our future plans and did not notice the scenery through which we passed. In about fifteen minutes more we struck another view of the sunset, coming abruptly upon it at a turn of the road. It was still so beautiful that we could not forbear to look at it once again, although it was already twice burned in upon our memories. Suddenly, as I took my eyes off the molten splendor, I recognized the same old restaurant, with its whimsical gables, its weather-cock and all the surroundings complete, even to the bob-tail grays, pawing the ground and anxious to get away. The four ladies were just on the point of entering their carriage.

It was maddening. I would have given anything for a few Russian words appropriate to the occasion. Would that the head-porter were there! Oh, for one minute of Firkin! But I was powerless. I could only gasp, "Europeiskaya Gostinnitza! *Poshoi!*" at the same time shaking my fist at the driver. He understood me this time without a shadow of doubt. In about forty minutes we entered the court-yard of the Hôtel d'Europe. When the head-porter came forward to assist us in alighting, I explained to him, with some indignation, the absurd persistence of that ass in taking us to see the sunset three times running, when once was all we wanted of it. Contrary to my expectations, the head-porter did not interpret my emotions to the culprit, but calmly explained to me that everybody who went to the Summer Garden to see the sunset took it in three times before leaving the grounds. It was the regular thing to do. The circuit, which is thrice made, was part of the fashionable routine never omitted on any account. Though the excellent head-porter did not say so, I could read in his face surprise that I should complain of having had too much of a St. Petersburg sunset.

At 4.30 A. M. it is broad daylight. I happen to be awake, and I step to a window which overlooks the Nevskoi Prospekt. The vast Gostinnoi Dvor, in which we had shopped three hours on the stretch the day before and seen but little of its inexhaustible stores in that short space of time, is closed now. In two or three hours its thousands of shutters will be taken down, and its swarming population of proprietors, book-keepers, clerks, porters, and small boys will be getting ready for another day's business. The eternal lights burn at the beautiful Greek shrine in the square opposite. The roof of the little temple is covered with gold. Its shape is that of a Paris kiosk, but greatly magnified. A Frenchman seeing it for the first time would step into it and ask for "Le Figaro."

There are people abroad at that hour, and every one who passes this shrine bows profoundly before it three times, and elaborately crosses himself. A carriage drawn by two coal-black horses stops in front of it. A priest, with the tall, black rimless hat and somber sweeping robe of his order, descends. All spectators bow to him. He passes through the ever-open doorway of the shrine to a place where I can see gleaming gold and flashing jewels as the light of many wax-candles falls upon them. After a short absence, the priest returns, carrying in his arms a large square something. It is covered by a white cloth, but, as this is accidentally displaced for a moment, I see the face of the Saviour. It looks solemnly and tenderly out of the matted gold and precious stones which overlay it. Three women in black follow it in procession from the shrine to the carriage, with bent heads and slow steps. The driver removes his hat. The heads of all spectators are bared, for this is the principal Icon of the shrine near the great Bazaar, and held in the deepest reverence by all orthodox Russians. It is about to be taken to the priest's house for some solemn ceremony of renewed consecration. The carriage proceeds slowly along the Nevskoi Prospekt. Through the open window I see the priest holding the Icon upon his knees, and bending above it in the attitude of prayer. All beholders doff their hats, bow, and cross themselves as the adored object passes. A young officer is galloping down the street. He is dressed in the dandy uniform of some crack regiment. He wears a shako with a tall feather, and a gold chain about his neck; a long saber swings from his waist; the blue cape of his light overcoat is thrown back to disclose the rich scarlet lining. Even at that early hour his mustache is waxed to fine points. He looks like a lady-killer. I say to myself, "He will not bend his haughty head as the Icon goes by." I am greatly mistaken. He removes his shako, and bows to the pommel of his saddle. I notice only one man who pays no respect to the Icon—that brawny fellow sitting in a chair on the sidewalk, exactly opposite my window. His head rests upon his breast, and he is evidently fast asleep. He is the *dvornik*, or *concierge*, of the house in front of which he is taking his nap. He is supposed to be watching the premises for the protection of the inmates and their property. Perhaps he spends the whole night in slumber, after the custom of unfaithful guardians in all climes and ages. If so, the policeman, who is now coming slowly down the middle of the street, with a drawn sword in his hand, must discover the fact if he keeps his eyes open, and will perhaps wake the *dvornik* to a sense of his neglected duty by prodding him playfully. He glances at the slumbering man as he saunters by, but does not disturb him. Doubtless, requiring charity himself on that point very often, he is prepared to extend it to others. Soon after he has passed, the *dvornik* gives a slight start, raises his head, pulls a bottle from beneath his heavy cloak, takes a long pull at it, and goes to sleep again.

I hear the heavy tramp of feet. Soon a battalion of soldiers comes in sight. They are men of the medium size, young, healthy, and strong. They put their feet down firmly, but do not march well, because they have no music, not even a drum and fife. Their uniform is of a bluish-gray color, and they wear fatigue-caps of cloth, slouchy and unsoldierlike. Blankets are wreathed across the right shoulder, and hang below the waist in an enormous fold, like a piece of boa-constrictor. On their backs are knapsacks, with small tin pans externally attached. The men look about as well as the raw conscripts of other countries, and are probably good fighting material if well drilled and handled. At their head rides the commanding officer, a young fellow, whose bright face is clouded, as if he were leaving somebody or something highly prized behind him. He may only be leading his men to their morning drill in the exercise-grounds near the arsenal. But it is more romantic to suppose that he is on his way to Central Asia, and that he will engage in terrible skirmishes with the border-ruffians down there, perform incredible deeds of valor, capture a big chief, annex a province, and then come back to St. Petersburg laden with loot and glory, to receive promotion to the rank of major-general and the grand cross of St. George at the hands of the Tsar.

At that moment a still, small voice calling from the adjoining room breaks up this day-dream, and ends my early morning view of St. Petersburg.

CHAPTER XXI.

GRAND-DUKE ALEXIS — THE AMERICAN MINISTER AND HIS CHASSEUR—RUSSIAN PRESS CENSORSHIP — AN INDIGNANT BRITON — UNDISCOVERABLE NIHILISTS.

As I was shuffling some card-photographs at Daziaro's (print-shop on the Nevskoi Prospekt), I noticed three or four costume-portraits of the same fine-looking man. They were all full-lengths and very effective. The intelligent face seemed familiar to me; but in vain I tried to recall its owner. Neither the front nor the back of the photograph gave any clew to his name. Where had I seen that open brow with the curling hair, and those large, expressive eyes? I sought light from Daziaro. "The Grand-Duke Alexis," said he.

That sent my memory back over quite a gap of years to the time when a youthful scion of the house of Romanoff visited America and carried the hearts of my countrywomen by storm. They unanimously declared that he perfectly realized their ideal of a prince. That ideal was a most exacting one; for it was founded on fairy-stories, and the Arthurian legends. They knew nothing of princes in real life, or they would never have made their standard so impossibly high. But here at last was a prince who came up to it, with his stature of six feet two inches, his winning face, and his dignified yet cordial manner. I have heard that there are American ladies who sacredly preserve to this day the gloves they wore when they danced in the same quadrille with the Grand-Duke Alexis.

With my countrymen he also made himself a great favorite by his desire to please and readiness to be pleased. For these reasons—and because of the sincere friendship which has always existed between the United States and Russia—the Grand-Duke Alexis, wherever he went in America, had a heartier popular reception than any other prince of any stock who ever visited us.

I could not help feeling a desire to see him again in the flesh, after noticing how like his former self (except for the lapsed years) he looked in the pictures. The Grand-Duke Alexis had become the admiral of the Russian navy. I thought how fine he must look in the full-dress uniform of his rank. I had more curiosity to see him than the Tsar himself, who is the rarest spectacle now vouchsafed to the eyes of the stranger, as he sticks close to his palaces and private shooting-grounds. I found myself unconsciously on the watch for the sailor-prince as I rode about the city. Sometimes I would see an officer of commanding stature approaching us in a barouche at a dashing gait, and would say, on the impulse, "I do believe that's our friend." "Who? Who?" "Why, Alexis, to be sure!" "Oh, no, it's somebody else." This happened very often, for showy officers in stylish turnouts are not uncommon sights on the Nevskoi Prospekt.

One day while standing in the spacious vestibule of the Hôtel d'Europe, I noticed the people about me taking off their hats. Looking up, I observed before me the Grand-Duke Alexis himself. The well-remembered features were there, minus the high, open brow which was concealed by a great cocked hat loftily plumed with green. Tall as he was in America, he seemed to be two or three inches taller now. His dark-green uniform—probably an admiral's—fitted him well. He looked more princely than ever. I took off my hat to him, but he did not notice it, and, in fact, he returned nobody's salute as far as I could see. "He used to be more democratic in America," I said to myself. "But that was to please us. He is in Russia now, and the case is different."

At that moment the excellent head-porter, who

was always rendering these delicate attentions to the guests, whispered in my ear—" *Voilà l'embassadeur Américain !*"

Never was pleasing illusion more rudely dispelled to make room for profound wonderment. So this resplendent being was the American minister to Russia. What was his name? Oh, yes, I remember—Lothrop, of Michigan. And that magnificent uniform? He must have been a general of volunteers at home, and so is entitled by act of Congress to wear it on ceremonial occasions abroad. A good idea, though some Americans who have no uniforms to wear may ridicule it as pompous and fussy. I have no doubt that the Russians are a great deal more impressed by all those buttons, feathers, and gold lace, than they would be by the plain black suit which I had supposed that Mr. Lothrop always wore. By-the-way, I wonder to what arm of the service Mr. Lothrop belonged? I don't remember about that dark-green and that particular shape of hat.

Just then a gentleman in complete black who had been following the American minister, drew up alongside of him, and I could contrast the two styles of dress to great advantage. Prejudice apart, there could be no doubt that Mr. Lothrop looked more like a Minister Plenipotentiary and Envoy Extraordinary of the United States of

America in his military garb than he would have done in civilian's clothes.

Can I believe my eyes? The minister is actually taking off his hat and bowing very respectfully to the somber-coated person by his side. Do my ears deceive me? He calls him "Your Excellency," and seems to be receiving an order from him like a servant. The next instant a gentleman approaches the less conspicuous of the two figures and says to him with a Chicago accent, "The American minister, I believe?"

"Yes, sir! What can I do for you?" he kindly asks.

And then I know that this gorgeous person is attached to our quiet American minister as *chasseur*, and that it is his business to herald the approach of that functionary. It is a practice found to be very useful by our highest grade of representatives abroad; and that American must be a ferociously uncompromising republican who would object to this inexpensive but effective display of rank and dignity on their part.

One afternoon while sitting in the reading-room of the Hôtel d'Europe, looking over the last number of "Punch," and trying to extract a laugh from it, I became aware that a gentleman near me was desirous to open conversation. Out of my side-eye

I could see a monocle glaring at me, with suppressed feeling behind it, and I knew by the fidgety motion of a pair of hands, holding a newspaper aloft, that the owner had something to say if I would lend him an ear. I laid down "Punch," and turning toward the stranger saw at once what was the matter. He was exposing to my gaze a newspaper—the London "Saturday Review," I think it was—several pages of which had been badly mutilated by scissors. Bits of various lengths had been snipped out of its reading-columns. I immediately recognized the work of the Russian censor, specimens of which I had seen before. The man who displayed this mangled "Saturday Review" for my inspection was English. Seeing that he was somewhat excited, I resolved to tease him a little for fun, though the indignation which blazed from his face was honest, and certainly not without cause.

"I know that this is a land of tyranny," said he, "but I'm an Englishman and not afraid to speak my mind. Isn't that an outrage?"

"I beg your pardon," said I; "what is the trouble?"

"This paper sent me by a friend; see the holes in it!"

"Ah! yes, he has picked out the plums for his scrap-book, and sent you the leavings."

"My dear sir," said the Englishman, dropping his single eye-glass in his emotion, "you don't understand; this is the beastly work of the Russian Government. See!" and he handed me the paper. I glanced at the damaged pages, and observed that the cuttings had been made in articles about Russia. The job had been neatly done. The censor had evidently read everything in the paper concerning Russia, and had scissored out all the passages that were uncomplimentary. The rest of the context was allowed to stand.

"And, to make it worse," said the Englishman, "the paper was detained in the post-office here five days at least. There's the original wrapper with the London post-mark."

"Yes, I see. The censor wanted to do his work thoroughly. He is more conscientious than most public officials, I should say."

"Conscientious, indeed! It was done for the express purpose of annoying an Englishman."

I was about to reply that perhaps the parts of the articles cut away had been written for the express purpose of annoying the Russians, but I forbore.

"And here is another style of mutilation," he continued, handing me a copy of another London paper. "What do you say to that?"

He opened a sheet which showed at intervals

large square or oblong patches, apparently a mixture of lampblack and oil applied by a coarse handstamp. The reading-matter beneath was effectually obliterated. These daubs looked like woodcuts badly printed.

"An illustrated paper?" I said, playfully. "Anyhow, this kind of cuts is better than the other; you get your paper whole, you see," and I smiled.

The Englishman felt hurt by my frivolous treatment of his grievance. "It doesn't seem to strike you exactly as it does me," said he; "and yet, I should think that, being an American, you—"

"I know what you are about to say," I interrupted. "Of course, I uphold the liberty of the press as much as you do, and equally detest this tampering with the mails; but then I don't expect to find the same measure of freedom here that I find in the United States or England. The Russian Government maintains a strict censorship of the Russian press. And, in order to be consistent, the Government also *pretends* to take great pains to keep out of the country all printed matter that it does not like."

"Pretends, my good sir?" cried my English friend. "But it *does* keep out all such matter— as you have seen from these two specimens."

"How about this?" said I, taking up the clean

and whole copy of "Punch" from the table. "This contains two or three jokes at the expense of Russia. And there are the 'Illustrated News' and 'Graphic,' 'Figaro,' 'Charivari,' 'Indépendance Belge,' 'Fliegende Blätter,' 'Kladderdatsch,' and—can I believe my eyes?—the great London 'Times' itself! All regularly taken here and filed. You will find plenty of hits at Russia in these papers, and not one of them has been cut or blackened with a stamp. I can swear to that, as I have been looking all through them."

"Yes, I know," he answered. "But these all come that way, because they are addressed to the Russian proprietor of the Hôtel d'Europe. The outrage—for so I must still call it—is inflicted on me because I am an Englishman."

It still gave him so much pleasure to imagine that he was a martyr because of his race that I hesitated to undeceive him. But I thought it better to correct his erroneous opinion by saying that, if he would ask the head-porter, through whose hands all the mail-matter came, he would find out that the newspapers addressed to all the transient guests of every nationality at the hotel were treated in exactly the same way. The letters, he would ascertain, came through straight enough, and showed no signs of tampering.

"That last is true," said he.

"And, as for the papers," I continued, "I am told that a line from your embassador or your consul-general addressed to the Russian Post-Office Department, or even a call at headquarters from yourself, will cause their prompt delivery undisturbed. Why not try it?"

"I would not condescend to ask the favor!" was the haughty reply.

"Well, then," said I, shrugging my shoulders to imply a desire of closing the somewhat unprofitable conversation—"then I am afraid you will be obliged to put up with it. For my own part, I am free to say that, while I am in a foreign country, I will not hurriedly condemn laws and usages which happen to be unlike those in America. When I don't like it, I will leave it."

"I fancy you Americans think better of Russia than we Englishmen do."

"Perhaps so," was my reply, as I buried myself once more in the pages of "Punch," and resumed silence.

Our English friends can not at least complain that they are denied freedom of speech in Russia. On the railroad-trains, in shops, in the hotels, and in the public streets, I have heard them talk as boldly and freely against the Tsar and his system as if they were at home. I have sometimes thought it would be only becoming in them to speak a little lower, or else tone down the severity of their criticisms while experiencing in their own persons the actual toleration of the government they so fiercely denounce.

Before entering Russia, I had stuffed myself—my mind, not pockets—with books, magazine articles, and newspaper letters about the Nihilists. From such sources of information I had learned that the Nihilists represent all classes of Russian society—peasants, priests, soldiers and officers, noblemen, and even the imperial family. It was said that ladies of rank, wealth, and refinement were among the most active propagandists of Nihilism. These reports had taken so strong a hold of me that, on striking Russian soil, I began at once to look about for some signs of the presence of this widely spread and terrible doctrine.

Among our fellow-passengers from Berlin to St. Petersburg was a lady accompanied by her maid. She had a *coupé lit* for her exclusive use, through the window of which I could see her from the platform of stations where we alighted for refreshments. She always shrank into a corner of her carriage, as if to escape scrutiny. I noticed that her chin was disproportionately large, and that her lips were firmly pressed together. Some one told me that she was of high rank in Russia. Whereupon the whimsical thought possessed me that here, perhaps, was one of those aristocratic female Nihilists of whom I had read so much. The absurdity of the idea did not prevent me from keeping an eye on her.

At the frontier station this lady's actions were so strange that I watched her with a "fearful joy." She was profoundly agitated. Her face was pale — even her resolute lips sharing in the ashen hue—and she strode up and down the *salle d'attente* unceasingly, as if to walk off her nervousness. She had three large, black, strongly bound trunks, marked with Russian initials in white paint. I knew they were her trunks by the anxious glances which she threw at them from time to time. Once, when the porter let the corner of one of them fall heavily to the floor, I observed her start. "Perhaps it contains dynamite," I said to myself, half-laughingly.

When her turn came for the formalities of the *douane*, she stepped forward with a boldness which was well assumed. She and her maid assisted the Government officers in unlocking, unstrapping, and unpacking. Her apparent anxiety to have the search made thorough did not deceive me. The men went to the bottom of two of the trunks— either removing the contents or probing them with their long arms, or peering among them with trained eyes and smelling hard for tobacco and spirits all the time. They found nothing contraband. When they proceeded to explore the third trunk, the lady made a strong visible effort to conceal her emotion. "Now for bombs," I thought, "or Nihilists' tracts at the very least!"

It was fortunate for her that the custom-house myrmidons had not noticed her feverish anxiety. But they were busy at their work, not over-suspicious, and glad to be through with a midnight job which paid them nothing. So they slighted number three, simply removing and putting back a top layer of clothes. Then they closed the lid, and chalked all the trunks. I could see the mysterious lady heave a sigh of relief, which I could not help sharing with her, though it left unanswered the interesting question, What did she have in that third trunk?

Was it dynamite? Or revolutionary pamphlets and circulars? Or some innocent but dutiable stuff which the lady carried into her country free? I have seen the sex equally agitated on the docks of New York, when the goods which had been hid away were nothing more dangerous than smoking-jackets or meerschaum pipes or uncut velvet. So let us give the fair unknown Russian the benefit of the doubt, and imagine that the extent of her offense, if any, was smuggling in a costly French dinner-dress or *articles de Paris* dear to the female heart.

Perhaps there never was a more harmless fellow than the *mujik* who made our beds and blacked our shoes on the Russian sleeping-car which bore us to St. Petersburg. But that man had the high cheek bones, the long, unkempt hair, and the generally wild look which I had once noticed in the portrait of a notorious Nihilist printed in the "Illustrated London News." I did not then know that these were the characteristic Tartar features, seen all over Russia. On account of his resemblance to that portrait I found myself suspecting the *mujik* of Nihilistic tendencies. I once came upon him suddenly while he was sitting on a stool in a little recess, at the rear end of the car. He was muttering to himself, and pounding his knee with his brawny fist. How could I help thinking that he was heaping curses on the existing order of things universal, and that that self-inflicted blow of his clinched hand expressed, in a feeble way, his long-pent hatred of all human society? And yet it is possible that the poor man was only cursing his ill-luck in taking a counterfeit ruble for good money.

During our visit to Tsarkoé Selo, while making the tour of the palace, I noticed from a window a gentleman in uniform walking slowly through the grounds. He had in his hand a letter which he was anxiously scanning. Attracted by his soldierly bearing, I asked the guide who he was. "*Le Prince*" (something unintelligible ending in sky), "*monsieur*," was the response. Now, here was a prince at home, in the private garden of an imperial palace, his hair white, his port manly, his breast bearing decorations—the man of all men, one would say, least likely to risk the assured good things of this life by linking his fortunate self to the Nihilists. And yet the book-writers and the newspaper correspondents had told me that the head and front of the awful conspiracy was to be found among the palaces of the empire. I owe an apology to a presumably loyal and devoted subject of the Tsar for permitting myself to suppose, for one second, that the prince, whose name I deeply regret my inability to spell, was perhaps " boss " of the Nihilists, and that the letter in his hand was written by some fellow-conspirator in Warsaw or Moscow. Thus unjustly suspicious does one become, after reading so many real or pretended revelations about high-life Nihilists in Russia.

Next day at the Hôtel d'Europe, while I was looking over the bill of fare for luncheon, I observed that my waiter—a typical Russian in aspect—hovered near me more closely than usual, and his appearance indicated that he had something to say to me privately, in the French which he spoke with some difficulty. He had heard us talk about America, and he doubtless knew my nationality. Now, it is to Americans that the revolutionists in all parts of Europe turn with full confidence for sympathy. They make no mystery of their hatred of kings and emperors when they get hold of an American ear. I have thus become the repository of several confidential opinions about crowned heads, which, if they had been known to the police, would have caused the arrest and punishment of the speakers. Therefore, when I saw this quiet-looking Russian waiter edging up, I said to myself: "He is going to whisper his longings for republican institutions. It will do him good to relieve his feelings. I am afraid he is a Nihilist. He looks like one. I must condemn him for that, of course, but I will not deny my sympathy for the oppressed, even in the heart of Russia."

As these thoughts floated through my brain, the waiter stooped down to make his mysterious communication. I cocked up my ear to hear him more distinctly. He said, in a half-whisper, "*Monsieur, il y a des* fish-balls *aujourdhui.*" And that was the whole of his tremendous secret. Well, I was glad it was nothing more serious and laughed heartily at my groundless misgivings.

It seems that the accomplished manager of the restaurant had lately added "fish-balls" to the extensive list of his special dishes for particular days. It was a flattering concession to American tastes, made, I presume, at the original suggestion of some Bostonian visiting St. Petersburg. In due time, probably pork and beans and brown bread will be introduced there through the same reforming agency. Supposing that I was an American, the waiter illogically inferred that I was fond of fish-balls. His hesitation in making the announcement arose from his imperfect acquaintance with French, and his still deeper uncertainty as to the exact pronunciation of "fish-balls."

This amusing incident cured me of my propensity for surmising that this or that Russian man or woman might possibly be a disciple of Nihilism. There may be a great many Nihilists in Russia, and they may belong to all classes of society; but, if the secret police can not find them out, we may be sure that strangers making hasty visits to the country are not likely to be more successful in the search.

CHAPTER XXII.

THE HOLY CITY OF RUSSIA.

THE "sea of fire" which Napoleon saw at Moscow was replaced for us by a sea of green roofs as we neared that city at 10.30 A. M., July 23d. The sight of a real sea could not have been more refreshing. We had been traveling fourteen hours by express from St. Petersburg. We could have read coarse print by twilight as late as 11 P. M., and then again as early as two in the morning. It was possible, therefore, to see most of the country through which we passed by simply raising the curtain of the sleeping-car window. But the more we looked at the flying landscape the less we liked it. The scenery was that from Wirballen to St. Petersburg over again—flat, boggy, densely wooded, in places well cleared and cultivated, in others with plenty of cattle reclining in the fields, but lightly dotted with houses. Nothing except mountains compensates for the absence of human life. We could have shouted for joy at the first glimpse of that broad stretch of pea-green, two stories high. From its surface, as from a body of water, rose domes, turrets, spires, towers, battlements innumerable. There were bulbous forms which we compared variously to onions, radishes, or turnips. These were mostly plated with gold, which shone intensely in the keen light of day. Others were silver or indigo-blue or red, and still others matched the green from which they sprang. The churches of Moscow are five hundred strong. Each of these may have half a dozen steeples. The effect of the whole is bristling. The city looks like "many-spired Milan" on a large scale, except that the domes interject an element which one misses in the Christian West. The place of the Kremlin is at once identified by the thicker growth of bulbs and needles which we see near the center of the great city. The terms "eccentric," "whimsical," "grotesque," "bizarre," "barbaric," are used by some of our fellow-travelers to express their feelings. We do not quarrel with their epithets. We can only say that for us there can not be too great a contrast between the church architecture here and that which we have seen in other countries of other religions. We thank the Tartars—if they are the responsible parties—for originating all those odd shapes which cluster in the fold of the Kremlin.

At the station we were received by a man wearing a long blue robe girded at the waist, trousers tucked into his boots, and a sort of smoking-cap with a band of peacock's feathers. If he could have spoken a word of English or French or German, the charm of this splendid apparition would have vanished instantly. He was delightfully Russian from top to toe. When we said "Slaviansky Bazaar" (name of the principal hotel here), he knew what was meant. He conducted us to a carriage, to which were harnessed four white horses abreast, all decorated with bells and tassels. It was obvious that this sort of thing was not universal in Moscow, for we saw no other men in the streets dressed in that way, and few other horses thus caparisoned. All the more were we obliged to the proprietor of the Salviansky Bazaar for treating his guests to the revival of old Russian hospitalities. At the hotel we were sorry to see waiters in the claw-hammer coats and white neck-ties of Delmonico's. But then, again, it was a pleasure to find a smooth-faced boy with his long hair parted in the middle and a tunic of such a cut and length that he looked externally just like a girl. When one finds these things at Moscow after traveling thousands of miles for them, he begins to feel rewarded.

We have been in pursuit of good, genuine Russian dinners in and out of the hotel, and are prepared to say that they fully equal the best French combinations in appetizing and nourishing qualities. At some of the restaurants you must read or speak Russian or starve, unless you can make the waiter understand that you will take a dinner at a fixed price. It is delightful to find a race with the moral courage to invent dishes of its own, with names which a Frenchman can not understand. The soup, to begin with, would be incomprehensible to a Parisian *chef*. Two portions of it would make a square meal. It is hot, slab broth, with a large chunk of meat (not a knuckle-bone) in the middle of it, inviting the knife to cut and come again. With this succulent dish is served pastry, looking like Yankee "turn-overs," stuffed to the bursting-point with meat hash. Croquettes and balls of meat—with delicious sauces—figure in almost every dinner. The conventional "joint" of other countries—beef, mutton, or veal—is not wanting, and the Russians so far accommodate themselves to our prejudices as to give us chicken and salad—but the latter in the disappointing form of pickled cucumber, while we are sighing for a little crisp lettuce. I had almost forgotten the fish, but then the fish is served out of place. Here it comes, third on the list, following a meat dish. For dessert, one has the fruit of the season. Just now the strawberry is in its zenith. They bring us a rosy pile, which we are expected to eat out of soup-plates with table-spoons. Cream is plenty, but powdered sugar scarce. I send for more. The waiter is polite, and goes for it.

When he returns, I am conscious that he is looking me hard in the face. He wants to see what manner of man it is who requires to qualify his sour berries with so much of sweet. He had previously been looking just as hard at my blue gaiters. I am beginning to discover that gaiters are as rare here as fez caps in Broadway. In fact, I have the only pair in Moscow, and should be glad to believe that the universal gaze directed at them is not one of secret derision in this land of boots. As we are now through with our dinner, we will dismiss that subject, only adding that, if one must have wine, he can get something pure, light, and nice, the product of the Crimea or Caucasus. In settling my score, I give something to the waiter, as a reward for his spotlessness; for, at the first-class restaurant where we have just dined (Moskovskia Traktir), he is dressed in complete white, relieved only by a little red cord about his waist. This shining habit is unstained by a single drop of soup or gravy, although he has been whisking plates and tureens off the table the moment we were through with them.

On Sunday we were wakened early by a grand crash of bells. As almost every one of the hundreds of churches has a set of four or five bells, you will understand that, when all ring together, they compel a hearing. None of them are very near us, and the sound of the harshest was mellowed by distance. They were of all pitches, from the deepest bass to the shrillest treble. I could not make out a tune in all the noise. The bells are not rung as chimes. Each one seems to work "on its own hook," and to be striking a continuous fire-alarm. After listening to the clamor for half an hour, one feels like turning over for another nap. But the attempt is useless. The bell-ringers are as punctilious in their performances as if these were the most essential part of religion. They will not shorten the prescribed hours of this labor by a single second. Among the profound notes that come booming over all the green roofs, I fancy I hear the voice of a monstrous brazen-throated creature whom I patted on the back the other day. He is kept in the stronghold of a tower within the Kremlin about one hundred and fifty feet from the ground. Without vouching for measurements, I should say he is twelve feet wide at the flare or rim and fourteen feet high. His tongue weighs about two tons. Sounded with the ferule of my umbrella, he gave a little muffled roar. The man in charge offered to tap him gently with the ponderous clapper swinging there. But I did not care to hear him more clearly at short range, and declined.

But one would willingly pay a number of rubles to hear the Tsar Kolokol struck, if that dethroned monarch of all the bells could be set up again. But there he remains, mutilated and silent forever. The pictures of the great bell of Moscow had not prepared me to see how neatly it had been broken. The detached fragment, which now stands by the side of the ruined bell, might have been cut from it with a knife, so straight and clean are the lines of breakage. One would think that it might be put back again and the last trace of a scar be obliterated with solder. But that would not restore its voice to the bell. For it has ten or a dozen cracks, some of them many feet long, and each one has spoiled it. If there is any considerable percentage of silver in this bell—as seems likely on inspection, and if it weighs two hundred tons, as we are told—it would be very valuable as old metal. But it is still more precious to Moscow as her unique and most interesting treasure.

The ordinary bass voice is often little better than a growl or huskiness of the throat. No one thinks of calling it musical. But I never heard tenors that thrilled and charmed me more than the basses at the Temple of the Saviour. This is the costliest and most splendid church in all the Russias. Its outside is marble and gold. Its inside is a lavish display of the precious metals thickly set with gems. Every fine quarry in the empire has contributed its best to compose the tesselated floor, the wainscoting, and the columns of the marvelous structure. It was built to commemorate the defeat of the French invasion of 1812, and was only recently completed, after forty-six years of consecutive work. As one walks about this stupendous church, and transfers his admiration from one object of beauty and richness to another, his attention is suddenly called off from everything by a burst of musical thunder. It floods the interior like the crash of a great organ. He looks all around, and can not see what causes it. Somewhere in an elevated and hidden choir, or behind the massive gold altar-piece, are the singers. The voices are all basses. There are three or four distinct "parts," some pitched so much higher than others that they seem relatively to be tenors. Each note—even the lowest—is clear and firm. It has the sweetness of a flute with the sonorous volume of a bassoon. The concealed performers are uttering responses to the gorgeously attired priests, whose own voices are deep and melodious, and worthy to take part in this noble choral service.

I wait for half an hour, hoping that the singers will execute some long and formal piece. But they do not, and I retire, having learned for the first time of what a bass voice is capable in sacred music.

Although the Russians spend so much money to celebrate the failure of Napoleon, they really admire the audacious genius of the man, and make no secret of it. In every palace and museum I have visited at St. Petersburg and Moscow I have seen full-lengths or busts of him in marble, bronze, or oil. Some are originals, others are copies. One painting, entirely new to me, represents him with brown hair, banged. In the Treasury of the Kremlin the guide shows you two camp-beds which Napoleon left behind when he evacuated Moscow. He is always indicating to you the street by which Napoleon entered or withdrew from the city, the steps up which he walked, the doors through which he passed, the chairs in which he sat. You would think that he was a Russian hero. The people still point with a certain pride to the marks of cannon-shot and bullets, and say, "Napoleon!"

Of all the Russian sovereigns, next to Peter the Great, Catharine the Second seems to have been the most extraordinary. The tourist is continually running across her statues, her portraits, her crowns, her jewelry, her silverware. There is more of her personal property and reminders of her of one kind and another on show than of any other Romanoff, man or woman. The best things in all the palaces, the treasuries, and the sacristies were hers. If you see a string of pearls, each perfect and as large as a hazel-nut, even before you have pointed it out, your guide says, "Catharine the Second." If there is a scepter with a particularly large diamond in the top, and the handle knobby with rubies, emeralds, and sapphires, you know who wielded it without being told. To the physical courage of a man she added the delicate æsthetic tastes of a woman. Other rulers may have been more extravagant than she, but Catharine the Second understood how to make boundless wealth contribute to the production of artworks that still live to be admired. The goldsmiths, the silversmiths, the lapidaries, the sculptors, and the painters found in her their most intelligent patroness. In their turn they did their utmost to perpetuate her memory. Stone and canvas, metal and ivory agree in representing her as tall and stout, with ample brain-power, a full lower face, and a most imperial port. She was one born to command, and she would have reduced men to vassalage by her indomitable will if she had not gentler arts for managing them. In

St. Petersburg stands a magnificent bronze image of the Empress, of heroic size. Seated at the base of this lofty figure, on a pedestal running all about it, are nine gentlemen, also in bronze. Their postures are sentimental or statesmanlike or warlike. The guide-book tells us they were favorites of Catharine the Second. In that capacity, perhaps, they thought they could manage her. But they were mistaken. A woman who, when in full army uniform, looked like the most gallant of generals, was not putty in the hands of any favorite. In that amazing collection of odds and ends known as the Treasury, inside the Kremlin, there is an equestrian portrait of Catharine. She bestrides her horse like a man. In front of the picture are two saddles, made for her use and presented to her by some tributary princes or neighboring potentates, who wanted to keep on good terms with her. Her horse, already burdened with her generous weight, could not have shared her admiration of the saddles, for they are heavy with all kinds of precious stones, numbered by the hundreds; and the stirrups and the shoes which the poor beast must wear in her honor are of solid silver.

In a corner of the room where I am now writing, just below the ceiling, is a framed, silver-gilt picture of the Saviour facing the east. The Virgin and Child look down from a similar position in the adjoining bedchamber. Every room in this great labyrinth of a hotel has just such an object of reverence which the pious Russian can not fail to see as he crosses the threshold. To this he pays his homage of signs and bows. He does it a thousand times a day in the streets, where these emblems confront him at every turn. He does not expect people of other religions to conform to any of his notions. He allows them to walk freely about the churches and stare through opera-glasses, in a languid way, at objects which to him are sacred, and to be approached only in a spirit of abasement and veneration. But there is one shrine in this city before which it is expected that every foreigner will remove his hat. If he fails to do so, he is thought an ignorant, boorish fellow, and may be hissed and hooted. It is the fine, large Icon of the Master, which hangs above the Redeemer's gate (Spasköi Vorota)—one of the entrances of the Kremlin. Immemorial custom has made it obligatory to take off the hat when entering this gate and keep it off till the entire width of the wall is traversed. The cabman would let his horses run away before he would neglect this hallowed usage; and if the Tsar himself should fail to comply with it, he would start a revolution.

CHAPTER XXIII.

THE MOSCOW FOUNDLING ASYLUM.

The foundling asylum (Vospitàtelny Dom) is as well known in Moscow as the Tsar Kolokol. Any droschky-driver can take you there by the shortest cut, if you engage him by the "course." Every *mujik* in the streets can and will direct you to it with the greatest pleasure. He may think that you want to adopt a child out of it, or to put one into it. As a man of Moscow, he is interested in both those operations. Let me not be misunderstood. The foundling asylum is not intended to receive only children born out of wedlock. It is indeed a refuge for those poor little waifs. Many a baby, over whom the Moskwa would otherwise close its dark and swift waters, is saved to become a good soldier for the Tsar or a modest and prettily dressed house-maid, simply because the newborn could be put by the mother within the folds of the foundling asylum and none be the wiser. She has only, in the darkness of night, to place the child in a sort of cradle attached to a door outside of the building, and pull a bell. This gives a signal and starts some machinery. The door revolves on its hinges, landing the little stranger on the inside. At the same time, a nurse responds to the summons and takes charge of the baby. If the mother has left any bit of a trinket tied around its neck, or a letter, or a card pinned to its dress, or anything else to identify it, she can claim her own at any time afterward, on proving her maternal rights. If she wants to keep her painful secret forever to herself, she may be sure that her child will be well fed, neatly clothed, taught to read and write, cared for in health and morals, and trained in the religion of the Greek Church, till he or she is old enough to be apprenticed, or adopted out by some respectable citizen, and put in the way of an honest living.

But the most frequent patrons of the asylum are married folk. If they have more children than they can rear, they turn over the surplus to the state—more often as a loan than a gift. They know that the good doctors and nurses of the institution will do all in their power to preserve the little lives unharmed. At the end of five or six years they are more likely to find their Nicolaievitch or Feodorovna well and happy, than if it had run the dreadful gantlet of scarlet fever, cholera infantum, and diphtheria in their own squalid homes. It is a misfortune to feel obliged to surrender a child to such a corporation, though the biggest of souls animates it. The parents are to be pitied—perhaps blamed—but it is not a disgrace to them.

I said that anybody in Moscow could pilot you to the foundling asylum, but you must know the Russian word for it. The landlord of your hotel will give it to you, and you may commit it to memory, or write it down by the sounds. It will not bear the slightest resemblance to the name of a foundling asylum in French, German, Italian, or any other language of which you may have a smattering. The surname of the present writer has always appeared, when chalked in script on the blackboard directories of Russian hotels, as "Tymour," or something to that effect. It reminded him of that monster in history—Timour the Tartar—and such a liberty taken with his patronymic was not at all agreeable.

But to get on to the foundling asylum. Before presenting myself at the visitors' door of the vast building, I took an admission-ticket from my pocket-book. This ticket is made of flimsy paper, about four inches long by three wide; it bears a portrait of the Tsar, a number of Russian words, and a facsimile of somebody's signature. It is popularly known as the "ruble." When a man has this between his thumb and finger, so that it can be seen of men, it will take him through doors that are locked and bolted to all other forms of passport. The same gratifying effects follow the exhibition of the shilling in England, the franc in France, the lira in Italy, the mark in Germany, and the florin in Austria. The door was opened by a dignified person. He loomed up so very large that I thought my ruble was a little too small for his measure; so I did not offer it, but crumpled it suddenly in the palm of my hand. The tall man looked as if he did not expect or desire a "tip." Speaking in French, he kindly asked me in, and I followed him.

I was just in time to see something very interesting. We entered a room at the end of a short passage. At that moment a poorly dressed old woman was in the act of unrolling a huge bundle of shawls and wraps. Over her was bending a matronly person with a very sympathetic face. My polite guide drew near to this group of two, and I stood at his elbow. The old woman peeled off the clothes as if she were unrolling a mummy. Nobody spoke a word, but I heard a faint cry from the center of the mysterious bundle. Then I knew that this was the reception-room for babies, and that here was the newest of the comers. A moment more, and a child was sprawling before us in its unadorned beauty. It lay in the middle of the heap of shawls as in a soft nest, which it was loath to quit. As it made another little piping cry, a tear moistened the old woman's eye, but she showed no other sign of agitation. I surmised that she was the grandmother of the baby, and had come to discharge a duty for which the mother was ashamed. The secret—whatever it was—was confided to the care of the good matron alone, not even my guide being allowed to share it. Then a little Greek cross of filigree silver was handed over as a keepsake and means of identifying and reclaiming the child.

These preliminaries over, the matron touched a bell. In response, there came a woman bearing a steelyard scale, and a measuring-tape. She held the scale aloft with a firm hand, and the matron lifted the baby gently from its nest and placed it in the large bowl-like receptable for weighing. Between its bare pink flesh and the cold metal there was a thin sheet of soft cloth. The baby performed its part bravely, for it lay perfectly quiet, while the matron rapidly adjusted the weight till the beam hung true. She could not have done the job more carefully if she had been selling the baby at a hundred rubles a pound. The exact weight was then entered in a great ledger.

Next came the nice measuring of the head—all around just above the eyes—and its length through the ears from crown to chin; then the girth of its little body below the arms; and, finally, the candidate was raised aloft again and turned in every direction in the strong light of a large bay-window. The aspirants for the honor of the princess's hand in the "Arabian Nights" were not more critically inspected for blemishes. The object of this minute examination of the body was to note birth-marks, if any. Not one was found, as I can certify, who witnessed the operation at short range. This over, a small ticket or medal made of hard wood, numbered 11,283, and attached to an India-rubber cord, was hung about baby's neck. It would receive a name later on; for the present it was only a numerical expression. Thus ended the first stage of baby's initiation. At that point, the old woman whom I provisionally call "grandmother," left the scene, carrying the pile of shawls and wraps loosely upon her arm. If she felt any emotions in parting with the child, she completely stifled them.

The baby, still stark naked, but not shivering in the warm air of the room, was then carried away. The guide beckoned me to follow it with him, and I did so. We entered a small bath-room where were a nice porcelain-lined bath-tub, of baby size, with silver plated stop-cocks, a showering apparatus, sponges, soap and scrubbing-brush all complete. A stout woman, with fat arms bared clear to the shoulder, officiated at baby's first bath, and I was expected to see it through. It is one of the penalties of visiting public institutions anywhere with guides, that you are in their hands and must go the rounds. But I had become interested in baby's fortunes, and found myself watching the soaping and sponging and scrubbing without being much bored. If that baby takes all the ills of life as bravely as it took the water in its ears, and the soap in its eyes, then there will be one angelic disposition more in this wicked world. It sputtered a little, but never cried or sniveled once. After it was all wiped dry and powdered with a flour-dredger, the stout woman shouldered her charge and led the way to another room. I found myself really curious to see what would happen to baby next. So I followed, with the guide at my heels.

We were now in the dressing-room; there was a large wardrobe with glass doors; through these I could see baby-dresses hung on pegs. They were variously trimmed with blue, red, and yellow ribbons, and I soon found myself wondering which color would fall to baby's share. Thus concerned in its affairs had I unconsciously become. On shelves in the wardrobe were displayed little stockings, soft knitted shoes, and caps. There was plenty of clothes on hand for every emergency. The woman reached up and took down a long, white dress trimmed with yellow. Now I had noticed baby's eyes and they were blue; so I took the liberty of suggesting, through the guide, that the ribbons ought to match the eyes. The hint was graciously adopted. If any future visitor to the Foundling Asylum of Moscow should happen to observe the fine blue eyes of No. 11,283, he will appreciate my good taste in matching them with the ribbons, which, if worn out, I trust will be renewed.

"And, now," said my guide, "you must see the baby nursed." I murmured a few modest objections. I did not wish to intrude upon such strictly private functions. The nurse would not like it, etc. The guide smiled, and said I must follow the baby. So we passed through another doorway, and entered the nurses' room.

It was a long apartment, spotless as to wooden floor and whitewashed ceiling. Along one side was a row of strong, wooden cradles; on the other side were the nurses' beds with frames of iron. The sheets were snowy and the pillows without crease. There were ten or twelve nurses present, each one rocking a cradle or holding a child to her breast. Ruddier and more robust women I never saw. They were mostly under thirty years old, I should say. The contour of their faces was more oval than the type of head seen between St. Petersburg and Moscow, and they were handsomer in other respects. They were dressed for business in neat and appropriate costumes, less scanty and more reserved than one sees at the opera.

Inquiring, I learned that the best nurses come from provinces south of Moscow, and that most of these were of that select class. As we entered they arose, still nursing their babies, and courtesied to us gracefully. At first, I felt that I ought to apologize for disturbing this large but peaceful family. The nurses, however, soon put me at ease. They took the visit quite as a matter of course. They could not have been less self-conscious had I been an artist, and they professional models. As we passed down the line, the guide chucked some of the babies under the chin or patted their heads. Not to be singular I did the same thing. Each nurse seemed to think the act complimentary to herself, as well as to the baby. I dare say, if her own chin had been chucked, she would not have taken offense. But we did not try it.

Near the end of the line stood a nurse, who had no baby in her arms. The cradle just behind her was empty. Death had removed its little tenant. She was the destined custodian of the neophyte in blue ribbons. I was glad of it. In looking at her honest face and healthy complexion, one felt sure that she was not to blame for that loss in the fold. The nourishment she supplied must have been life-giving. On that broad and generous bosom there was room for twins. As she saw the baby borne toward her, she knew what it meant. Her large eyes shone with pleasure. As the baby stopped opposite her, both reached out their arms. It was an act of nature and spontaneous. That nurse and that child were made for each other. Its own mother could not have folded it to her heart more tenderly. I felt that I had no right to push curiosity further. I was satisfied that baby's fortunes, so far followed with interest, had reached one happy stage. As I turned to depart, the last sounds I heard from baby were faint gurgles of satisfaction.

My initiation into the mysteries of the foundling asylum was now complete. I would gladly have stepped out of window on to the green grass, with that touching picture of suckling innocence still in my mind. But a guide, like a sentinel, must go his rounds. So I was taken by moral force through other rooms full of nurses and babies, whom I passed in review. The prevalent quietness of the infants was surprising. Those who were awake were not crying. Like everybody else in the building, they appeared to be on their good behavior during my visit. One touch of human nature—if only the clinching of a tiny fist—would have been a relief amid all that angelic display of sweet temper. It made one suspect that they had been dosed with something to keep them quiet. I was glad to pass on to the laundry, the hospital (with only two or three little inmates) the kitchen and the pantry, till finally we came to a refectory. There was a tableful of children large enough to sit and ply the spoon. The oldest of the thirty or forty could not have been more than six years. They were boys and girls, simply and neatly dressed in uniform style. They all rose as we entered, and held up their spoons in salute. It was a pretty sight and more confusing to the visitor than one would think. Such courtesy seems to demand a better response than a bow. A distribution of sugar-plums or of small coin would seem the proper thing. But this is not allowed; so that, all we can do, besides bowing, is to walk around this company of little people, and smile at them in a vague, benevolent way. Through the guide I begged them to be seated. They did not need to be asked twice, for they were hungry, and

I had interrupted them in the act of eating what looked like hasty-pudding and milk. It recalled my own early fondness for that dish, and I would gladly have been invited to join the simple repast, even at the risk of spoiling a keen appetite for the forthcoming elaborate dinner at the Slaviansky Bazaar. It was a pleasure to note the size of the bowls. They held an honest quart apiece, and had been so scrupulously filled that some of the children stopped plying their spoons before they got to the bottom; others rapidly emptied their bowls and polished off the interiors. For those greedier ones there was still a supply of sweetened bread in stacks, waiting a signal to be passed around. It was plain that the older children, as well as the babies themselves, were objects of a provident care which would shame many parents. Not otherwise can I explain the bright eyes, contented faces, and chubby bodies I saw in that refectory. Many of the children were strikingly good-looking. I recall the seraphic face of a five-year-old girl, with large black eyes, and a perfect mouth, and two dimples dotting cheeks of rose-leaves. And one of the boys looked almost like a twin brother of the child in the arms of the Sistine Madonna. There was the same dreamy, far-away gaze in his eyes. I wondered how parents could abandon such beautiful children to the care of other people.

This was the climax of interest at the foundling asylum, as the guide then candidly informed me upon being questioned. It was much against the good man's wishes that I tore myself away from him. But, I hope, when I pressed a humble gift into his hand, that he felt the more reconciled to my departure, though it is only due to him, as to all of his class whom I met in Russia, to say that they have the rare tact of not appearing to want one's money. One always feels a little delicacy about offering *pour boires*. But the truth binds me to say that they are never declined.

CHAPTER XXIV.

RUSSIAN EPICURISM IN TEA — THE JOLTAI TCHAI, OR YELLOW-FLOWER BRAND.

BEING at Moscow, I improved the occasion to look up the yellow-flower tea—the Joltai Tchai—of which I had read and heard much. Travelers, claiming to be veracious, have told us that this tea is the first picking of the young and tender leaves of the choicest plants in China, and that it is brought overland on the backs of porters. I have seen pictures of men in Chinese dress climbing up mountains at angles of 70°, with chests of the precious tea strapped on their shoulders. The object of this incredible toil, we were assured, was to avoid a sea-voyage, in which the damp, salt air would impair the exquisite flavor of the Joltai Tchai. The story went that this tea could always be known by the presence of the small, yellowish-white buds or flowers of its native stalk scattered through it, without which, as the quack advertisements say, "none is genuine"; though it always seemed to me that that proof must be a fallible one for all those people outside of China who had never seen a tea-flower, and that, anyhow, it would be easy to cheat them by mixing the real blossom with poor tea. But these same enthusiastic authors proceeded to give higher and more subtile tests for Joltai Tchai. They declared that, when a package of it was opened, it exhaled the most delicious of perfumes, which filled a room on the instant. They did not compare it to any earthly or known odor, but left the impression that it was something heavenly, and therefore indescribable. Its flavor on the palate was vaguely mentioned as aromatic, delicate, and yet perceptible when diluted with any amount of water. The mental effects ascribed to this tea were no less remarkable. It was said that a cup of it, with only two teaspoonfuls to the ordinary pot, was equal to a pint of champagne for exhilaration, without the least after-clap of headache. As for those obfuscations of the intellect commonly known as "cobwebs," it would brush away the last filament of them from the nooks and corners of the stupidest minds. But we were solemnly warned not to take two cups of it at a time, under penalty of losing sleep for forty-eight hours. Its cost to the consumer in Russia was variously stated at ten to twenty dollars a pound. But a tea, half as wonderful as this, should be cheap at any price. I resolved to buy some of it.

I was so anxious to secure the authentic article, that I called upon an English gentleman, to whom I was referred, long a resident of Moscow, and speaking Russian like a native. He consented to accompany me to the only shop he knew of where the real Joltai Tchai could be obtained. We found it in a part of the city but little visited by foreigners. The shop was small, and three Tartar-like persons stood behind the counter. On the walk thither the Englishman had kindly explained that the Tartars were the most honest people in Russia —where honesty is the rule, so far as I know. He assured me that Tartars pure and simple were preferred before all other races for places of financial responsibility. They made the best cashiers, head book-keepers, superintendents, and managers. And when he said he was taking me to a Tartar tea-shop I felt as if I should not be robbed.

The three Tartars did not even nod at us as we entered, but only stood at ease to take our order. This was quickly given in Russian by my companion, who first, however, asked the price of Joltai Tchai by the pound. It was ten rubles (about eight dollars and thirty cents in paper money), which was less than I had expected, and I mentioned the quantity I would buy. One of the Tartars took down a small box from an upper shelf, opened it, and disclosed another box having a tightly fitting slide cover; this he removed, and brought to light a thick tin-foil wrapping, which being unfolded revealed tissue-paper, beneath several thicknesses of which lay the tea. Up to this time I had stood back, waiting to catch the all-penetrating odor of the Joltai Tchai at a distance, but it did not report itself. So I leaned forward, bent over the little chest, and took a good long sniff. Yes, there was a decided tea-smell, but no more searching or ravishing than that of the Oolong I had been consuming at home all my life. This was disappointment number one.

The required amount of tea was carefully weighed before me. I could watch it as it was shaken out of the chest into the capacious scale. It looked about the color of green tea, with a yellow shade in a side-light, and had no points of distinction except the presence of many shriveled-up, dirty-white buds. These were yellow only to the eye of faith; and that was disappointment number two.

After the tea had been weighed with great particularity, the Tartar removed it to the back of the shop, to do it up in a package with many thicknesses of rice-paper and tin-foil. I could not help fearing that, when out of my sight, the man would substitute a far inferior tea for the costly Joltai

Tchai. But when the Englishman, speaking from his past experience with the race, said, "You can trust him," I felt completely reassured, paid my bill, thanked my English friend for his assistance, and returned to the hotel with my treasure. And here let me give the sequel of my experience with Joltai Tchai.

It was not thoroughly tested for its supposed remarkable qualities till I returned to the United States. Russian lovers of Joltai Tchai will here object that the trial was not a fair one; that it should have been made on their soil, before the tea had crossed any salt-water. There is force in this suggestion. But it seemed a pity to break a package so shapely, and intended to secure the contents completely against the harmful influence of the elements. And then, too, all the tea I drank in Russia was so excellent that I did not want any better there. At home it was the subject of many experiments, which go far to establish the following conclusions: The yellow-flower tea is delicate to a fault; so much so that persons accustomed to the rank and adulterated teas of commerce find it insipid. It is like the finest old Johannisberger or Château-Margaux as compared with heady new wines; no one but a professional tea-taster can appreciate its high grade. Its odor is markedly not different from that of any other tea, except as one may say it is more "tea-like." Its unique excellence lies in its clarifying and cheering effect on the mind of the drinker. It disperses a headache like magic, and mental anxiety as well. If one were possessed of "blue-devils," I should expect two stiff cups of Joltai Tchai to send them scampering.

If it is worth, as some think, two or three dollars to extract a few fleeting moments of joy from a bottle of champagne, then one should not grudge thrice as much for a pound of yellow-flower tea, which will insure him perhaps some hundred hours of innocent exaltation. And, as for sleep, I have not yet lost any from its use, but prefer not to drink a strong infusion of it late at night.

Like any other high-grade tea, where the object is not to disguise the flavor of the herb, it is best without sugar or cream, or even the slice of lemon beloved by all Russians. But these ingredients, unless too freely employed, do not rob the tea of its slightly peculiar taste, or impair its virtue as a most agreeable tonic or stimulant. Connoisseurs in teas prefer to treat it with fresh, actually boiling water poured directly on the tea in a sunken cylinder full of holes set into the pot. The clear infusion passes through this perforated cylinder, and it should be drunk immediately afterward. But other persons less critical like it better when the boiling water is poured on the tea at the bottom of the pot, and then allowed to draw a good five or even ten minutes on the stove itself, or, better still, on the iron shelf for hot plates above it. This treatment makes a stronger decoction, but tends to substitute rankness for delicacy of flavor. But it brings out some of the valuable properties of the tea which do not apparently respond to the other and more superficial method. On the whole, the verdict of the majority of those who have tried it both ways is in favor of the drawing process. Under no circumstances does it acquire a bitter taste. And yet, after all that I have said in favor of Joltai Tchai, it is a fact that nobody who drinks it seems to think that it is anything extraordinary till told so. And I must say that I am sometimes in serious doubt whether my high opinion of the tea is not the work of pure imagination.

CHAPTER XXV.

A HUNT FOR MALACHITE AND LAPIS-LAZULI IN THE GOSTINNOI DVOR.

An American's pride in his importance as a customer is apt to get a bad fall when he enters at random a shop in Moscow. At St. Petersburg he has noticed that his patronage was not greatly coveted in the vast bazaar opposite the Hôtel d'Europe on the Nevskoi Prospekt where he made most of his purchases. He missed the assiduous, almost servile, attention to which he was accustomed in London, Paris, and Vienna. But in Moscow the shop-keepers carry their indifference a point further. They act as if they wanted to repel American customers. This is because we are confounded with Englishmen, and, as such, are not liked. Dressing and speaking like Englishmen and too often imitating them in tricks of manner, Americans are only naturally mistaken for a class of foreigners with whom Russia has perpetual feud. As Moscow is the heart of Russia, the anti-English feeling is strongest there. Americans soon find this out, whenever they walk the streets or visit the great bazaars, from the icy atmosphere that seems to surround every Russian like a nimbus. At the great hotels the Englishmen are welcome, because the landlords are superior to local prejudices when their guests pay well. At least one porter or waiter who speaks French is kept on hand for their convenience. At some of the larger and higher-priced shops of Moscow, they are also treated with some of the consideration paid to them in Western Europe. But their room is undoubtedly more desired than their company by the Russians at large. And Americans, except where they can make their nationality known, suffer from the same antipathy. I give my own experience.

I wanted to buy some articles made of malachite and lapis-lazuli. Having seen in the churches whole pillars rising from floor to ceiling veneered with those beautiful green and blue stones, I imagined that both of them would be abundant and cheap in the heart of the empire where they are mined. Much to my surprise, the manager of my hotel could not direct me to any shop for such purchases. He advised me to try an immense bazaar near the Kremlin. Its Russian name, as nearly as I can give it in English characters, is Gostinnoi Dvor. The district of the city in which it is situated is the Kitai Gorod (Chinese town or quarter). I took his advice, starting out just after breakfast one fine morning, and determining to give all of twenty—possibly thirty—of my precious minutes to the search for lapis-lazuli and malachite.

The bazaar is a great, covered market divided into innumerable stalls. Each stall has its show-cases thrust in front, containing the choicest of the goods for sale, usually ticketed with prices in rubles and kopecks. These are given in figures to be read of all men. Just be' ind the show-cases stands a man or woman on the alert. In the rear of the little booth is the proprietor, sitting on a three-legged stool before a ledger. On either side of him rise tiers of shelves packed with his reserved treasures. As I started to go down the narrow passage-way between two rows of these stalls I observed the long perspective of men or women waiting for customers at that early hour. I almost dreaded to run the gantlet. My object was to go through the entire bazaar; "mark down" the shops at which lapis-lazuli and malachite were exposed for sale, with a note of the prices, and, after I had found just what suited me, then to come back and buy it on the best terms I could make.

To escape being teased to purchase the clothes, boots and shoes, kitchen utensils, mouse-traps, fancy soaps, cutlery, and thousands of other things I did not want, I kept to the middle of the passage-way, walking fast with head down, but looking out sharply at the corners of my eyes. These swift side-glances took in not only the strangely various contents of all the shops I passed, but also the looks of the people in charge. I was much astonished to receive no particular notice from them. They looked at me as at a passing dog or cat, but not one of them nodded or beckoned. And not one even began to tidy up his things with a wisp-broom, or change them about ostentatiously, as the shopman in other lands often does when a possible customer comes in sight. The Russian face is generally considered inexpressive. But I never knew till then how blank it could be. Once in a while, however, I noticed a lowering of brows and a slight protrusion of the lower lip, which looked very much like disdain. I did not then know that I was mistaken for an Englishman, and that I could not have chosen a place for shopping where our insular friends are held in such large measure of dislike as in that truly Russian bazaar.

Two pretty girls, dressed in bright colors, with silver skewers in their hair, were selling flowers at one of the stands. I stepped up to buy a buttonhole bouquet, and selected one, tendering a ruble for change. I was anxious to see if either of the girls would offer to pin it to the lapel of my coat, as flower-venders often do elsewhere. To propitiate them, I said "American." This single word has been known to produce wonderful effect on occasions. But it was thrown away here. These fair creatures were of the peasant class, totally ignorant of any language but Russian. It is doubtful if they had ever seen an American to know him. To them I was only an Englishman, and therefore it was that one of them sheered away from me, and the other pouted, and I was obliged to pin on my own *boutonnière*. Now, I was indeed vexed, not guessing the real trouble.

I determined to compel some of these people to notice me. I stepped up to a counter, picked up an old copper frying-pan, and rapped it sharply with my knuckles. This meant in the sign-language, "How much?" I had a note-book and pencil in hand, and intended to intimate by dumb-show that the proprietor should jot down the price there. The frying-pan, when smitten, sounded like a gong, and made quite a noise. This was all the better for me, as it was sure to bring down the man who sat back there on a high stool, and was the only occupant of the shop. He descended from his perch, but it was with a scowl, as if the harsh sound had disturbed his meditations. Looking at me, he seemed instantly to make up his mind that I did not want to buy that ancient frying-pan on any terms. And this was true. But I was not prepared for what he did. He just took the utensil gently by the handle, gave it a little twist to detach it from my grasp, and then laid it down on the counter. It was as if he had said, "No more of that, please." I stalked away as majestically as possible, without any attempt at explanation. Broad faces with high cheek-bones were on the grin all about. It would have been a real comfort to know that I was mistaken for an Englishman.

I walked fast down the middle of the aisle, resolved not to stop again till I saw some stall at which jewelry and ornamental knickknacks were on sale. For about a thousand feet farther it was a monotonous stretch of useful articles to wear or to eat or to furnish a house withal. Then I came to a corner round which was another passage-way about a quarter of a mile long, also lined with shops. And I may as well explain here that, at regular intervals of a few hundred feet, other alleys just as full of shops branch off criss-cross. The bazaar is of the distracting chess-board pattern; and the man who started out, as I did, to see the whole of it, in order to miss no good chance of buying some malachite and lapis-lazuli, had a bigger job in hand than he dreamed of.

Far ahead, I saw strings of gilt beads dangling in front of a shop. Hurrying on, I found that it was full of ear-rings, breastpins, chains, crosses, and all the other kinds of jewelry in vogue everywhere. The objects were mostly of silver and gold. There were real diamonds, rubies, emeralds, and pearls. Putting on my best smile, to propitiate the owner, who, like all the others, did not seem to want to have anything to do with me, I peered into his show-cases and ran my eye rapidly over the contents. Among them there was nothing green, but emeralds, or blue, but sapphires. Still, I was not discouraged, for there were miles or more of shops under that vast roof, and sooner or later the desired objects must be found.

After a smart walk of about five minutes more, through files of apathetic Russians without seeing what was wanted, I came upon a colony of Jews, and warmed up to them at once, when they bowed and beckoned to me. It was evident that they were anxious to trade, and had no prejudices against supposed Englishmen. Several of them dealt in jewelry and works of art; and, as luck would have it, there was a huge object made of malachite exhibited conspicuously on a shelf in front of one of their stalls. It was shaped like a punch-bowl, of about one gallon capacity. I pointed to it with my cane. The man took it down for me. It was a masterpiece. The fragments of malachite of which it was composed exhibited the various green shades of the stone, and the characteristic wavy lines. The pieces were so carefully selected, and the joining was so nicely done, that the colors and the lines ran together making a perfect whole. At first sight, one could not believe that this punch-bowl was not carved from a single piece of malachite. There was no need of asking the Jew his price, for it was ticketed plainly enough two hundred and fifty—the figures standing for rubles. This would be about one hundred and twenty-five dollars, counting the ruble at its then gold value of fifty cents. I might have bought it at a third or perhaps a half off, and was strongly tempted to try for it. But its size, the trouble of carrying it round in a trunk, and, not least, the high duty which would be levied on it in New York, were enough to restrain me. I looked all over his exposed stock, but could see no more malachite and not a sign of lapis-lazuli. It then occurred to me that, being a Jew, he might have traveled, and have some knowledge of the world's great languages. So I threw scraps of French, German, and English at him in succession. To all he only shook his head, and expelled from his chest a few of those deep gutturals which I had already learned to recognize as pure Slavic. Like most Russians, whether Jew or Christian, he had never been out of his country, nor spoken to a foreigner. Nothing so deeply impressed me with the immensity of the Russian Empire, and the isolated condition of her people, as the fact that so few of them, and those only the well educated—even in the two great cities, St. Petersburg and Moscow—understand a word of any language but their own. I nodded good-by to my Jewish friend, whose kind manner showed that he regretted as much as I that we could not find a common ground for exchanging ideas, and went on with the search.

It might have been half an hour later when I saw, shining through the window of a show-case, a pair of deep-blue sleeve-buttons. I stepped up and examined them closely. The shade of blue was indigo. The surface had a fine, hard polish, and reflected to the eye those little star-like points of light which, in the true lapis-lazuli, seem just buried beneath its surface. The beautiful stones were heavily mounted in gold. They were exactly what I wanted. The ticket linked to them bore the figures twenty-eight—rubles, of course. This was not too high for genuine lapis-lazuli sleeve-buttons, gold mounted in the best style. The pleasant looks of this Russian proprietor seemed to invite me to tarry and trade.

Forgetting for a moment that he could not possibly understand English, I pointed to the lovely objects, and said, interrogatively, "Lapis-lazuli?" To my great delight he nodded and smiled. That was a "Yes," all the world over.

"Is it gold?" I asked, in reference to the setting, at the same time repeating the question in French. It was plain that he understood the one or the other language, for he nodded and smiled again. To find some one at last who could catch my idea was indeed gratifying. Anticipating my wish, he then removed the sleeve-buttons from the show-case and put them in my hand. I turned them over and examined them minutely. Though unfamiliar with the best tests for lapis-lazuli, I knew that, like all natural stones, it should have a cold touch, and not warm readily in the palm. I held it for a moment, when it became heated in contact with the flesh. Then I strongly suspected it to be paste. A solid gold setting should be heavy of its size. This one was very light. I decided that the sleeve-buttons were not a bargain at any price, and laid them down on the counter.

At that instant I was startled by a voice at my elbow, which said, "Those just suit me, if you don't want 'em."

I turned and saw a plethoric Englishman, who looked flushed and panted as if from over-exertion. "Fact is," said he, "I've been chasin' up and down this blarsted bazaar after lapus-lazerlee more'n two hours, and this is the first lot I've struck. I don't want to take 'em away from you, you know. But I've promised to buy a pair of just such sleeve-buttons for a friend in London."

"You are welcome to them," I said; "but"— and I was about to give him a friendly hint to examine the goods very carefully before buying.

"Thanks," he said, interrupting me. "Twenty-eight rubles, I see by the ticket. I'll try him at half-price," he added in an undertone for my ear.

Then, raising his voice at the shop-keeper, he cried, "I'll give you fourteen, and not another ruble." The Russian certainly understood that much of English, for again he nodded and smiled mechanically as usual; whereupon his customer thrust two ten-ruble notes at him, in evident anxiety not to lose a great bargain. As he did so, he said to me in a side-whisper, "Now I've got 'em, I don't mind telling you that a cousin of mine paid thirty rubles for a smaller pair than them at Nijni-Novgorod two years ago."

Now came a surprise for our hasty English friend; for the shopman, with a bewildered expression of face, handed back to him one of the ten-ruble notes. Then he opened a till and scooped out a quantity of change—some paper and some silver and copper. I now shared the Englishman's amazement, and we both looked on, silently wondering what would happen next. Finally, he deliberately counted out seven rubles and ninety-two kopecks, and pushed them toward the Englishman. This made the price of the sleeve-buttons only two rubles and eight kopecks, or about one dollar and four cents of American money. Here, indeed, was a stupendous bargain, unless the lapis-lazuli were only paste and the gold pinchbeck.

The latter proved to be the case, as the Englishman and I readily perceived after giving the sleeve-buttons a more minute examination than we had hitherto bestowed on them. The figures on the ticket, when critically inspected, turned out to be 2 with a dot followed by an 8. This meant two rubles and eight kopecks, but the dot was so faint that we had both failed to notice it at first. The Englishman had rashly taken it for granted that the materials were genuine without asking any questions. He had no cause of complaint against the seller, for he had not been cheated. To persons who wanted such imitations, they were worth the low price charged. The fact was, as the Englishman and I agreed on comparing notes, that the

Russian had not understood one word of anything either of us had said to him. He had simply nodded and grinned, as a matter of civility, trusting that, when the business came to close quarters, the meaning could mutually be made clear. This habit of nodding, as the equivalent of "Yes," is very common among people in all parts of Europe, who have not the faintest idea of what you are asking them. They take the chance that "Yes" may be the right answer, and perhaps they even say "Yes" to you in whatever language they speak, in order to keep up the illusion. I have been a hundred times misled—and often greatly to my annoyance—by this nod or spoken assent of coachmen, porters, and tradesmen in all parts of Europe.

The Englishman realized the impossibility of explaining matters to the jewelry-dealer, and of getting his money back. He accepted the situation philosophically. After the goods had been carefully packed for him in a little pasteboard box, he put them in his pocket with the simple remark, "Good enough present for somebody, you know."

We then separated with a friendly hand-shake, he to return to the Hôtel Dusaux, where he said he was stopping, and I to pursue my researches for a stone almost as elusive as the philosopher's.

"I've done the whole bazaar, and I know it's no use," were his parting words. But I determined to see for myself; and it was not till the end of two hours more that I gave up the hunt in despair, wearied and foot-sore.

But I had better luck when I returned to St. Petersburg. There I had the pleasure of inspecting several small but choice stocks of malachite goods, and purchasing some specimens at reasonable rates. I saw a few pieces of lapis-lazuli—undoubtedly genuine—but not one as handsome as the imitation sold to that Englishman in the Gostinnoi Dvor of Moscow. The prices asked for them seemed always far too high for their intrinsic beauty. So I left them all in their show-cases on the Nevskoi Prospekt, to meet the possible demand of other Americans for that kind of stone.

CHAPTER XXVI.

THE PEACOCK-FEATHER MYSTERY—MANAYUNK AND THE OLD MASTERS—HIS FRUITLESS SEARCH FOR THE KREMLIN—THE MOSCOW RAG-FAIR—THE PETROVSKY PALACE—DINING IN THE GROUNDS.

THE Russians are semi-Orientals in one respect. They are not as sternly utilitarian as we of the West. The man with the long, blue tunic corded at the waist, and the cap decked with peacock-feathers, who received us with speechless effusion at the Moscow railway-station, was ornamental, not useful. He did not take charge of our hand-bags or shawl-strap. That was done by another man, who wore no peacock-feathers. He did not drive the carriage and four (white horses abreast) from the station to the hotel. He sat by the driver's side, erect and imposing. I was moved by a powerful curiosity to know what he did, except to impress the stranger with a sense of barbaric splendor.

Whenever I had occasion to leave the hotel, I

always found one of the pair (for there were two of these magnificent retainers) at his post on or near the door-steps, gazing into vacancy. On my return I never failed to see the peacock-feathers vibrating above any crowd of servitors or visitors who might be sunning themselves in front of the Slaviansky Bazaar. But what did this man do? Such was the question that haunted my practical Western mind. I decided to watch him and find out.

One morning I took my station for this purpose near the entrance, where I could observe his movements at my leisure. The taller and finer-looking of the two was on duty (if such it can be called) at that hour. The feathers in his cap were quite new, and their gold and green eyes gleamed iridescent in the sunlight. His long, blue tunic was nicely brushed, and his boots were highly polished. There he stood, almost motionless, save when he shifted the weight of his body from one leg to the other. He was in a position where he could be seen by everybody who entered or left the hotel. While I remained there on the watch, some trunks were brought in, but he did not lend a hand. Other trunks were taken out to the sidewalk, but he held aloof from them. He neither gave nor received orders. His patient attitude and his calm stoicism reminded one of the North American Indian. Only once did he exhibit any sign of interest in mundane affairs. That was when a horse-fly or blue-bottle buzzed about his head in a very provoking way. He could not conceal his annoyance; and, when the insect alighted on a door-post near him, he leaned over and killed it with a quick stroke of his huge palm, and instantly resumed his erect position. At that precise moment I caught his eye, and smiled at him. But he did not smile back. That would not have been dignified, and dignity was apparently his sole object in life.

My observations were here interrupted. A young man whom I had previously noticed loitering about the hotel stepped up to me, and asked in a pleasant voice, "Are you an American, sir?"

I knew at once that he was a compatriot, and judged from his accent that he was a Philadelphian. He was a nicely-dressed, wholesome youth, and I warmed to him.

Being assured that I was an American, he began to talk freely, as if he had lawful claims on my time and attention, and I was glad to give him both, although he broke into an interesting investigation and caused me to leave a problem forever unsolved.

"Can you tell me if there is a picture-gallery of the old masters in Moscow?"

"Nothing to speak of. The only collections of old paintings worth seeing in Russia are at Petersburg."

"Sure of it?" with a pleased expression in his eyes.

"Perfectly."

"You can't imagine how glad I am!"—and his face testified his joy.

"Why?"

"I don't mind telling you, seeing that you are another American. My aunt is a great admirer of old china, old furniture, and old pictures. She has plenty of money, and her house at Manayunk, Philadelphia, is just full of 'em. I'm her only nephew. But I am boring you, perhaps."

"Not at all," said I, really interested, and curious to know why he rejoiced over the absence of the old masters from Moscow. "Fire away."

"Thank you. Well, you see, my aunt would give anything if she could come to Europe, and go through all the galleries that tire me so"—and he heaved a sigh. "But she's afraid to cross the ocean. So she made me promise that I would go and see the most famous pictures of the old masters—the *she-durvs*, they call 'em—and describe 'em for her in my letters, the best I know how. It's no fun, I assure you, but then she's my aunt."

"And you her favorite nephew" (with a smile).

"Exactly. And I want to repay some of her kindness. For she is real good to me. Of course, I don't pretend to judge 'em for myself. All I have to do is to praise 'em to Auntie. I can't lay it on too thick for her. It was a big job at Petersburg, you bet."

"Why at Petersburg?"

"Because there's such an awful lot of the old masters there—the real, genuine things. I must have seen sixty or seventy Rubenses at the Hermitage; and about an acre of Rembrandts, and, as for the Van Dycks, they made me sick. Do you know," he continued, speaking low, as if imparting a great secret, "that a man can get to hate Murillo, if he sees enough of him?"

I replied that I could understand his feelings of satiety. "The full soul loatheth the honeycomb," etc.

"I forgot to say that the old fellow I loathe most of all is Botticelli. And he's the very one Auntie is craziest about. She has collected all the photographs of his pictures she could get in America and I am adding to the stock all I can pick up in Europe."

"But there are not many Botticellis in the world. At least, I find them scarce. That old fellow, as you call him, can not trouble you very much."

"That's it," said Manayunk. "It's the scarcity of Botticellis that gives me the bother. You see Auntie told me not to miss a Botticelli on any account. I have to look over all the pictures for the names of the artists to be sure I don't skip him. At first I trusted to the printed catalogue, but some of 'em are old and not corrected up to date; and then, again, the pictures are changed about, and the numbers get mixed."

"You are conscientious at any rate, and do not neglect your aunt's commission."

"Yes. She is very much pleased, she writes me, and thinks I'm becoming a good judge of the old masters. That's because I puff 'em so, I suppose. But I tell you, I'm right glad of a rest here. All I really had to see in Moscow was the Kremlin and the big bell. I've seen the bell, but isn't it strange I can't find the Kremlin?"

"Can't find the Kremlin?" I echoed, in amazement.

"At all events, the droschky-drivers can't or won't take me to it. Kremlin, I am told, is a good Russian word, and I should think the Russians ought to understand it. The first day I came here, I jumped into a droschky, and, said I, 'Kremlin!' The man nodded, and off we went like a flash.

Just at the head of the street, we passed through an opening in a wall and came into another part of Moscow. It is full of churches and buildings that look like palaces, but I don't care about them any more. I didn't know the Russian words for 'big bell,' but the driver went to it without my asking. When I had looked at that long enough, I said 'Kremlin' again, very plain. The driver nodded, and away we went. He must have taken me through miles of streets, and I was expecting every moment he would pull up at the Kremlin. But no, he kept driving on, until, after about half an hour, we came round to the big bell again. I called 'Kremlin' at him once more, and he grinned and waved his hand about in a sort of general way. I never saw anybody so stupid. So I yelled 'Slaviansky Bazaar!' at him, and he brought me home. Perhaps, now, you can tell me how to find the fortress, prison, or whatever it is, they call the Kremlin."

"Here is where you feel the want of a guide-book," said I, gently. "If you had one, you would find that the Kremlin is not a single structure, but is the name of a great inclosed space with two miles of walls. All those palaces and churches of which you speak are within the Kremlin, and important features of it. The poor droschky-driver was showing you the Kremlin all the time to the best of his ability."

Manayunk looked a little sheepish at this explanation, as it reflected on his want of intelligence. "Thank you," said he, hurriedly, at the same time consulting his watch, and, without another word, he bolted into the street.

When the visitor becomes satiated with the splendors of Moscow, he may find it pleasant—for a change—to make a tour of the rag-fair or old-clothes market. The site is an open space of about two acres in the heart of the city. From dawn till dark, in fair weather, it is filled with eager traders, who come there to buy, or sell, or barter. The second-hand goods are generally so well used up that they may be placed on the dirty cobble stones without receiving further injury. There they remain arranged as neatly and compactly as possible, with the proprietor standing guard over them and ready for business. Only a few of the traffickers have stands of any kind for the exhibition of their wares. The use of these is reserved for the more aristocratic merchants, who occupy sheltered places alongside the ancient wall, whose towering height affords a shade for them during several hours of the day. It is among the multitude who spread dilapidated treasures on the ground that the most amusing incidents are to be noted by the inquisitive stranger.

Articles which are thrown away by Americans as wholly valueless would be offered in the Moscow rag-fair and find ready purchasers. Nothing would seem more unlikely to be bought than a single boot, the mate of which had been lost. But I saw one of extraordinary size—No. 15, I should say— which was the center of quite a gathering. The boot had been brilliantly polished for the occasion, and I supposed at first that it was the specimen sign of some enterprising *mujik* prepared to "shine 'em up" for ten kopecks. Then I noticed a man measuring the boot by the standard of his own foot, to see if it would suit him. It was about an inch too long. He shook his head. Other spectators with large feet stepped forward, and made the same personal comparison with the unmated boot. One man thrust his stockingless foot into the yawning leather, and rattled round in it for a minute, much to the amusement of the bystanders. Then he gently kicked it off, and evidently dismissed all thought of buying it. The boot was unpatched, and not run down at the heel, and it seemed a great pity that an article in such superior condition should go unbought. The proprietor, whose only stock in trade was this solitary boot, was getting anxious, when relief unexpectedly arrived. A strapping fellow, about six and a half feet high, elbowed his way through the throng to see what was going on. The instant his eye rested on the boot, it gleamed with surprise. He placed his own foot by the side of it, and lo! it was a perfect match! I could see in his face astonishment that another boot could be found as large as his own. The seller at once saw that he had a probable customer before him. Then began a lively chaffering between the two in Russian, in which the spectators took the keenest interest, acting the part of chorus to the principals. It ended in the sale of the odd boot at a price to me unknown. The buyer took it in his hand and walked off with it. Perhaps to this day he is trying to find a mate for it ready made. The chances must be strong against his success in that search, even in the old-clothes market of Moscow.

I saw on sale a dress-coat of which one of the tails had been torn away. It may have belonged to a man of fashion, or to a waiter, before its immediate descent to this low destiny, and, in either case, the history of that lost tail would doubtless be interesting. It was taken up and minutely inspected by several persons, and then carefully dropped on its assigned place in the dirt. But its owner did not seem discouraged, for he knew that, sooner or later, some man would present himself who, perhaps, had purchased the missing tail from some other dealer, and was looking for the rest of the coat. Among the other bargains offered were frying-pans without handles, and handles without frying-pans; tables and chairs that needed only two or three legs apiece to make them useful; coffee-mills minus cranks, and thermometers with smashed bulbs. Asparagus and tomato cans, empty and battered, such as would be tossed into the garbage-barrel or gutter in the United States, were in great request. A little pile of them vanished in five minutes.

I was only a looker-on. The merchants seemed to understand the motive of my presence among them, for they wasted none of their appeals on me —with one exception. This was the case of a man who had one of Lincoln and Bennett's best London hats for sale. It was but little worn, and looked good for many years of service on the head of some conservative middle-aged gentleman who does not approve of novelty and gloss in his hats. I was wearing a Derby at the time; seeing which, the dealer ventured to suggest by signs that I should try on the stove-pipe pattern which he held enticingly toward me. Taking me for an Englishman, he supposed that I would be glad to acquire a London hat at a price doubtless far below the original figures. He implored me by gestures to put it on. I had not the remotest idea of buying a first- or second-hand hat of that shape while traveling, but, to please him, I consented to see if it would fit me. A large number of idlers looked on approvingly while I made the trial. The hat was decidedly too small, and was returned to the dealer with a shake of the head made as emphatic as possible. Whereupon he did exactly what I have seen done twenty times by hatters in various parts of America. He took that undersized hat and began to stretch it with his hands one way and compress it another way. Then he drew it over the cap of his knee till I thought he would have split it up the side. Then he bowed, and handed it to me again for another experiment. I made the politest signs of declining; and, as he pressed the hat upon me with increased ardor, improved the opportunity offered by a gap in the crowd and slipped away from him. As I withdrew, I could hear murmurs of disapproval among the bystanders. They thought I ought at least to have tried on the hat once more after it had been so carefully enlarged to suit me.

The country roads in the environs of Moscow are not kept in good repair. They abound in depressed places, which become miry pits or pools after a heavy rain. The one which is least exposed to these criticisms is that leading to the Petrovsky Palace and Gardens, a few miles from the Kremlin.

A French guide and interpreter whom we had secured for a day or two recommended us to visit the Petrovsky Palace, because Napoleon occupied it for a time after the heat and smoke of burning Moscow had driven him beyond the walls. It was there the Emperor took his last look at the gilded domes and spires of the holy city as they glowed in the crimson light. It was from this palace that he sent, by relays of swift couriers to Paris—as if bad news does not travel fast enough without whip and spur—the intelligence of the burning of Moscow, and the forced retreat of the grand army through the snows. Our French guide thought it would give us great pleasure to see the identical room, chair, table, ink-stand, and pen which were involved in the production of this famous dispatch. But we had heard of Napoleon at every turn about Moscow so far, and were quite willing to forget him for a few hours. Therefore, we at first declined the proposition to go out to the Petrovsky Palace, until it was further explained that a good dinner could be had in the gardens adjoining. Then we resolved to make the trip, the day being pleasant.

The ride outside the city walls is not interesting until the Palace Gardens are reached. These are laid out with the forethought and tended with the scrupulous care which one always sees in the public grounds of Russia. Visits to the parks in that country go far to compensate one for the absence of more natural, diversified scenery. We spent a pleasant hour or two among the winding roads and footpaths, obtaining many views of the palace from different standpoints. It is an old-fashioned building, with an air of homely comfort reflected from every brick. If hoarded memories of twenty or thirty other palaces in Europe had not interfered, we should hardly have been able to resist the importunities of our guide to behold more relics of his adored Napoleon. At 6 P. M. dinner was much more to our liking than the exhibition of rooms in endless succession, however thickly crowded with souvenirs of the great.

Our man's promise about a good dinner was fulfilled. The restaurant where we pulled up for the momentous transaction is small but nicely kept. The meal was served in a pretty little garden in the rear of the premises. The walls were masses of climbing-plants in full bloom. Venerable trees kept off the still warm rays of the declining sun. A fountain shot its sparkling jet high in air, and the crystal drops tinkled musically as they fell back into a marble basin. Our round table was spread under a mighty oak. Sparrows of the unadulterated English type hopped familiarly about us, as if expecting crumbs from the forthcoming feast. They were the tamest of birds, alighting on the tops of chairs almost within reach. At times they seemed to dare one to drop a pinch of salt on their tails, preparatory to catching them, according to the method recommended in childhood. As the dinner, besides being excellent, was lengthy and in quantity superabundant, there was plenty to spare for the companionable sparrows. They flocked to us from all parts of the grounds, and at one time the chirping congregation could have been numbered by the hundreds. There was nothing particularly Russian about the dinner, except the soup, which was serious and important. From this dish the central island of meat and the stuffed pastry-ball are never absent. The occurrence of a meat *entrée* between the soup and the fish is another invariable departure from the Western *menus*. There was an abundance of sauces served upon meats which we had been accustomed to eating quite dry or in their natural gravy. Where all was good, no one item—the soup excluded—lives in my recollection. But I shall not soon forget the honest, delicious wine of the Crimea. A little experience with the Russian vintages had impressed me favorably. They have not the taste or the heating after-effect of the French wines which are now so commonly fortified and otherwise doctored all over the world, and not least in France herself—and, worst of all, perhaps, in Paris. So I ordered (through the Russian-speaking guide) a bottle of a Crimean brand. It was an accidental, but fortunate, choice. The wine was red, and had the general taste rather of Burgundy than of Bordeaux. But it had a bouquet of its own; it dwelt pleasantly upon the palate, and it produced those salutary effects of gentle warmth and cheer of which good wine may still be capable if not abused by the drinker. But one may travel thousands of miles in Europe and not find many wines of which this high praise could be justly spoken.

The English sparrows—pests in America—were so friendly and affable in their way that we were reluctant to leave them. But we finally bade them farewell with a parting largess of crumbs, and returned to Moscow by the light of the setting sun. As we quitted the pleasant restaurant, the proprietor and several of his staff flocked about to see us off, and looked an unutterable good-by with a kindness of manner which touched our alien hearts. ·I took pleasure in thinking that this mark of courtesy was paid to our nationality. The guide knew that we were Americans, and doubtless had mentioned that fact to the people at the restaurant. There may be many Russians still ignorant of

America and Americans, but, among the vast majority in every part of Russia who are aware of the friendly relations which have always existed between the two nations, our countrymen are sure of a cordial welcome.

CHAPTER XXVII.

A COMEDY OF PASSPORTS—MYTHICAL POLICE ESPIONAGE.

TRAVELERS are told that, the farther they go into Russia, the more they are subjected to police espionage. Whenever at St. Petersburg I casually alluded to the informality of the passport examinations, any English tourist with whom I was conversing would be sure to say, with a knowing smile, "Wait till you get to Moscow." "But, my dear sir," I would rejoin, "the time to be strict is when one is entering the country. The object of requiring passports, as I understand it, is to guard against returning Nihilists and dangerous characters generally. I do believe that any other man could have come in on my passport, for nobody attempted to identify me by my own—perhaps flattering—description of myself. When it was finally handed back to me at Wirballen, the only sign that it had been inspected was a little round stamp next to the *visé* of the Russian consul-general at Berlin."

"Just like the rascals," an Englishman once said to me, lowering his voice a little. "I wonder if in America you ever heard the song about 'The Spider and the Fly'? 'Come into my parlor,' you know, and all that sort of thing."

I told him that it was not entirely unfamiliar to me, at which he seemed surprised.

"Well," he continued, "Russia is the spider, and you are the fly. She will bleed you in your pocket if not in your veins." He stopped to laugh at his own joke. "It's easy enough to get in; but, when you want to get out, and go to the police-office for a permit, you'll see—"

He did not say what would be seen; but the vagueness of his unfinished remark implied something terrible.

I had heard that the rooms at Russian hotels assigned to foreigners were all provided with Judas-holes, through which an EYE watched the inmates with the hope of surprising them in the act of loading up bombs with dynamite. The thought of this scrutiny was horrible. I could not help glancing uneasily around my apartment to discover the treacherous orifice. The stucco-work next to the high ceiling seemed to be a mighty snug place for a spy-hole, the dark shadows and the festooned cobwebs lending themselves to its concealment. Once I seized an umbrella, and stood on a chair tip-toe, and reached up just far enough to punch the ferule into a spot which had crumbled away a little and looked like a hole. If there was an EYE on the other side, its owner must take the consequences. I heard no scream as the weapon pierced the ceiling. As it was withdrawn, a shower of fine plaster followed, powdering my hair in the true style of the last century. The absurdity of this incident dispelled, once and for all, any real fear of being watched in that way.

If the St. Petersburg police took any notice of my comings and goings, I was unaware of it, though always seeking to discover some indication of their surveillance. At the Hôtel d'Europe I had surrendered my passport to the head-porter by request, and it pleased me to think that I was not neglected by a paternal government. Next day, when it was politely returned, it bore no fresh pen-mark, seal, or stamp, or even the impression of a dirty thumb, to show that it had been opened. Since the police did not seem to be looking after me, I determined to look after the police.

The execution of this design was reserved for Moscow; for it is in that city, according to the best obtainable information, that the odious features of the Russian police system may be seen at their worst. That is the phase of it with which I most ardently desired to become acquainted. I wanted to see the originally immaculate passport still further soiled. It was really provoking that, up to the time of reaching the Holy City, the following were the only indorsements upon it, as translated from the Russian:

No. 4,710.

Seen at the Imperial Russian Consulate for going to Russia.

BERLIN, July 3/13, 1886.

Consul-General, KUDRIAVTZEFF.

And, adjoining, was the stamp affixed at the frontier, containing in a circle the words " Seen at Verjbolovo (Wirballen) when coming, July 5/17, 1886."

At Moscow, the passport, having been surrendered at the hotel as usual, came back next day with two Russian superscriptions. There was a formal entry as follows :

July 11/23, 1886.

City precinct. In the house No. 9, presented and recorded.

For the captain (signed),
RALIKHIN.

The other was personal and cordial, and produced a gentle thrill of gratitude in the bosom of the recipient of the courtesy :

July 11/23, 1886.

It is permitted to John Bouton, an American citizen, and wife, to remain in Russia until January 5/17, 1887. For further stay he is bound to obtain a passport, under the regulations established for foreigners wishing to live in Russia.

For the senior clerk (signed),

VOLYNIA.

(*Gratis.*)

The omission of my middle name was noticeable. At first, I explained it on the theory of official carelessness, from which no country is exempt. Then I remembered that, in the Russian nomenclature, there is no recognized middle name, except that derived from the father. This is constructed by adding "*vitch*" (son of) to the father's Christian name. In the case of the present writer, it would be *Nathanaelóvitch* (son of Nathaniel), and thus it appears in the Russian version of the title-page of this book. And the present place may be as good as any to give the English pronunciation of the first six Slavic words there displayed. They read, "OKOLNYM POOTEM VŬ MOSKVOO — EPIKOORÁY-SKOYE POOTESHESTVEEYE."

Except for the slight immaterial defect already noted, the police indorsement at Moscow defies the most unfriendly criticism, even of Englishmen.

Here is a favor extended to me without asking. It exacts no conditions. It clothes me with a six months' residence in Russia, and with all the protection of her laws. And to this truly hospitable concession is attached no stamp requiring the payment of any fee. Great is my surprise to see, instead of the customary *timbre*, the familiar word "*gratis.*" I rub my eyes hard and look again. Yes, it is no accidental combination of Russian characters reading "gratis," and meaning something widely different. It is the good old Latin word, English by adoption, and known even in faraway Russia, which we often see coupled with samples of garden-seeds, or specimen newspapers, or bits of dress-patterns, or something else seeking free introduction and circulation. But one may travel round the world, and find not many places, if any, besides Russia, where this welcome word adorns government paper in lieu of a stamp for fees. It is like a shake of the hand, and makes one feel at home among strangers.

And this same word "gratis" started another train of thought not wholly complimentary to the United States. Up to this time my total outlay to Russian officials, for the privilege of entering and moving freely about their country, footed up less than forty-five cents. But my American passport had cost me five dollars from first hands. True, that without this magic document I could not have entered Russia. But had I not been intending to visit that empire, I probably should not have taken out a passport, for in previous trips to Europe it had been found as superfluous for exhibition purposes as a college diploma. In point of fact, therefore, I had paid our State Department, for the right of going to Russia, more than ten times as much as Russia herself had charged for throwing her doors wide open! Now, it seems to me that a government with an annual surplus which encourages the most foolish extravagance and waste, might afford to discard this tax upon those of its citizens who desire to go abroad. The American passport-fee should be abolished, if for no other reason than because it deters our people from visiting their good friends, the Russians. I wonder if the boast "*Civis Romanus sum*"—that warning to all the barbarian world not to molest a Roman citizen—was uttered by a man with a five-dollar passport stuck in the folds of his toga?

Notwithstanding this most agreeable incident at Moscow, I could not forget the unpleasant things reported about the Russian police system. I could think of no surer way to ascertain the truth than to go to police-headquarters, observe the manners of the chief and his subordinates in their official den, and note their treatment, not merely of an American citizen, but of natives whom one might chance to see there. For this purpose a good occasion soon presented itself. Instead of profiting by the gracious permission for a six months' stay in Russia, I was ungratefully meditating an early departure; and, in order to leave the country without hindrance, must secure a police permit. With this business as the pretext, perhaps the depth of the mystery could be plumbed.

One morning, I mentioned this purpose to one of the hotel staff, who could speak a little French or English as required, and who stood for all we ever saw of the "administration," except the cashier in the settlement of bills. He raised his eyebrows and shrugged his shoulders, expressing at once surprise and dissuasion. Then he explained in a dignified way that the guests never visited the police bureau in person—that the house had "an agent," "a representative," "a man" (these were some of the descriptive phrases used), who was authorized to act in such delicate matters, with the consent and indeed with the wish of the police, and that this person would take charge of my passport, and save me a great deal of time and trouble.

But my mind was made up to interview the chief of police, and so I cut short the conversation by peremptorily requesting the call of a droschky. The man smiled, with another shrug of the shoulders, and, beckoning to one of those boys whose smooth chin, flowing hair parted in the middle, pork-pie cap, and long, blue tunic strapped tightly about the waist, make them look like girls, spoke to him in Russian. I followed the little fellow to the sidewalk, where he ordered the droschky for me, explaining the destination to the driver, and then he started off on a run.

As usual, the carriage dashed through the streets like a meteor. But, however great our speed, I always saw on the sidewalk, just ahead, the girlish dress and streaming hair of the hotel-boy. I wondered what imperative business caused his race against time—or was it against the droschky? Not the latter evidently, for in a few minutes he disappeared down an alley. A quarter of an hour later, after quite a circuit of stony streets, we entered a little court-yard, and halted opposite a door with a Russian inscription on the lintel. The driver signaled me to descend and go in. Opening the door, I saw before me a narrow stairway, and, at the head thereof—the hotel-boy. His round, innocent face was flushed, and he puffed audibly. That last half-mile had nearly done for him. He looked down and beamed at me as I climbed the steps. I playfully shook my finger at him, at the same time taking my passport from a side-pocket.

With a roguish laugh, he snatched it from my hand and scampered away before I could stop him. I followed as fast as possible through some half-lighted passages into what seemed an anteroom, where I caught a glimpse of his flying blue tunic and tossing locks as he entered a larger apartment beyond. Before me was a soldier or policeman (convertible terms in Russia), who motioned me to a seat, which was a rude bench. Upon my heels, as I entered the anteroom, trod another policeman, who drew up inside as if awaiting further orders. To a casual observer, ignorant of the truth, I should have appeared to be under arrest, with these two sworded *gorodovois* mounting guard.

I could do nothing but wait till the boy had executed the commission of obtaining my leave for departure, for which it was then evident he had been privately sent from the hotel ahead of me, contrary to my expressed wish. So I philosophically improved the occasion to look about the place. From my position one could see into the adjoining large room. There, at a square table, sat a middle-aged man with a refined face, a mustache artistically curled, and a delicate white hand, on the little finger of which sparkled a large diamond that shone to great advantage as he raised it to his lips and withdrew or replaced a cigarette. Before him was a pile of papers, which he was signing, or indorsing, or stamping with official seals, and looking somewhat bored as he performed that automatic task. Men came and bowed to him deferentially, and took orders which issued languidly from his lips between the whiffs. That imp of a boy stood in the background, with the precious passport opened out wide, so that I could see the spread-eagle water-mark (about two feet square) through it against a window. He grinned as he caught my eye, and, though I now feared that he had baffled my cherished design of penetrating the *sanctum sanctorum*, I could not help smiling back at him; observing which act, one of the policemen standing near looked hard at me as if to check the display of any levity in that place. So I became grim again, and fell to contrasting the stylish and genial appearance of the police magnate yonder with the serious, gruff, heavy-bearded, and cruel-eyed person who would have seemed (according to English reports) the most natural occupant of that chair.

Meanwhile my curiosity was also excited in another quarter. Just in front of me, within a space inclosed by an iron railing with an elaborate pattern of cross-bars, was a little crowd of Russians. They were all looking by turns at me and at the two policemen. "Can it be possible," I thought, "that they — evidently prisoners themselves, penned up there and awaiting orders which will consign them to dungeons or to Siberia—suppose me also to be under arrest? I certainly detect in their faces marks of sympathy and fellow-feeling."

I study the motley group at leisure. One of the number may have been a student, for he had a thoughtful face; but I was pained to remark a fierce expression in his eyes, as if he had absorbed the deadly virus of Nihilism. "R. sh boy! most likely implicated in the latest plot (for full particulars, see highly imaginative dispatches in the London press) for assassinating the Tsar. And there is a young girl with a pretty face; another Nihilist, probably—the misguided student's sweetheart, it may be. They say that women are the most fanatical disciples of the new dispensation. By her side stands a priest of the Greek Church in his cylindrical black cap and full robes, which he has disgraced by some offense—trivial, let us hope. But he, too, may be a Nihilist, for we are told that the gospel of anarchy draws some recruits from the ranks of the priesthood." A soldier in fatigue-dress, and some other men or women whose station in life one could not fix, composed the rest of the company behind that grill, all (perhaps) arrested for alleged Nihilism. This gave them, in my eyes, a tragic interest which the common ruck of misdemeanants would have lacked. Who can tell what they thought of me, as they reciprocated the curiosity bestowed upon them?

Engrossed in these interesting speculations, I had clean forgotten the object of my visit until recalled from the reverie by the apparition of the ever-smiling boy. He stood before me with the passport open, and pointed out a new streak of inscription running down the back. It had been obligingly furnished without any further information about my identity than he had supplied. Thus ended ingloriously the only opportunity which had presented itself to learn from personal observation anything about the police system of Russia. I folded the passport with a sigh, and thrust it into its pocket. As I did so, one of the *gorodovois* courteously indicated that my departure was now in order. His long forefinger pointed to the door.

As I rose to go, an official-looking personage came out of the chief's audience-room and walked briskly to the little knot of expectant culprits behind that iron railing, which needed only a roof to make it a cage. I halted a moment to see what would happen next. The Nihilists began to look anxious, and I shared their emotions. What followed was interpreted to me by gestures which could not be mistaken. The official personage shook his head at the group, as if he were denying them something. They seemed to entreat him. He only shook his head more determinedly. As they persisted in trying to overcome his objections, he brandished both hands at them in a manner which plainly said: "It's no use; go away; out of this now!" And this with so much energy that the party in the pen instinctively fell back; and, as they did so, the door behind them was flung open, disclosing, not a perspective of cells as I had expected, but an outside stairway, the blue sky, and a tree in leaf, all belonging to the free world, into which they hastened for the labors or pleasures of the day! Putting this and that fact together, I was impelled to the conclusion that these people were, after all, not Nihilists or offenders of any rank, but only respectable citizens of Moscow, who had called at the chief's office to lay some request before him, and that he had either decided to deny it, or else had put off their reception to another day. And I never came any nearer than this to identifying a Nihilist in Russia.

Translated into English, this final indorsement of the passport reads as follows:

July, 15/27, 1886.

On behalf of the local police, there is no objection to John Bouton and wife, American citizens named in this passport, leaving Moscow for abroad. Captain of the city precinct,

(Signed) DVORONIN.

There was quite a galaxy of stamps affixed, making a total charge of ninety-five kopecks—less than fifty cents gold value. The hotel assumed the payment of this fee, and, adding a trifle for the services of its "representative," or "agent," or "man" (the small boy), inserted in my bill a lump item of one ruble fifty kopecks on "passport" account. And I advise all American tourists to transact this kind of business by proxy instead of wasting droschky-fares in unproductive visits to the chief of police.

CHAPTER XXVIII.

SUMMER WEATHER IN RUSSIA—ST. PETERSBURG AND MOSCOW ENOUGH FOR SIGHT-SEERS—M. KATKOFF AND HIS GAZETTE—TSAR AND PEOPLE—REPUBLICAN POSSIBILITIES OF THE COSSACK.

AFTER one has packed trunks, paid hotel bills, bought railway-tickets, procured a supply of rubles and kopecks from his banker, and made every preparation to leave Germany for Russia, it is discouraging to be told that he has chosen the wrong season for visiting that country.

"The winter, sir, is the only time to see Russia. St. Petersburg is like a furnace in July. It is a rainless month. The streets are never watered, and when the winds blow—mostly from the south, making the air still hotter—you are smothered with dust. The mosquitoes—"

But I had heard enough. It was too late to back out from the Russian trip, and I did not care to know the worst. So I interrupted the speaker with the question, "When did you leave St. Petersburg?"

He colored a little. "Oh, I have never been there myself! No money would tempt me to go to Russia before December, at least. I am only telling you what everybody knows. The books are full—"

"Of probable misstatements on these points," said I, finishing the sentence for him. "I know that English writers are unanimous about the heat of a St. Petersburg July. But then Englishmen complain of every temperature over 70°. Americans are less fond of cold weather. I will learn the truth for myself. Good-evening."

The man with whom I held this conversation looked like a professor in some small Western college. I had met him by chance in the rooms of the American Exchange at Berlin. Overhearing me say that I was bound to Russia that night, he had proceeded to draw upon his large store of book-knowledge for my benefit. His positive manner was probably borrowed from the classroom; and I have no doubt he was pained because I did not take his advice on trust, with many thanks, like a docile pupil.

As an American accustomed to "summer heat," I declare St. Petersburg to be very comfortable in July. Neither there nor at Moscow, four hundred miles farther south, have I seen more than 80° F. registered in the shade, and the mid-day temperature touched much lower figures during my stay. Clothed accordingly, one may ride or walk in the open air at high noon, and revel in the bright sunshine unharmed. There were several rainfalls which were more than showers. They cooled the air to the point of chilliness, and effectually laid the dust. At no time were the streets swept by the wind with the sirocco-effects described in some English books. Even the largest open squares were free from the predicted nuisance. Dressed in light woolen, and armed with an umbrella against the sun or the rain, the American will have no occasion to carp at the Russian weather in those months when his compatriots at home are fleeing for coolness—and not always finding it—to the mountains and the sea-shore. Contrasting his comfort with the sufferings he would have undergone in New York, Philadelphia, or Boston, he can feel only gratitude for the endurable summer weather of St. Petersburg. He is unvexed by mosquitoes and the flies are well-behaved.

A Russian winter may be all that Gautier paints it; but, if that brilliant Frenchman had been thin instead of stout, with less inside room for the storage of solids and liquids as a sure defense against Arctic rigors; and, if he had been obliged to look after anybody besides Gautier, he might have hesitated to take the journey whose record gives so much pleasure to readers. And, remember, his point of departure was Paris, not New York. A trip from America to St. Petersburg, merely to verify Gautier's impressions there, would hardly pay for the cost, time, and trouble. Americans prefer to pass the cold months in Italy or Egypt or the Holy Land, or some other sunny clime, and leave to more adventurous souls the pleasures—such as they are—of a Russian winter. Everything that the ordinary tourist cares to see can be seen in July as well as in January. The Winter Palace in St. Petersburg is closed in summer, it is true, but the Hermitage, with its glut of pictures and *bric-à-brac*, is open. So is Tsarskoe Sélo, a little distance outside of the city. There are many other palaces in or about the capital, mostly accessible in summer. Private, if not public, admittance can be had to every museum and library. The Tsar may be absent during the warmer months, but the visitor would probably not get a look at him or any of the imperial family in winter. If the nobility are also missing, the innocent American does not know it, as he has no means of telling a prince from a plebeian. If the entire court and all the fashionable element are away, St. Petersburg has not been carried off with them. And that city, and, still more, Moscow, are at all times so full of interest on a hundred accounts that one does not pause to think whether their attractions would or would not be greatly heightened by the presence of snow six feet deep on a level, or by the return of the Tsar from Peterhof or Gatschina.

Russia is fortunate in the possession of two great capitals. St. Petersburg is the civil and Moscow the religious center of a double administration. Paris is the only city of France that most Americans desire to visit. That city is, indeed, France in the sense that Parisians claim for her; and the rest of the republic is but a matter of detail. Similarly, St. Petersburg and Moscow are Russia. By sojourning a few days in each city, one can gather sufficient, if superficial, knowledge of the Russian people, their religious and secular institutions, their amusements, their business ways, their modes of living, to correct a host of errors into which prejudiced authors have led him. If he is a student of natural history, an ethnologist, a profound investigator of social problems—if he desires to see with his own eyes how the exiles fare in Siberia, or whether the petroleum-wells of Baku are running dry, or how the railway to Merv is getting along—he may spend many months in Russia acquiring interesting information. But, if he wants a good time, with the minimum of discomfort, while he is packing away in the odd corners of his brain the things most truly worth knowing about Russia, let him stick to St. Petersburg and Moscow. There he will find hotels first class in all respects, easy carriages, and French (if not English) newspapers. Unless he is a critical analyst of race peculiarities, he will be satisfied with the many varieties of Russia's population which he sees in Moscow alone. And, as to souvenirs of the country, he will, perhaps, be more fortunate in picking them up at bargains in the Gostinnoi Dvors of the two capitals than if he hunted and chaffered for them at the crowded and noisy fair of Nijni-Novgorod.

In the restaurants and reading-rooms one often notices little groups of Russians earnestly scanning the columns of a newspaper in their own language. It is a large, four-page sheet, usually accompanied by a supplement. Perhaps one will read, and the others will listen. At times they seem deeply interested, hanging upon the words that are uttered as if they were revelations of the greatest moment. The expression of their faces is unbroken by any trace of levity. They lay the paper down, and seem to be discussing what has been read. Sometimes one observes marked signs of dissent from some member of the group, but more commonly there is an apparent agreement with those sentiments of the journal which have provoked the debate. Seeing the same scene enacted with trifling variations a number of times, I became anxious to learn the occasion of it, and then I ceased to be surprised.

The paper is the "Moscow Gazette" ("Moskovskeeya Vedomostee"), edited by M. Katkoff, the man who wields an influence in Russia second to no subject of the Tsar. We are told that the Russian press is fettered and crushed, and here is an editor more powerful, for good or ill, than any statesman of the empire. Holding no office, reaching the mind of the Tsar only through his printed columns, he disputes with M. de Giers (Minister of Foreign Affairs) for the confidence and support of their common master. And, hardly less important, he makes himself felt, through the widely distributed "Gazette," among the most thoughtful circles of Russia. In all the foreign offices of Europe his opinions are carefully studied, being regarded as the earliest and best indications of the drift of Russian sentiment. For M. Katkoff is, above all things, a Russian. He is the champion Panslavist. He advocates the federation of all branches of the great Slavic race. It is his policy that keeps alive the national jealousy of Germany and Austria. His eyes are fastened on Bulgaria, Roumania, and Servia, where the Slavic population is a strong element. Galicia and Bohemia in Austria, Posen in Prussia, and independent little Montenegro, are among the regions embraced within the wide sweep of his Slavic sympathies. A union of the Slavs for any purpose, and on any scheme of protection extended by the great Empire of the North to the federated provinces, would end in their consolidation with Russia under the government of the Tsar.

Italy and Germany have each been substantially unified on the same principle. If it is admissible in those two cases, why not in that of Russia? Panslavism, ably upheld in the "Moscow Gazette," can never be unpalatable to the Tsar or the people, for it strongly appeals to patriotism and national pride. Therefore, M. Katkoff is permitted to display zeal in this direction even to the point of excess. It is only when his feelings betray him into undue hostility to some power—Germany or Austria, for example—with which the Tsar desires to keep on good terms, that the Panslavist leader is called to order. But the rebuke takes only the form of a summons to St. Petersburg, where he has an audience, and is readily restored to the favor which he had only nominally lost. The existence of such a paper, which is not a government organ, and yet passes as such among most of its readers—which can be approved or repudiated at pleasure, just as circumstances may require—is a great convenience. It must be understood that no editor would enjoy the license given to M. Katkoff if he were in the least degree politically unsound or disloyal. The strength of his position lies in his intense, unselfish devotion to Russian interests, his passionate adherence to the autocratic system, and his burning hatred of all those revolutionary elements that would precipitate changes for which Russia is not prepared.

A foreigner thrown among Russians, who can not speak his language, is worse off than a visitor to a deaf and dumb asylum, the inmates of which can make their opinions known by writing or by signs. One may travel all over Russia, and learn nothing more of the political ideas of the common people than when he entered it, if he depends on them for enlightenment. His only sources of information are educated Russians, who can converse in his own tongue, or English, French, or German residents who have lived in the country long enough to understand the people and have outgrown their native prejudices. It is from such persons that I gathered a few impressions, which went far to modify views formed upon the strength of unfriendly English publications.

It may sometimes be true, as the proverb says,

that "to hear the news, you must go away from home." But this can hardly hold good in the case of reports relating to the Tsar's personal character and habits. It is much more likely that the assertions about his intemperance, insanity, and brutality, which appear in the London "Times," are fictions, than that such alleged facts should be totally unknown among intelligent people in St. Petersburg, where he lives. I sought in vain for any corroboration of the reports that the Tsar ever has the delirium tremens, or is under the influence of liquor, or exhibits signs of madness, or has a violent temper and is abusive to his ministers and courtiers. Nobody with whom I conversed had ever heard any rumors of this kind, except as they originated from known reports in the foreign papers. These were invariably denounced to me as malicious inventions. Old English dwellers in Russia expressed themselves warmly on the subject. They felt ashamed at the wholly unfounded and outrageous libels heaped by the press of London on one who, so far as they know, is truly temperate, free from any taint of lunacy, mild and reasonable in his intercourse with all. They spoke of him as a "family man," having a German fondness for wife and children and the simple pleasures of domestic life. They regretted that he observed so strict a seclusion; but admitted that he was forced to be very circumspect in his movements in order to escape the fangs of the Nihilists. All my informants pitied the Tsar and still more pitied his subjects, who are, in large measure, deprived of that direct personal cognizance of their needs and wishes which might prove so beneficial to them if the Nihilists would permit it to be freely exercised. It also follows, from this comparative isolation of the Tsar, that the powers which he delegates are undoubtedly in many cases abused, and the facts are never brought to his paternal knowledge.

For the Tsar is not only the executive and the law-making power of the state, head of the Church, fountain of justice, commander-in-chief of the army and navy, but, more than all these, he is father to his people. His subjects owe him, in theory, a filial respect and obedience; and, with the exception of the Nihilists, they are dutiful children. The relation is an Oriental one, which we of the West can not understand. But it is powerfully operative in Russia. It has not been really weakened by anything that the Nihilists have done, but, on the contrary, strengthened. This would be proved any day by the spontaneous and almost universal response of the Russian people to any call for sacrifice which their father should make upon them.

Some foreign writers profess to fear that the Tsar will plunge his country into a causeless war, in order to find an outlet for national discontent. But the only discontent which troubles Russia at present is that of the Nihilists, who are irreconcilable. No war in behalf of some Slavic race, or to extend the boundaries of Russia, or to possess the Holy Places, would have their sympathy. They would still plot against the life of the one man whose murder, according to their shallow view, might bring about that chaos which is the desire of their hearts. The assassination of Alexander II did not promote the cause of Nihilism in the least; but, on the other hand, led to the adoption of severer though unsuccessful measures for its repression; and there is no reason to think that the removal of the present sovereign would be of any advantage to the cause of anarchy. The Tsars live in their successors. The mighty empire which has weathered the storms of a thousand years is not now at the mercy of a dynamite bomb.

The undoubted tendency of Russia is now toward what is commonly spoken of as a "constitutional government." This is not following a general demand of the people. They seem to be, as a rule, quite indifferent to it; but it is believed to be favored by the Tsar. His life, aside from the dreadful menaces of Nihilism, is made a burden to him by the enormous and steadily increasing responsibilitics of his position. As a conscientious man, these must press upon him heavily, no matter how much he seeks to distribute them among the ministers who are but his creatures. If he could be assisted in his great work by a national body, in some sense representing the people, and if his ministers were made responsible in fact instead of being purely clerical functionaries as at present, the diabolical aims of the Nihilists would be frustrated more surely than they could be in any other way. The blind hate which now seeks the life of one man only would then lose its concentration. It would then be necessary to kill or terrorize a whole ministry, or a majority of delegates—a task, the difficulty of which would probably impress the most unimaginative of Nihilists. One might almost predict the disappearance of Nihilism as an organized danger in Russia, if constitutionalism could somehow be grafted on the old trunk. (See APPENDIX.)

The fifty years assigned by Napoleon as the period during which Europe would become either republican or Cossack, passed away, leaving his prophecy unfulfilled. But his own France is a republic, and more liberal principles have been incorporated in all the imperial and monarchical governments of Europe. If there is a drift discernible, it is toward republicanism. By the word

"Cossack" Napoleon meant that absolutism of which Russia was the most remarkable example of his day. But the Cossack himself is now in the stream with the rest. It will be perhaps only a question of time when he will be as well fitted for and desirous to adopt republican institutions, as the man of any other race in Europe. Who can say that, wherever the Cossack of the future goes, he may not carry with him the germ of republicanism? It is this possibility which lends to every sign of liberal development in Russia a tremendous significance in the eyes of Americans. And if Russia still clings by preference to her venerable paternal system, that is no reason why our ancient friendship for that great country and people should be impaired.

CHAPTER XXIX.

RUSSIAN FINLAND — STOCKHOLM — THE LARGEST KNOWN METEORITE—THE DJURGARDEN.

It takes some time to get the confused impressions of brilliant Moscow out of one's head; and, until this is done, one is in no fit condition to judge of other cities. The gold, green, blue, yellow, and red of Moscow left images in my brain which shifted about for days as with turns of a kaleidoscope. Entering the capital of Sweden by water on a bright August morning, I saw it at its best. Stockholm is a handsome city in its own right, and that guide-book writer who first called it the "Venice of the North" owes an apology to the Swedes for instituting an unfortunate comparison. There is plenty of water in and about Stockholm, but no intricate network of canals, no rich tint, no mellow antiquity. Comparing Stockholm with Boston, one would not be so far out of the way. There are resemblances in the hilly grounds on which the two cities stand, in the central dome and the tall spires, in the crooked and converging streets, the stone buildings, the trimness and cleanliness of everything, the all-pervading air of prosperity. The American who happens to know Boston feels at home here at once. Even when he has just arrived from Moscow, and misses colors in the roofs of Stockholm, he is soon somewhat consoled by the many-colored native dresses which he meets at every turn. These are worn by the women of Dalecarlia. In coming to this city to live, they keep on wearing the showy costumes of their native province. Their head-dress is either a sort of liberty-cap in blue or an exaggerated smoking-cap in red, attached somehow just above the nape of the neck, and always on the point of falling off. The rest of the dress is a mysterious composition of bandanna handkerchiefs and bunting of divers hues. Chains, spangles, beads, and embroidery cover all. There is nothing like this in the Russia I have seen. It is the prettiest sight in all Stockholm. But to go back a space, and tell how we got here.

We left St. Petersburg in a clean and stanch little boat at 6 P. M. Before stepping on board, I drew my passport from its envelope and held it ready for the final ordeal; for, in theory, every stranger is scrutinized as sharply on leaving as on entering the empire. I was wondering where, on the broad surface of the dear old American eagle, room would be found for still another and positively the last inscription, seal, or stamp. But again, much to my disappointment, nobody evinced the slightest curiosity to examine the document, either at the gangway of the boat or during the voyage of some hundreds of miles which we afterward made before quitting the jurisdiction of Russia. Perhaps, if I had been a Nihilist, my departure from the country would not have passed unnoticed. But my personal experience on this and previous occasions, when a police supervision might have been expected to make itself apparent, convinces me that it is a formality much neglected, except when an attempted assassination of the Tsar excites the authorities to spasms of real vigilance.

The passengers—about thirty in number—assembled on the upper deck to take last views of St. Isaac's dome, the spire of Saints Peter and Paul, and the other landmarks of gold which loom above the horizon when twenty miles away. In half an hour we had scraped acquaintance and crystallized into sets, which continued unbroken all the voyage. Among those aboard were a Siberian family, a Chilian, a Belgian, a German who had won the hand of a London lady, married her at St. Petersburg, and was then on his wedding-journey; a Nijni-Novgorod merchant, several Finns, and a number of Norwegians and Swedes. Every language of Northern Europe was spoken on that deck. If one person could not talk directly to another, he could do it through the medium of an interpreter. And gestures eke out the meaning at the point where words fail. We were a merry party, without asking or caring to know one another's names.

Cronstadt—the sea-defense of St. Petersburg—was reached about 8 P. M., and everybody inspected the fortifications which are called (by the Russians) impregnable. To me they seemed old-fashioned and fragile. Some of the forts are of stone or brick, with cannon in three or four tiers. If a 500-pounder, working from a monitor at short range, could not knock them about the ears of the defenders, I am much mistaken. The real dependence of Cronstadt is probably the torpedo, and nobody yet knows exactly how much that is worth. Toward eleven o'clock, when the twilight had faded out, there was a general disposition to retire for the night. The cabins of the Stockholm boats are small but comfortable. Before the two sofas are transformed into beds, they are downy enough. But, when they are rigged up with sheets, blankets, and pillows, the inmates discover bones and buttons inside of them. They are very trying on tender ribs. The cabin-doors have neither locks nor bolts, and many persons do not even shut them, trusting to the screen of a curtain which lets the air freely in and out. As the numbers of the rooms do not show when the doors are ajar, this arrangement gives rise to amusing mistakes, of which we hear some particulars the next morning.

In crossing the Gulf of Finland the water was rough for a few hours, and the pitching motion of the vessel disturbed the equilibrium of all sensitive interiors. In the morning some of the friskiest of our company of the night before did not report for coffee at 7.30 o'clock. When they did appear at nine or ten, they were silent, if not sad. I can only say that they missed some coffee which was wonderfully good. It was served with an assortment of bread, sweet biscuit, and cakes. This light refreshment kept one alive till nine, when those who could pull themselves together dived into the little dining-saloon and had their regular breakfast. The most important part of this meal —Swedish fashion—is the "trimmings." You are expected to fill yourself at a sideboard before you sit at table. I counted twenty different dishes set out as appetizers. Among them were cold boiled lobsters, eels in jelly, several fish-salads reeking with oil, head-cheese, slices of sausage, pickled tongue, potted meats of nature unknown, cabbage, beets, onions sliced with vinegar, bread, butter, and cheese. The true Swede, when in "good form," attacks all these viands *seriatim*, and makes a hole in them. But, before he does anything, he fills a large wine-glass from the colorless contents of one or more decanters, which tower above all other things in a great caster. These hold gin or *kummel* or other fiery spirits. After ten or fifteen minutes thus spent on his feet, he is ready to appreciate the beefsteak and potatoes and the ham-omelette and other substantials which are tendered to him when he sits down.

We reached Helsingfors—the present capital of Russian Finland—about noon. For several hours before coming in view of the town, we had passed between numberless rocky islands. These kept off the winds and waves, and after a while everybody was on deck and feeling well. The practical joker (no company on shipboard is complete without one) did not miss his chance when the famous white-roofed church of Helsingfors hove in sight. As belated passengers thrust their heads above the companion-way, he would seize them by the hand and drag them to the bow to show them that it had been snowing during the night! To those not in the secret the illusion was complete, and there was an instinctive movement to button up coats. There was a great church on a hill, and every roof, gable, and cornice where snow could lodge was apparently covered with it. The church could not look whiter in the dead of winter. This snow-effect is the work of design. It is paint—a study from nature; and, if Helsingfors were distinguished for nothing else, this unique church would make the place worthy of a visit. But all of us who went ashore to spend the day—as the boat would not start again before one o'clock the next morning—found much more there. The rides and walks were pleasant; the parks large and full of flowers, with fountains playing, and we could dine and sup in the open air, with music by the best band of the garrison, which is always kept strong at Helsingfors. Although the people of Finland are submissive to Russia in many respects, they are quite independent in others. Russia humors them to the extent of permitting home-rule in all matters local, and even allows them to coin their own money. This concession suits the Finns more than the traveling public. You are obliged to change your rubles and kopecks into marks and pennies —all reckonings being made in the latter money. I should say that Finland has the best of the bargain. Russia protects her and makes business for her, and in return exercises a sovereignty which strikes the stranger as merely nominal.

By one o'clock, A. M., the last of the wanderers had come aboard, tired out with his or her pleasurings on land. But all were ready for another frolic of four hours when we arrived at Abo— the old capital of Finland, and still strongly attached to the Sweden of which that country was once an appanage. But here, as elsewhere, among the Finns, the Russian yoke is hardly felt. There is not much to see or do in Abo, except to visit an old castle and church, and dine at a pretty little restaurant within hearing of the steamer's whistle. This was all very unexciting when compared to our revelries at Helsingfors. No one was sorry when the screw again buzzed, and we were heading in a southwest direction for Stockholm. Abo is the farthest northing we have yet made. According to my tattered map, it is about on the latitude of the Shetland Islands. It must be bitterly cold in winter, but on the day of our visit the weather there was just on the verge of warmth. Except for a light wind, it would have been uncomfortable in thick clothing.

The third stage of the trip—from Finland to Stockholm—is uneventful. We sleep through the larger part of it. The morning finds our craft threading a multitude of islands. Many are richly cultivated. As we approach Stockholm the pilot steers carefully. Navigation is difficult for natural reasons, aside from the swarm of steamboats, ships, and yachts. The Swedish flag, mainly a yellow cross on a blue ground, is voted a beauty by all on deck. Our hastily formed impressions of everything are favorable. We think well of the custom-house men, who, while not neglecting their duty, give us as little trouble as possible, and do not look significantly at the palms of their hands. So, after a journey which has used up the best part of three days, we begin to see the sights of which I spoke in the opening paragraph of this chapter.

The greatest curiosity in Stockholm is Professor Nordenskiöld's meteorite. He found it in Greenland many years ago, shipped it to this city, and presented it to the principal museum, where it occupies the post of honor. It is the largest messenger from the skies of which I have any knowledge. Some of the guide-books make a woful blunder in mentioning the weight of the mass. They put it at two hundred and fifty tons. This is the truth multiplied by (say) ten or more. But an aërolite of twenty-five tons is still a prodigy. It would cut up into a hundred of such pieces as are now the pride of separate collections in the great cities of the world. Its bulk is about that of a New York hackney-coach, minus wheels and box-seat, and it would resemble that ugly object in shape if it were not flattened and narrowed on one side. It is iron of the specific kind called meteoric, with a definite proportion of nickel in its composition. The intense heat to which it was subjected in passing from the celestial regions through our atmosphere scorched it terribly. It is blistered all over. This is a kind of heaven's artillery before which the biggest red-hot shot of human invention sinks into insignificance.

There are many treasures of art and science in Stockholm which even the most hurried of travelers should not fail to see. There are churches which, though bare and cold when contrasted with those of Italy or of Russia, are interesting by virtue of their tombs, their pictures, statues, wood-carvings, and historical associations. On every side the inquisitive mind may gather knowledge. But I think most tourists will agree with me that for pure entertainment nothing yields better return than a dinner in the Djurgarden. At one of the great restaurants in that beautiful park you may dine perfectly in a shaded corridor and watch the ever-fluctuating crowd of well-dressed, light-hearted people, and hear the finest selections from the musical masterpieces of all nations. These are rendered by a military band which might be safely sent to America to compete with the best of ours. When the wind and muscle of the performers give out, the music does not cease. As the last strain of one band dies on the air, a second band, just as good, continues the programme, so that there is no break in the feast of sounds. The two sets of musicians "spell" each other, till all the hearers have had enough.

CHAPTER XXX.

BY RAIL TO CHRISTIANIA—FARE ON THE ROAD—NORWAY'S CAPITAL—THE VIKING-SHIP—AN INLAND TOUR.

"Twenty minutes for dinner!" supper, or breakfast, as the case may be. The conductor on the Swedish or Norwegian railways announces this important fact to English-speaking travelers in the sign-language. He spreads out all his fingers and thumbs twice. It speaks volumes to the hungry man. He jumps from the train to the platform of the pretty little station. He enters a room where he finds the feast all spread, but no waiters. Behind a desk in a corner sits a woman calmly knitting. Her business is only to take the money. The guest's business is to help himself. It is fortunate for him if he has been through the same ordeal before. For that mighty soup-tureen, with a ladle in it, does not contain soup. It is full of delicious whipped cream, destined for the strawberries or raspberries which form a mound by its side. Another tureen, exactly matching it, is the one into which he should first dip. He should go down deep and stir up the rich sediment. With a pint of this soup at his disposal it matters less what he eats afterward. He can have fish, two kinds of meat, various side-dishes, pastry, cakes, bread, cheese and butter, tea, coffee, and bottled ale, besides berries and cream (the latter in soup-plates always) all at discretion. It rests with himself whether he will clear the board. When he has satisfied his appetite, or eaten out his twenty minutes, he hands the industrious woman at the desk one krone and a half—about forty-two cents of American money. She barely looks up from her work, sweeps the coins into the till, and resumes the clicking of her needles with an expression of impatience. At first it seems as if this "self-help" system were extremely liberal on the part of the caterer. But after trying it a number of times I find that about half of my twenty minutes is spent in choosing dishes, changing my plates, knives, forks, and spoons, and these are never handy. It also occurs to me that I am saving the establishment the expense of a waiter; and, on the whole, I would prefer to pay a little more, and be helped by somebody else. These meals, occurring at intervals of a few hours, pleasantly break the monotony of the long rail-ride from Stockholm to the

Norwegian capital. The scenery is a succession of ponds—full of lilies—birch-forests and hay-fields. After the first hundred miles of it one cuddles into the corner of his seat and waits for the conductor to make the invariable signs at him to rise and eat.

Approaching Christiania and looking from the car-window, I think I see the British flag everywhere. It is the red and blue of Norway—resembling at a distance the colors of England. Norway, though under the same popular king as Sweden, has her own flag. Are those London policemen at the station? They wear cloth helmets, have their numbers in metal on their standing coat-collars, carry sheathed clubs, and only dispel the illusion when they give mild orders in an unknown tongue. They motion us to go into a room where custom-house officers are in waiting. For reasons good unto themselves, but incomprehensible to the traveler coming from Stockholm, the Norwegian authorities put the baggage through a second inspection. For all I know, the good King Oscar himself may be obliged to stand this sort of thing every time he rides from one of his capitals to the other. Though the ceremony seemed absurd and needless, I determined to spare the officials all possible trouble. I unbuckled the straps, unlocked the trunks, opened them, took out the top trays, folded my arms, and awaited developments—strong in innocence. Great was my astonishment when the custom-house man looked at me, but not at the trunks, and asked simply, " Clothes?" I nodded, whereupon he stooped and leisurely replaced the trays, locked and buckled up the trunks, and chalked them without another word. Before one could even thank him, he had vanished.

As we rode through the streets to the hotel, the likeness of Christiania to London was repeated in the yellowish fronts of the two-story houses and the extreme cleanliness of the streets. What, therefore, could be a better name for the principal hotel than " Victoria "? It looks just like one of those great, rambling inns which are the delight of Americans in the midland counties. It is a labyrinth of halls, little passages, and stairs. On every landing-place is a black or white bear or other wild beast artistically mounted. To come upon one of these at dusk for the first time is startling. Elk-horns, walrus-tusks, and every imaginable trophy of the chase, are displayed in nooks and corners. We see at once that this free museum is intended to please our English friends who come to Norway in the season to hunt and take in Christiania on the way. We hope they find that all the game has not already been shot and stuffed for the hotel.

At the royal palaces, both here and at Stockholm, visitors have a free run of the family rooms.

Among themselves, kings, queens, and princes are just like other people. No well-to-do household among Oscar's subjects contains a larger collection of personal photographs and little souvenirs of relatives and friends than may be seen at any one of His Majesty's homes. Only the cabinet-portraits, cheaply framed and hung on the walls or stuck into card-racks, are those of the Emperor William, or the Prince of Wales, or the King of Denmark, or some other sovereign or prince with whom Sweden and Norway are on the best of terms. Fans, pipes, snuff-boxes, and all sorts of *bric-à-brac*, which have been presented at Christmas or other times, are displayed on *étagères* or under glass. I dare say that the pin-cushions, antimacassars, and tidies one sees in the more private rooms, are the gifts and the work of princesses, at the least. It would be hard if royalty could not act like the commonalty once in a while and enjoy things which are simple and cheap.

The King has artistic tastes with a strong patriotic bias. He prefers Norwegian pictures for his Christiania palace. No others are to be seen there. Some of them are crude, but all show originality, and there are a few pieces which, by their truthfulness and vigor, would make a sensation in any *salon*. In front of one of these people spontaneously collect and stand in horror and wonder. It is an old-fashioned sea-fight, not one of the modern scientific kind, where the combatants are at long range and almost invisible to one another. The crafts engaged are a Viking-ship and a vessel of some power with which the ancient Norsemen were at war. The former stands high out of water at bow and stern. The latter is more clumsily built— scow-shaped. The two are in dead-lock, and the crew of one is boarding the other. Every man on both sides is wielding an axe, pike, or short sword, and carries a knife in his teeth. There is a desperate resistance, but the Viking fellows are surely overmastering their enemies. The deck of the doomed ship is red with blood, and so is the water all about, as the victims of the terrible combat sink to their death. One lingers spell-bound before this picture till a cough from the guide reminds him to move on.

Every one should see this remarkable painting before or after paying a visit to the special wonder of Christiania. It is the fortune of that city to own something which is unique in archæology. This is a practically perfect specimen of the Viking-ships with which the fierce sea-robbers of the North made their descents on the English and French coasts eight hundred or a thousand years ago. It was recently dug out of a burial-mound of blue clay, where it formed the sepulchre of the chief who owned and commanded it. The surrounding earth had preserving qualities; and so the wood-work of the ship, the iron bolts, part of the iron anchor, some of the cordage, bits of the sail, spears, swords, and shields were recovered in good order. The remains of the interred hero had evidently been removed for some purpose in the distant past, as there were traces of a hole through the mound and then through the wooden tent-like inclosure where the body had been placed. The hull is beautifully modeled—about seventy-two feet long, fifteen and a half feet broad, and three and a half feet deep inside. There are holes for thirty-two oars, many of which were found within the hull. They are of various lengths from eighteen feet downward. The helm is attached by a rope to the right side of the vessel near the stern-post. Pieces of the single mast—which carried a square sail— are shown, but its height is unknown. The general shape of the ship reminds one of a Venetian gondola, than which nothing could be better designed for speed and offensive qualities. The crew, from the elevated position, fore and aft, could easily jump down to the vessels they were assailing; and they could, by the same arrangement, more surely repel boarders. It takes but little imagination to people this black, rakish hull with the original pirates standing erect and prepared to leap on their prey, and in their midst some fair-bearded giant whom they adored and would follow to the death. Such a ship as this may have witnessed such scenes of bloodshed as are depicted on that canvas in the King's palace.

Fiords, lakes, rivers, waterfalls, snow-mountains, soft, rounded hills alternating with low but savage precipices, cultivated and peaceful valleys—these are characteristics of the scenery in Eastern Norway. We desired to take an easy trip into the interior, admitting us to the heart of the country, with the minimum sacrifice of comfort. The problem was how to get a good miniature impression of the natural features of this region in four days? Fortunately, there was (and still is, I hope) a man in Christiania able to solve this problem to the entire satisfaction of the anxious inquirer. His name is Bennett. He cashes your drafts, he outlines your excursions, he furnishes you with carriages, horses, and drivers, he sells you books, carved wood, old Norwegian silver, and other curios; he is universal purveyor and everybody's friend. I went to Bennett and laid my wishes before him. Would he be good enough to plan a little outing, say of four days, warranted to afford some slight idea of picturesque Norway?

The worthy man listened to the request with

as much apparent interest as if I had been the first person who had ever asked him that familiar question. Squaring off at a sheet of paper, he rapidly drew the skeleton of a trip which was at once adopted on his recommendation. Luckily, he had a carriage on hand, which was just the thing for the bad weather then threatening. It was a stout four-wheeler, with a high seat for the driver and a hood which came forward like that of the old-fashioned chaise, and a thick leather apron for the further protection of the inmates. There was a spare seat for the hand-bags and shawls, and a roomy box in the rear for extra harness and a small trunk if required. But we proposed to dispense with any luggage larger than a valise. Everything that Bennett suggested I at once agreed to.

Presently he said, "Of course, you want a guide, to speak the language, and save you trouble?"

"Never, Bennett, never!" said I, calmly but firmly. There is something more unpleasant than the worst of rains in the idea of having a man constantly perched before one, cutting off what little view he might have, and showing him things he does not want to see. I remembered bitterly some of my experiences in Switzerland and Russia, and determined to abandon the trip rather than take along such an incumbrance.

Bennett smiled sweetly, and shrugged his broad shoulders. "As you please," said he. "Perhaps you can manage to get along with a copious phrase-book, giving the Norwegian and English in parallel columns, you know. I have a fine pocket-edition cheap."

"Never, Bennett, never!" I repeated. "I just happened to look into one of those phrase-books this morning. The reader is told to consult the rules for pronunciation of Norwegian words, and be sure to apply them carefully; otherwise he would not be understood by the natives. I tried it on the word *skyds* (English, 'posting'). May I drop dead if it wasn't pronounced *shoss!* No, Bennett, no! I will never have anything to do with a language like that!"

He laughed pleasantly again, like one who is accustomed to dealing with highly eccentric persons. "And pray, sir, what will you do?"

"Bennett," said I, "have you, or could you get for me, two or perhaps three pounds of the copper coins *öre*—pronounced *ouray*, I believe?"

"I have a barrel of 'em at your disposal."

"But I want only enough to fill up my outside pockets. And could you supply me with twenty or thirty notes of one krone each?"

"I understand," said he, "and I am sure it will work. There is no language like ready money, after all. But it is the last that most people think of trying."

It took but a few minutes to cash a draft on my bankers in London. I received enough copper *öre* packed in small *rouleaux* to fill two pockets, and stuffed my wallet with single paper kroner. Then I knew I was prepared for any emergency arising from ignorance of the Norwegian tongue. Besides these smaller resources, there was a due provision of larger currency which can never come amiss.

CHAPTER XXXI.

A BABY KUDSK—TYRI-FIORD—HÖNEFOS—LAKE SPIRELLEN—DINNER AT A SANITARIUM.

NEXT morning (August 9th) we made an early start, with Hönefos as the objective point for the day, the hotel there having been highly recommended to us. The postboy (*kudsk*) who was to drive to the first station on the route, two hours distant, was not a boy, but a man. And that was a damper upon the enthusiasm with which we should have set out; for all the authorities on Norwegian traveling assure one that the drivers are invariably real boys—when they are not girls. Much of the charm, and most of the risk, which is itself a delightful excitement to some people, of carriage-riding in Norway, is always said to consist in the fact that you are in charge of a joyous child, whose infantile ways divert you, when there is nothing else worth looking at. As we had already journeyed over a part of the road in a little ride we had taken out of Christiania some days before, we would have been glad to extract some amusement from the driver. At the next station there would be a change on the box-seat, and we were hoping for somebody a little smaller and less obstructive of the view, than postboy number one. But we were not prepared for what happened. I had settled for my mileage up to that point with the *skydsskaffer* (station-master), paid the overgrown postboy the gratuity in *öre* which usage decrees to him, the tired horses had been taken from the pole and fresh ones put on, and we were impatient to be off again, when a little chap climbed up to the box-seat. He looked six or eight years old. I supposed he was the youngest brother of the driver, who had not yet appeared. His toes, by stretching, just touched the dash-board. The child was so very young that we thought of asking him to take part of a spare seat inside if he wished to ride to the next station. We waited five minutes for the driver, when, what was our amazement, to see the reins handed up to the mite! He took them in his baby-hand like an old coachman. Then he prattled something in Norwegian. In reply he received a whip-stock with about three inches of lash. He looked at it scornfully, and flourished it in the air to show that it would not "crack." The poor little fellow wanted a real whip, with a thong about ten feet long, which he could snap as he passed every house, like his father and his grandfather, who were somewhere on the road that same day. But the station-master had no better whip, or was unwilling to trust the child with one. He ordered the carriage on. I saw a tear steal down the cheek of Toddlekins, and heard an infantile sob, but he suddenly checked himself and made a scarcely audible noise with his lips, and the horses, hearing that signal to go, flew down the road. I stood erect for a while, ready to jump to the box-seat and seize the reins; but in a very few moments both the mite and the horses had my entire confidence.

The animals knew every inch of the road, and were perfectly trained. They went fast or slow in the right places, and they turned aside enough for every passing cariole or *stolkjærre* (cart with seats for two). Perhaps the horses should have all the credit for that highly satisfactory drive. But we preferred to think that we owed our safety and pleasure to the baby *kudsk*. At the foot of every hill he would jump to the ground—I always felt like lifting him down—and, while the ponies were struggling up, he would, in the gravest and most knowing manner, inspect the state of the harness and the wheels, and be sure that everything was right and tight. He was a model coachman, seen through the wrong end of a telescope. When he had clambered up to his seat again and all was going well, he would look in a distressed manner at that mockery of a whip; he would repeat the motion of cracking it, and when the miserable apology for a lash would not make the slightest noise, his lip would quiver and he could hardly hold in his tears. We were sorry that we had no candy to give him at the end of the ride, but made up for it in small coin. If he had been a shade cleaner, I might have kissed him for his mother, at parting.

At this second station, Holmedal, we commanded a view of the Hols-Fiord, a branch of the larger Tyri-Fiord. It is a ribbon of fresh water winding between crags and wooded slopes and would pass for a lake in any other country but Norway. It has no direct connection with the salt-water, violating my preconceived notion of a fiord, which I had always supposed to be a true arm of the sea, thrust far up into the land like the fiord of Christiania, at the head of which stands the beautiful city of that name. But one soon comes to learn that the same sheet of water is called a fiord or a lake according to the caprice of writers about Norway, who are at swords' points on all subjects. Lake George (New York), or the Italian Lake Como, would pass for a fiord in Norway. But, aside from questions of nomenclature, there is no disputing the loveliness of Hols-Fiord or of the nobler Tyri. We looked down upon a mirror, which perfectly reflected the green hills and the beetling rocks that composed its frame. There was not wind enough for sailing, and the surface of the fiord was unvexed save by a few fishermen's boats lazily rowed through the smooth water. The original lotos-eaters, stretched along the ground covered with dry-pine needles in the rear of the house, would have been loath to quit the idyllic scene. Nothing less imperative than a luncheon would have called us away from it. We would have been more grateful for the savory stew of mutton served at that meal, had we known that we were soon to be put on short rations of meat. The one article of food that never fails is the egg. The trout are left to flash their speckled sides in the brook, instead of gracing the table. And by the road-side, millions of bushels of delicious strawberries rot unregarded! All the women and girls are busy in the house, and all the men and boys are guiding and driving the mob of tourists. Thus the hen— which can scratch for her living, and needs to be watched only for her eggs laid in the neighboring barn—becomes the unfailing reliance.

At the Holmedal station, a man who was resting there, on his way to Christiania, recognized the carriage as his own. Bennett had hired it of him, and sublet it to me. The owner learned from me that I had agreed to send it back from Odnæs to Christiania, by rail or steamboat, at my own expense; whereupon occurred to him the brilliant idea of getting me to sell it for him for his standing price of four hundred kroner (about one hundred and twelve dollars). I thought he was joking, and dismissed his proposition with a laugh. While we were lunching, the man resumed his journey. On re-entering the carriage, I found upon the seat a paper written in Norwegian, and signed by a name and address. It proved to be a document authorizing the bearer (myself) to sell the carriage at Odnæs for four hundred kroner. Nothing was said about paying the money to the signer; that was taken for granted. I was interested in gratifying his wishes, to the extent of fifteen kroner—that being the freight-charge on the carriage from Odnæs back to Christiania. I tried to make the sale, but without success. Such instances of confidence in perfect strangers are, it is said, not rare in Norway.

A boy about ten years old here took the reins. He was so much larger and maturer than the preceding youngster, that he looked a man in contrast. He had a whip with a long lash, which he cracked continually, till I was impelled to check his exuberance of spirits. He also had the fault—which it seems impossible to correct in the Norwegian *kudsk*, old or young—of urging the horses downhill at a headlong gait. They all seem to think that this must give the greatest possible pleasure to the riders. It is, indeed, agreeably exciting at times, when the road is free of stones and sunken places. But we were journeying along the side of the Tyri-Fiord at a good height above it, and did not want our attention distracted from its calm, sunny bosom. In the post-luncheon mood, we would fain have rested half an hour each at some of the points. But, as this would have delayed the arrival at Hönefos till an unseasonable evening hour, we took in the scene on the wing. At one elevation we seemed to survey the whole expanse of the Tyri-Fiord. It was apparently landlocked. Not till one examines a map does he discover that a long strip of water—Drammenselv—links it to Drammens-Fiord, which in turn leads up to the Christiania-Fiord. And this is the only tenure by which the Tyri holds the title that is so misleading to travelers. But, whatever its classification in geography, it is one of the most picturesque pieces of water in Europe.

The tourist's principal motive in visiting Hönefos is to see the waterfalls. He wants those falls "neat," as one may say—that is, unmixed with baser things. If he could realize in advance the number of saw-mills for which these falls supply the power, he would probably stay away from Hönefos. His idea of a fall is of a body of water which has nothing to do but tumble gracefully over rocks with a tremendous roar and a following cloud of spray. If he is an American, and has seen Niagara, he is sure to be very exacting in his requirement for waterfalls. When such a man first beholds the cascades of Hönefos, his feeling is one of disappointment. The saw-mills stand so thick as to cut off the view of the foaming, white water at many points. The bubbles that are borne toward him by the raging current are flecked with the fine dust of wood. With the roar of the water is mingled the sound of buzz-saws.

But one soon adjusts himself to the conditions of the scene. The falls are so attractive that, when he has studied them a little while, he ceases to note the planks, the boards, the shingles, which are piled up on the banks of the Bægna River, and the dust that whirls past him on all the surface of the water, and he no longer hears the saws as the teeth eat their way through the hard Norwegian pine-logs. By shading his eyes with his hand, he can shut out the mills which occupy the middle distance, and imagine himself in the presence of Nature before man had harnessed her up for his use. And when he inspects the branches or side-issues of the cataract, he finds some as untamed and free as any mountain-brook. In these he sees the natural fall of the waters over rocks of their own choosing, uncontrolled by dams and sluices. The Bægna is about an eighth of a mile wide at the place where it takes a sheer plunge of thirty feet, and then races away in rapids. The best view may be had in safety from a bridge immediately below the falls.

The village of Hönefos is compact and businesslike. But there is a Garden of Eden at the north end of it. This is situated at a bend of the river, where one can see the falls in the distance and hear their deep roar free from the under-tone of the saw-mills. By a wise choice, Glatved's Hotel has been placed there, and the tired wayfarer knows not which to praise the more, the quiet comfort of the well-kept inn or the restful charm of the lovely grounds in which it stands. They are laid out in walks, lined with flowers and fruit- and foliage-trees. In shady spots stand little tables and rustic chairs for the use of those who like to eat or drink *al fresco*. But that sort of thing, though very romantic, is quite out of the question at nightfall, with the mercury down to 55° Fahr. So we took our first meal at Glatved's in the pretty dining-room, and a very good supper it was. I distinctly remember the crisp trout, the broiled chicken, the snowy bread, and a dish of huckleberries with cream. There were few guests at that season of the year, English for the most part, friendly and affable to us Americans. Our sleeping-room was large and clean, and opened on a broad balcony facing the river. There in the morning was served a capital breakfast. The sun shone brightly. The distant falls sparkled. The roar of the water was a musical bass. Birds flew among the trees and butterflies hovered over the flowers. If all things were steeped in rose-color, who can say how much of it was owing to the strong, fragrant coffee, with whipped cream, the dainty lamb-chops, the fried potato-shavings, the *omelette au confiture* with its purple heart of raspberry-jam?

We had hoped to be favored with a girl instead of a boy as driver to the next station on the route — Heen. After our experience the day before, we felt that anybody who could sit on the box-seat and hold the reins could manage trained ponies in use on Norwegian roads. A girl could safely be trusted with them. But to our great disappointment, a lout of a boy climbed up in front, and off we started for Heen — with the injunction (from the young woman who settled our bill and saw us off) ringing in our ears— "Stop at the Captain's!"

The road to Heen was sandy and hilly most of the way. There were more dashing falls at Höfsfos. And we found, in the depths of a pine-wood, stunted bushes with just such blueberries on them as the people of distant New Hampshire and Vermont were doubtless picking that very day. It is one of the pleasantest incidents of foreign travel to come across wild flowers and fruits identical with those of America.

The Captain's at Heen is the only name given to the roomy house belonging to the commander of the steamboat that plies between that place and Sörum on Lake Spirellen. We reached it about 1 P. M., at the moment dinner was going on the Captain's hospitable table. As our carriage was destined to accompany us up the lake, that was the end of the land-ride for the present, and we were glad of it. The Captain greeted us as we alighted. He is a square-shouldered, resolute man, who speaks English well. Instead of ordering some one else to do the work, he put the carriage with his own hands on board the steamboat, which was then lying at her wharf close by and ready to leave. The Captain's dinner was a good one, as ten or twelve persons who sat about the board all agreed. Soup, fresh eggs, two kinds of meat, pudding, strawberries, cheese, coffee, and wine and beer for those who ordered them, satisfied every rational expectation.

We all boarded the little craft in a contented frame of mind. The day was cloudy, but not damp or cold. Our course, for several English miles, was up the Bægna River, in the teeth of a tremendous current. At times it ran like a millrace. The boat could make headway in some places only by closely hugging the shore. Occasionally we would see logs, that had slipped their moorings in the lake beyond, coming down the middle of the stream with frightful velocity and threatening to punch holes in the bow. The steersman smoked his pipe as calmly as if sitting by his own hearth. If any log ever touched the hull, it glanced off harmless. There were moments when the boat refused to mind the helm. Then the Captain, who stood hard by—pipe in mouth also—would put his great hairy hands on the spokes, and she minded quickly then. Presently we entered upon that expansion of the river known as Lake Spirellen. It is the Tyri-Fiord over again—in its alternately tame and wild environments—but the current still ridges itself in the center of the lake, and only near its shores can the boat make six or eight knots an hour. No landings are attempted, but passengers and freight are taken off or put on by flat-bottomed barges, which require powerful rowers to hold them against the stream. We killed time watching these struggling craft, or gazing through the crystal water down to the grassy bottom, which our keel almost scraped.

It was nearly dark when we landed at Sörum and the boat tied up for the night. We all hurried ashore, to try our luck at a new hotel whose unpainted sides showed a beautiful wood-color against the dark background of hills. There was in its newness a promise of clean beds, and wholesome, if homely, fare. The beds proved to be good, and the fare was undoubtedly satisfactory to persons, if any, who happen to prefer hard-boiled eggs to meat. For it was the five-minute egg that formed the staple of supper and again of breakfast. The eggs were always brought on in heaping platefuls wrapped up in hot napkins and deceiving the eye with the promise of something better than themselves, till the cloth was removed by a waitress, disclosing the standard food of the smaller inns of Eastern Norway. But the bread, butter, and cheese were very good, and there was a choice of tea, coffee, and chocolate. What the Sörum hotel lacked, even more than meat, was modern improvements. It is the want of these that makes the traveler, who has outlived his passion for roughing it, think at least twice before he makes up his mind to enter upon an extended tour of the interior of the country. The most primitive New England farm-house of twenty-five years ago was better off in these respects than any Norwegian hotel we have seen outside of Christiania.

The third day of the excursion was the one to which we had looked forward with the greatest pleasure; for the route from Sörum to Odnæs was said to traverse some of the finest scenery in Eastern Norway. We were promised a succession of high mountains, some snow-clad, waterfalls leaping down precipices, and valleys unsurpassed in loveliness stretching between the frowning heights. Throw in a lavish supply of lakes and rivers, with Rands-Fiord as the goal, and you have the seductive features of the journey as we had fondly dreamed of it.

But the day opened with lowering weather. The air was full of moisture. It seemed like a sponge just waiting to be squeezed a little to give down rain. There was a good twelve hours' ride before us to Odnæs. So I determined to be off early. Everybody else at the hotel who was bound in the same direction was equally anxious to get away. Breakfast was ordered for us at half-past six, and, even before I had attacked my ration of hard-boiled eggs, I interviewed the head-hostler upon the subject of horses for the carriage, which had been drawn up before the hotel during the night. He was a Norwegian who did not speak a word of English; and, if he had spoken it as well as myself, we could not have conversed at any length, he was so beset by people all wanting their carriages and horses immediately. Thus far in our progress from Christiania I had not had occasion to test the persuasive power of the krone. The humble öre had been good enough for the trivial exigencies that had hitherto arisen. Taking care not to be observed by others, I held up one of the enticing bits of paper so that the head-hostler could see it. Then I said "Odnæs," and displayed seven fingers.

Sure enough, at 7 A. M., sharp, there was the carriage with two fine ponies attached, and a bright-looking lad in the seat, waiting at the door of the hotel for me. Other persons, who had previously ordered their carioles or *stolkjærres*, looked on in amazement. They had been coaxing and scolding the poor man, but had evidently not thought of my simple expedient to secure his attention.

We set out in fine style, with much cracking of the whip, all for effect, however, as Norwegian horses need only a hint—which sounds like uncorking a bottle, and is made by the lips of the driver—

in order to display their speed. They stop with equal readiness in response to a buzzing sound emitted between his teeth. The road was good, and that was fortunate, for we went at a frightful pace over every short level stretch, and just the same down-hill. Some of the hills slope at an angle of forty-five degrees. But this made no difference. The horses dashed down one with a speed that did not slacken till they had proceeded some distance up the next hill. They would climb this at a fast walk, and at the top would be fresh and ready for another plunge. After we had taken several of these dives and come up safe and sound, the sensation of anxiety about consequences wore off, and we enjoyed the delirious rush. They recalled the excitement of tobogganing and swinging. But they did not permit that survey of the scenery which one ought to take leisurely in Norway. Whether we went fast or slow mattered but little that day, however, for the rain soon began to fall in torrents. It was a steady down-pour, which taxed our utmost resources in leather aprons, waterproofs, shawls, and umbrellas. We were obliged to close the sides of the carriage with oil-skins which had been provided by the ever-thoughtful Bennett. Thus almost hermetically sealed up, we missed the charms of the landscape, save when, at rare intervals, we would make a little chink through the folds of the envelopes and catch tantalizing glimpses of it. The driver—poor boy—must have been soaked through his heavy top-coat to the skin. He urged his horses at their topmost speed, to gain the station where some other luckless fellow must take his place. We reached it in about three hours, and found it full of travelers, rained in. Bed and board there were out of the question, in the crowded condition of the station, and our only recourse was to go ahead.

Here the omnipotent kroner again came into play with immense effect. The exhibition of a few of them procured an immediate change of horses, and no less a person than the station-master himself occupied the post of driver. A full-grown man was very acceptable for that function in such weather. Small boys and girls were no more to be thought of. The station-master made himself as nearly waterproof as possible; and I hope was none the worse for his exposure to the storm, which continued unabated all the way to a certain Sanitarium at which we had been advised to stop for luncheon, instead of going on to the regular station for that meal. Never was advice better given, or more obediently followed. We found the Sanitarium a large, first-class house. It would be a haven of rest, even in the finest weather, after three hours of furious driving. As a refuge from the pitiless storm, it was welcome and delightful beyond description. Luckily, we did not want a room, for the house was packed full of summer boarders, who were said to be drinking or bathing in the mineral waters which are the chief attractions of the place. In whatever way they took the waters, they were undoubtedly deriving benefit from them; for when we sat down to dinner with about one hundred and fifty of the convalescent patients, we never saw such a display of ravenous appetites. The bill of fare was long. The waiters were nimble and attentive. The dishes were gigantic platters, heaped up with food and passed with the utmost dispatch down the long lines of hungry guests. As fast as these mighty trays were cleared of their burdens, others equally large and laden with steaming meats or vegetables would come to the rescue. A sturdy corps of white-aproned carvers, at an adjoining table, could be heard slashing away at the hot joints, trying to keep pace with the jaws of the patients, and were at last successful, however difficult their task.

It would not have been thought possible, but is a fact that, in the final stage of the repast, plenty of fruit was passed around and no takers. But then it must be explained that pudding, ice-cream, cakes, and a most toothsome dish, which I will now briefly describe from the best information procurable, had already made the circuit for all who wanted them. This novel delicacy, without an English name, is prepared as follows: A thin gruel is made of rice-flour, or farina will do. Into this, while boiling hot, a mixture of jellies is introduced—the greater the variety the better. Currant, raspberry, strawberry—whatever the good housewife finds on her pantry-shelves—are all dumped in together and vigorously stirred. The artful compounder studies how to blend the natural flavors of these jellies so that no one shall be in the ascendant. When the operation is an entire success, the eaters should not be able to distinguish any particular berry in the compost, but should enjoy a gustatory effect in which each of the jellies is lost, only to reappear improved in a new and delicious combination that defies analysis on the palate. It is eaten, hot or cold, with or without cream and sugar.

CHAPTER XXXII.

OMNIPOTENT KRONER—THE FAMILY PARLOR AT
ODNÆS—RANDS AND CHRISTIANIA FIORDS.

At the Sanitarium we scraped acquaintance with one of the ever-friendly English race. When he learned that we were bound to Odnæs that afternoon through the rain, which was still pouring, he expressed his sympathy. For he explained that it was impossible to get any accommodations at the only hotel there. He and a party of friends had been turned away from that house the night before, and had come on in the dark to the Sanitarium, where they were fortunate in securing the billiard-table—the only sleeping-place (except the floors) not then engaged.

As there was no prospect of a relief from the pressure at any place on the road while the severe storm lasted, we were in a quandary. But I had unfailing faith in the power of kroner, and decided to go on. We could not be worse off at Odnæs than at the Sanitarium, and, when there, would be so much farther on the way to Christiania and the home comforts of the Victoria Hotel.

If the day had been fine, the view from this watering-place in the hills would have been magnificent. It takes in a marvelous combination of peaks, table-lands, valley, lakes, and rivers. But none of these objects were visible through the rain; and, after many abortive efforts to catch glimpses of grandeur and loveliness which we had come so far to see, we shut ourselves up in the carriage as tightly as possible, and tried in vain to sleep.

The road to Odnæs was down-hill most of the way, and the drivers, whom we changed twice, made good time. After five hours of imprisonment in the carriage, relieved only by alighting at two little stations while fresh horses were put to the pole, we reached Odnæs. The moment we came in view of the hotel I realized how hopeless was the expectation of obtaining any bed there. Six or eight vehicles of different kinds were drawn up in front of the door. Others were squeezed into the small sheds near the large stables, the stalls of which had long been filled with horses, the later comers being tied to trees near the house. But the most convincing evidence of an overflow was the human crowd on the balcony, in the doorways and windows. Every pane of glass had its peering face. There were rows of people standing on tiptoe and looking over one another's heads at us as our driver brought round the carriage as near the front door as he could get. The countless lookers-on smiled sarcastically as they saw us about to alight. That unanimous grin suddenly decided my line of action.

The head-porter of the hotel presented himself at the door of the carriage. He had good manners, and spoke a little English. He deeply regretted that they could not give us anything better than a place on the floor, without bedclothes of any kind.

"Very well," said I, pointing to a neat little house—the only one in sight—"perhaps they can take us in."

"Varce soree, sir, but they been all full two day."

In this serious emergency, I must test the virtue of kroner. I handed one to the head-porter, and promised him three more if he would secure a bed for us in that cottage.

"I vill try, sir," he replied, with a slight shrug of the shoulders; but he spoke as one not without hope.

Jumping to the front seat by the side of the driver, he ordered the carriage on to the other house. We pulled up before it, and waited there in the rain while the head-porter went inside to interview the proprietor.

We knew from the exterior of the dwelling that it was private, and that lodging and board were provided by the occupants only as a favor to those who could not possibly be accommodated at the hotel.

In about five minutes, that seemed equal to fifteen—so acute was our suspense—the good fellow returned beaming with smiles, and followed by a man who looked a welcome which he could not speak.

The head-porter wore an air of mystery as he thrust his head into the carriage and said, in a low voice: "You vill have de best room—de parlor. Dey vill make you much attention. Don't say noting."

"Mum's the word," said I, not understanding the object of the last remark, and not caring to ask. It was evident, from the manner of the master of the house, that, during the last five minutes, he had been in some way powerfully impressed with a sense of our importance; and, in consequence, had consented to give up his parlor, which he had refused to all previous comers. I appreciated the courtesy, knowing from books how sacred in the eyes of all these northern races is the parlor—or best room—of the house.

The promised reward was slipped into the hand of the diplomatic head-porter. He smiled his thanks.

"You vill please be so goot to step out," he then said, taking his hat off in the rain to mark his profound respect for us.

We observed that this act had its effect on the man who stood looking down from the piazza, for he bowed in sympathy.

I do not to this day know by what highly colored representations the extraordinary privilege was obtained. I only know that, as if by magic, the prohibition was removed from this almost holy room, and two single beds—which probably were in use elsewhere by members of the family at the time of our arrival—were brought in. The proprietor, his wife, and three bright little girls all lent ready hands to transforming the parlor into a comfortable sleeping-room. As not one of them could speak any English, they only looked at us deferentially. In their eyes we were persons of great distinction—thanks, no doubt, to the lively imagination of our good friend from the Odnæs Hotel.

The parlor had a neat, home-woven carpet—a rare decoration in Norwegian houses—an excess of new furniture in mahogany and horse-hair, brightly figured window-curtains, and family photographs hung on the papered walls. Having arrived late, we were anxious to sup at once, and the head-porter had told them to hurry up. But they were desirous to show their respect in preparing a supper of unimpeachable excellence. We were, therefore, kept waiting and hungry for about an hour; and, during this interval, the pleasant landlady and her daughters frequently knocked at the door, and, upon being admitted, would courtesy, and proceed to bring in more towels, or water, or drinking-glasses, or something else supposed to be conducive to our comfort. Among the other offerings was a vase of flowers.

The supper would have been very good for persons who could not have too many hard-boiled eggs at once. They were the principal dish, and in the abundance of their supply we recognized a marked compliment. For ordinary persons probably not more than four eggs apiece would have been served. There were about two dozen in the bowl before us, covered by a steaming napkin to keep them warm. The only meat was ham unboiled and thin slices of sausage, which did not commend themselves to conservative palates. But berries and cream, the bread and butter, and, above all, the cheese were highly relished, and the only fault with the tea was what one finds everywhere—its weakness. We were waited on by the little girls, looking nice with their hair done up in ribbons, and long, snow-white aprons strapped about their shoulders. They watched us with great curiosity, and occasionally compared notes in whispers. Their manner indicated that they were overawed.

Meanwhile our presence in the house had caused no small stir among other guests, who filled every available nook and corner. It may well have surprised them to see the spacious apartment, which they had all longed to occupy at any price, finally given up to two persons, when, with close packing, it might have sufficed for a stag-party of ten. We were much stared at whenever we entered and left the room; and two Englishmen, after eying me closely awhile, tried to draw me into a conversation about myself; but I recalled the mysterious injunction, "Don't say noting!" and stood on my dignity. If there was any illusion of which we were reaping the advantage—if, for example, we had been represented by the romancing head-porter as a princely couple traveling *incognito*—it was not for me to assist in dispelling it.

After a good night's rest, we sat down to more hard-boiled eggs about six o'clock in the morning. We breakfasted thus early in order to take the steamer down the Rands-Fiord to the point of rail connection with Christiania. The rain had ceased, the air was temperate, and we could see all around us signs of the approaching departure of guests so long weather-bound at Odnæs. Most of them were going on to Sörum, over the road we had traveled the day before. Only two or three persons from the hotel—and none from the little cottage—were destined for the steamer.

The bill for our accommodation was presented, and proved to be reasonable. If we had unconsciously been posing as high and mighty personages, we were not unduly charged for it. When the family assembled on the piazza to see us off, their manners showed how much they appreciated the honor we had done them. May they never be made victims of a less innocent imposition! If, to keep up the character thrust upon me, I tipped a trifle to the daughters of the house, I hope to be pardoned for that much complicity in the fraud.

Our guide-book said that the Rands-Fiord was only six and a half miles long, and we had thoughtlessly supposed the miles in question to be English. But, to be sure of it, when we got on board I asked the captain (who spoke English fairly) what time the boat was due at the railway-station down the fiord. Looking at his watch—which then marked seven o'clock—he replied, "At half-past one."

"What!" said I, in amazement, "six hours and a half for as many miles?" "Yes," he answered, laughing, "Norwegian miles!" One of these equals seven of English measure.

There was some little delay in putting the carriage—the trusty companion of our travels—on board. It had been hauled down from the house where we passed the night, and hoisted to the upper deck of the baby-steamer, out of the way. This done, we began the passage of the Rands-Fiord, and found it pleasantly unexciting. It is almost a duplicate of Lake Spirellen, save that the water has less of a current, and the surrounding mountains are tamer. There is no apparent reason why the one sheet of water is called a lake and the other a fiord. They are both expansions of rivers, like the Tyri-Fiord heretofore described, and in no sense inlets of the sea, though they may empty into it by long and winding streams. We stopped many times on the trip to take on or let off passengers. With only a few exceptions, the transfer, as on Lake Spirellen, was made rapidly by small boats, which put off for the shore as we approached a landing-place, and did the business of shipping or unloading passengers and freight with neatness and dispatch. These transfers, often as they occurred, were in the nature of "incidents" of the voyage, and every person on board watched the operation for the twentieth time with unabated interest.

The great event of the day was a dinner served at 1 P. M. in the small cabin below deck. It was a solid meal, with varieties of meat, which we were glad to taste again after our short deprivation of fresh beef and mutton. Just before we reached our destination at the end of the fiord, the sun shone out with a splendor that rejoiced all hearts. It made the little dancing waves of the Rands-Fiord sparkle, and threw a warm flush over the dark hills on either hand. As we looked back on the water which had been traversed, it recalled the Tappan-Zee of the noble Hudson River as seen from Piermont.

At the Rands-Fiord station we took rail—the carriage following by the goods-train—for Christiania. This part of the route, though one from which the traveler expects the least, is no less interesting than the rides by carriage or steamer. The train passes through one of the loveliest districts of Eastern Norway. The line skirts the west shore of the Tyri-Fiord, affording glimpses of blue mountains not seen on our journey along the east shore. It passes through the old towns of Hangsund and Drammen, enabling the tourist to see occasionally from the car-windows houses and costumes slightly different from those he finds in the more modern and conventional Christiania. And then, with a mighty curve, the train follows the trend of the magnificent and properly named fiord upon which Christiania stands. The views here are very fine. From the height above the water one can look down on the calm expanse dotted with little islands, each one green with its patch of woodland, or brown with its ripe rye and barley. The sails of the pleasure-yachts and fishing-smacks gleam against the dark bosom of the fiord; and at intervals of a few miles along the shore are towns or villages where white houses shine from afar—proofs positive of the industry and thrift of the Scandinavian race. One may travel thousands of miles west and east, north and south in Norway and never behold a fairer scene than that which made everybody on the train thrust head out of window and gaze at it until a range of low coast-hills shut it from view.

CHAPTER XXXIII.

THE GOTHENBURG WHALE—THREE KINGS IN A BUNCH—NORTHERN OUT-DOOR LIFE—A STUDY OF WINDMILLS.

LET me tell my readers something about the pursuit of a whale under difficulties. At Gothenburg, Sweden, I learned that a stuffed whale, sixty feet long, could be seen in a museum of that city. Objects said to be whales in the act of spouting are often pointed out to one at sea. But they are usually miles away. They throw up jets which look in the distance like little puffs of steam or exploding beer-bottles. I always assented to the existence of those whales, to avoid controversy, but reserved my doubts. Here, at last, was promised on the dry land what had never really been seen by me on the ocean. So I lost no time in seeking out the museum. Entering it, I steered at once for the fish department. A single glance up and down the long room convinced me that there was not even a baby-whale among its skinny and foul-smelling treasures. An old woman, with a large brass plate—numbered—hanging round her neck, was the only other living occupant of the room. She was the custodian. I said, "Speak English?" She only shook her head. As I could not speak Swedish, I tried pantomime, which goes a great way in strange countries. First I looked round in astonishment, as if missing something that ought to be there; then stretched both hands as high and wide as possible, to imply that the thing wanting was of immense size; finally, made a noise like the fizz of champagne, and jerked both thumbs into the air. I flattered myself that all that meant a whale, if anything. But the old woman's face remained a wrinkled blank. She did not "catch on." A happy thought! I opened out both arms like a pair of jaws big enough to take in Jonah. She exclaimed, "Yaw!" with much energy, and took me to a corner of the room and left me in front of—an alligator, with a very open countenance. Still keeping my temper—though under extreme provocation—I made a fierce wiggle-waggle motion with both hands to represent a big fish that thrashes about a good deal with his flat tail. This time there could be no doubt that she understood me, for she piloted me into a side-show, where I brought up before—a shark. That was too much for my patience. Forgetting that the poor woman could not speak a word of English, I cried out: "How stupid! Why don't you show me the whale?" You should have heard her yell: "Oh, yaw, yaw! der vale, der vale!" Thus near was the Swedish word to the English one all the time I was wasting my best pantomime on her. In two minutes more I had descended a long corkscrew flight of stairs at the heels of the aged guide, and there, in a cool basement, found the monster upon the ownership of which Gothenburg is entitled to put on airs, for it is claimed to be the largest whale ever skinned and mounted. It is all of sixty feet long, and so thick in proportion, that twenty Jonahs could sit around inside quite comfortably. In fact, its interior is fitted up with seats, and may be hired by small parties who take a fancy to eating and drinking in a whale's belly. Alongside of the skin is the skeleton, also an object of great interest, looking like the frame of a schooner bottom-side up.

It is not often that the tourist has a chance to see three kings in a bunch. At Copenhagen we were just in time to witness the entry of the King of Portugal. He came to pay a little visit to the King of Denmark, one of whose sons, the King of Greece, was then spending a few days at the old home. I hope it is not very unrepublican to say that if I must look on kings I prefer that they should "act as such," and always be wearing their crowns and robes, and holding scepters in their hands like pokers. If they would ride on horseback, or in golden chariots, so much the better. These three kings sat in open barouches, like other people; and they had left their robes and crowns and scepters at home. But they were good enough to put on gorgeous cocked hats with fountains of white feathers, and coats plastered all over with gold which served as a background for decorations blazing with diamonds. It was not for me—as the stern and unbending representative of a republic—to scowl upon all those lovely gewgaws and that beautiful man-millinery. They seemed appropriate enough for an occasion of show. The philosopher accepts them gratefully, like any other free entertainment. Probably the three kings were bored by it more than any of the spectators. The King of Portugal is a middle-aged, stout gentleman with an expression of face amiable as far as it could be seen under a weeping-willow of plumes. To be born good-looking is a great initial advantage. Perhaps that is why the young King of Greece received so large a share of the applause. The reception was planned for the royal stranger. But the people of Copenhagen take a lively personal interest in their own dynasty. They follow its fortunes in all parts of the world, and, when any of its members return for a visit, they never fail to testify their pleasure. If King Christian of Denmark needed the indulgence of his people to any great extent, much would be pardoned to him because he is the father of so many good-looking children who have got on in the world.

These lucky children reciprocate the popular feeling at Copenhagen, and come back from their distant thrones at least once a year. Then there is a regular house-warming. The husbands and the wives and the babies are all on hand. The court photographer is called in, and pictures of the party are taken in a variety of combinations and attitudes. A favorite group is one in which the Tsar of Russia—the big brother-in-law—occupies the central position. He is a tall, bluff-looking man, with a laughing face. In a Derby hat and a shooting-jacket he would pass for a young English squire, without a care in the world. He holds by the hand—with a tight grip, one would say—the gentle Dagmar who shares his fate. By her side is one who looks almost like her twin-sister—the Princess of Wales—and the Prince himself is within touch. The tallest and best looking of all the men is the King of Greece, and his queen nestles up to him very fondly in the pictures. The Crown-Prince of Denmark is also there, doing credit to the family.

His wife, a princess of Sweden, with other desirable qualities, is rich in her own right—a fact of which the thrifty Danes remind you with pride. The youngest, Princess Thyra and her husband, the Duke of Cumberland, with the unmarried son of the King, make up the second generation of this great family party. The first consists of the parents—the still comely Christian and his wife—and the third generation is a mass of babies that I have never stopped to count. They swarm all over the steps of the palace where these pictures are taken. Some one of them is always wriggling about, just enough to blur the photograph at that point.

There is something pathetic in the way that the people of Copenhagen, Gothenburg, Christiania, and other northern cities make the most of their short summer. Flowers are very precious to them, since they can have them for so few months out-of-doors. We found every available foot of front garden brilliant with blossoms—the reddest and yellowest preferred. Every window in every house had its box of pinks, nasturtiums, marigolds, heliotropes, and mignonettes. For the time being the natives make believe that they are living in the tropics. They play with sun-shades and awnings as if they really needed them. They imitate the custom of Italy, and take their meals in the open air, as if it were not generally cool and uncomfortable there. I never saw an illusion better maintained. But I noticed that many, who carried the self-deception too far, paid for it in coughs and sneezes. It was not till we descended to the latitude of Hamburg, that we found it an unalloyed pleasure to sit under the trees in the edge of evening and dine. The good Hamburgers know how to live. They have established a first-class zoölogical garden in a shady wood, near the center of their city. They have stocked this garden with the most ferocious and delightful wild beasts, securely caged. They have organized a restaurant and *café* of an incredible feeding capacity. They have provided chairs for everybody. They have hired the best military band in Hamburg and bade it play every day free of cost to all comers.

We went out there to dinner one afternoon— between five and six o'clock—and saw a sight not yet so familiar that it has ceased to be deeply interesting. There were thousands of women and young girls, neatly dressed, sitting at little tables sipping their coffee or beer and nibbling their pretzels, and knitting or sewing "between whiles." Every one was talking or laughing. Between and under and over the tables, and constantly on the move, were the happiest of children, in numbers past counting. It was evident that this was the children's hour, and that they, with all their mothers and nurses, were having a good time. In the midst of the joyous tumult would be heard the bark of the seal, the roar of the lion, the squall of the peacock. Presently the men began to collect and to occupy seats not hitherto taken. Corks popped out of bottles and incense ascended from the deep bowls of pipes. The fathers had come to join their babies. Not a policeman was in sight, and there was no need of one. The only turbulent and dangerous creatures anywhere around were the wild beasts, and they were behind the bars. The music was exceedingly good—as it always is in Germany—and it was pleasant to watch the vast audience drinking in the sweet sounds with ecstasy and beating time with knitting-needles, pipes, beer-mugs, and everything else handy. But in some of the most delicate passages of favorite compositions, when the conductor was doing his best to quiet down the band, funny effects would be produced by the growls of the bears, which somebody was stirring up with a long pole.

Before quitting the colder lands of the North, let me not fail to mention the warm, luxuriant—almost tropical—tastes of her sculptors. After leaving Rome and Florence, one never sees as many marble Venuses, Cupids, Adonises, and Apollos as in the capitals of Sweden, Norway, and

Denmark. They are all new, and sparkle like loaf-sugar. At first, I thought they were copies of great originals in the Italian galleries. But they proved to be native conceptions of the old myths, wrought out with the patient art—if not the skill —of the true Greek. It would take double windows and red-hot stoves to make those gods and goddesses look comfortable in-doors in a Norwegian January. The costume of Eden is even less adapted to the temperature of the front yard. Imagine Venus in a snow-drift!

Coming by boat from Korsör, Denmark, to Kiel, Prussia, the passengers on our steamboat had the pleasure of reviewing a division of the German ironclad fleet. Attention was first caught by the rapid discharge of cannon from a man-of-war in the offing. We could see her balls strike the water. At the same time she was tacking to all points of the compass and making signals. We next came in sight of a torpedo-fleet. Each boat had a little smoke-stack, and hugged the water like a spider. With the most powerful glass the details of this fleet could not be made out at a distance of four or five miles. Then we passed two or three great black hulks, with a double row of teeth all round. These were war-ships of the ordinary type, and did not make one think very highly of the German navy. But, a few miles farther on, there was a change of opinion. Inside the spacious harbor of Kiel, and under the guns of the great forts, lay the flower of the ships upon which Germany will rely in her next war with a naval power. We counted twelve of them —all new and terrible. They comprised every variety of ram and battery, but we could not make out anything that looked like a revolving turret. One mode of armament is a favorite. It consists of two guns mounted to sweep the upper forward deck, two with the freest play on the starboard and two more on the port side. The guns are all of large caliber, of great length, designed for pounding at long range. Seen aft, these ironclads are very noticeable for their breadth of beam. They would float tranquilly enough, but seem deficient in speed. As they were all at anchor, we could not judge of that point. The skeletons of other vessels which promise to be, when completed, as formidable as those before us, were to be seen in the imperial ship-yards near by. Every country of Europe which has a navy is exercising it about this time. Germany is only in the fashion when she orders out her ironclads for mock-battles in the Baltic. But, though we all knew this fact, we could not help wondering what power she intended to impress with these exhibitions of her resources on the sea.

I suppose that few travelers trouble themselves to study windmills from the inside. Perhaps these structures are best regarded as artistic objects. They certainly set off landscapes very well. Standing on little elevations, flinging out their gaunt arms against the evening sky, they kindle the fancies of the beholder. A brain cooler than Don Quixote's might imagine them endowed with life. I confess to an ancient desire to know something of the internal economy of windmills. It was hard to understand how such slender, graceful towers could contain the machinery for doing any really serious work, and, still more, that the arms could have hurt Don Quixote very much when he pitched into them, lance in rest. Revolving lazily in a moderate breeze, they look harmless enough. An inspection of the works of one of the windmills on a hill-top in Bremen has enlightened me a little. That which looks so small and fragile at a distance, is a four-story house. It is at once a granary, a mill, and a residence. The miller and his family have in it their roomy parlor, dining-room, kitchen, and chambers. These apartments are all comfortably furnished, and so well isolated that the floating meal, of which the air is full in the mill itself, does not invade their home. I have never seen anything neater, snugger, and more generally habitable than the set of rooms which the miller's good wife was pleased to show us. When the wind stirred, there was no idleness on those premises. The arms—monstrous when measured from the upper platform—turned three great mill-stones, and had power to spare. The miller and his boys strained every muscle to feed the ravenous maws and bag the meal as fast as produced. Americans in Europe are too apt to think ill of the old-fashioned modes of working here. Windmills are often cited by them as specimens of antiquated notions. They would change their minds if they could see, as I saw, how simply, effectively, and above all how cheaply, a windmill can do useful work for mankind.

CHAPTER XXXIV.

DIAMOND-CUTTING AT AMSTERDAM.

THERE is something in the business of diamond-cutting that appeals strongly to the imagination.

It must be extremely interesting to see the precious stones at the mines disclosing themselves to the anxious seekers. Any chance blow of the pick may bring to light a mate for the Koh-i-noor, the Orloff, the Shah, the Sancy, the Pitt, the Hope, or any other of the great diamonds of the world. In a moment the digger may become a rich man. His occupation has all the excitement of gambling, with the essential difference in his favor that he can make a steady living at it, though he may fail to draw one of the capital prizes. Work in the diamond-fields of Brazil and South Africa is a legitimate pursuit, and, when well directed, wrests a subsistence from the stony earth as surely as from a corn-patch or a cabbage-garden. It is, perhaps, more seductive to the outside observer than to the fellow down there in the pit who does all the grubbing.

The traveler who can not make it convenient to go to South Africa or Brazil to see diamonds found, may, by visiting Amsterdam, see them cut. That old Dutch city—famous for its grave men, its plump women, its dikes, its canals, its quaint houses, its commercial push, its thrift and consequent wealth—enjoys the unique distinction of cutting the diamonds of the world. Within a few years some other cities have engaged in the business in a small way. But Coster, of Amsterdam, still handles most of the rough stones which reach Europe. At his establishment the Koh-i-noor was recut, and its latent fire fully revealed. He gave to the Star of the South—the largest stone ever unearthed in Brazil—the blaze of light which justifies its brilliant name. He may truly be said to find the real diamond under the dull, opaque crust which often hides its glow in the native state. He is even more the discoverer of its beauties than the man who picked it out of its gravelly bed.

If Baedeker had given me some account of Coster's way of cutting diamonds, I might not have taken the trouble to look him up in Amsterdam, where there are so many other things to claim the tourist's attention. But, in the absence of such information, I was impelled to seek it for myself.

In books one may see pictures of diamond-mining in Brazil, where the slaves are represented as toiling with shovels and hoes in rich gravel, while overseers stand in sentry-boxes all about, watching every movement of the men lest they may conceal some gem in their scanty clothing. He wonders if they keep up that kind of espionage at Coster's, where the opportunities for stealing diamonds must be very great. I supposed there would be some difficulty in gaining admission to a place where pecks of stones were lying round loose in various stages of treatment, and even the air was full of diamond-dust. This was romance. Now let us look at the reality.

Coster offers no obstacle to the inquiring mind. It is only understood that a small sum of money —a guilder (thirty-eight cents) is the proper size of it—must be paid to the superintendent, who turns it over to a fund for the good of the workmen. Every person who bears in his face and clothes evidence of his ability to stand that assessment is admitted and made welcome; and, if he has a lady with him, that is the best voucher of his pecuniary responsibility.

The man who piloted us about Coster's spoke English, and made himself agreeable. He first showed a handful of stones in the rough. As he tossed them down carelessly on a table, I thought they were bits of gum or grains of tapioca. Not one of them sparkled. Their hue was generally a dirty yellow; only a few were milk-white; some were cream-colored. Invited to examine the stones, I took them into my hand with some reluctance, and kept my eye all the time on the exhibitor, being afraid he might turn his head, or be called off to another part of the room, and leave me in possession of those treasures, with a blind confidence in my integrity. I trust it would not have been misplaced, but do not want to take charge of a handful of diamonds, even temporarily, for anybody else. There was no need of anxiety on this score, for the man's gaze was never once withdrawn from that valuable property.

It was hard to realize that those poor-looking scraps of mineral were diamonds—some worth one thousand dollars apiece when cut. Not one of them was a perfect crystal, a pair of pyramids set base to base, of which we see diagrams in the books. The edges had mostly been worn away by much rolling in water, as one would say, their general appearance being that of pebbles smoothed in a brook. But, on close inspection, remains of the original crystalline shape were always detected. Every diamond still retained rudimentary cutting edges, which are all that is left of the old sharp lines. As they rested in my palm, they felt cold as ice. As they struck against one another in moving them about, they emitted faint, musical sounds;

and their weight was remarkable for their bulk. These peculiarities would attract the notice of the most ignorant person. He would know that the stones in his hand were out of the common. But it would be safe to bet that, if they were thrown down by the quart in the streets among other stones, they would pass unnoticed by persons not familiar with the appearance of uncut diamonds. The experiment, however, is not likely to be made.

After examining this handful of diamonds, one has no desire to see any more in the rough. He could look at a cart-load of them without the least emotion. They do not excite that feeling of cupidity which is said to exist, however passive, in every human breast.

Our guide then led us into a room where we saw the first process of cutting. Several men were engaged in this work, which requires great experience, judgment, and skill. It is there that the shape of the polished stones is decided upon— whether it shall be a brilliant with many flashing facets, or a rose with but few. Here the faults, if any, of each stone are discovered by unerring eyes, and the defective parts chipped away. We stood by the side of one of the men while he disposed of what seemed a very knotty question. He held between thumb and finger a stone as large as a filbert. To the uninstructed eye it was a lump of gum arabic, with a certain symmetry of outline showing its old octahedral form. After turning it over and inspecting it critically, he put it in a little vise before him, and screwed the jaws tightly together. Then he took a light, sharp chisel in one hand and a small hammer in the other. He could not have looked more unconcerned if he had been about to crack an after-dinner walnut. My heart was in my mouth when I saw him apply his chisel to the diamond and give it a smart tap with the hammer. What if he should break the stone in pieces, instead of removing a defective fraction of it! The guide had said it was a twenty-carat diamond, and believed to be of the first water. But the operation, hazardous as it appeared, was easy to the skilled artisan, and was successful. He had struck the diamond exactly on the line of cleavage, and a thin piece fell into a box sunk into the table just beneath the vise, and intended for the reception of the chips. The man picked it out, and I saw at a glance that it was full of black specks. These were uncrystallized carbon, like coal-dust, the presence of which would have spoiled the stone when cut. He then showed me the freshly exposed surface of the diamond. The rough, yellowish scale of the imperfect portion having been removed, one could see something of the true sparkle of the gem, though its full luminous effect would be evoked only by the polishing process. Sometimes it is necessary to detach a spotty part by working in a direction other than the cleavage-line; then the hammer and chisel are of no avail. The operator resorts to a saw, which, strangely enough, is toothless. It is nothing more than a fine steel wire, perhaps double the thickness of a hair. This wire is kept moistened by olive-oil, in which diamond-dust has been mixed. As it is moved forth and back, saw-like, across the surface, the dust supplies the place of teeth, and the metallic thread slowly buries itself in that hardest of stones.

The truth of the adage, "Diamond cuts diamond," was made clear to us by the spectacle of six men illustrating it. Each man held in each hand a short stick, having at the end a socket filled with lead or some easily melted alloy. The diamond to be cut is partly sunk below the surface of this fusible metal while it is still in a molten condition, and just before it cools; and, when the metal "sets," there is the diamond immovably imbedded, with enough of its surface exposed to enable the operator to attack it with another diamond, which is fixed in another stick the same way. Each diamond is to cut the other, and thus two stones are simultaneously prepared for the market.

When the exposed parts of the two diamonds have been cut by each other as far as possible, then the soft metal in the iron sockets is melted, the stones are released and turned to bring the uncut sides uppermost, and the work proceeds as before. This is the most tedious stage of the business. One watches the men by the half-hour, and sees them make but little progress as they press one diamond against the other with all the power in their arms, and rub the two slowly together with a faint, crunching noise. If the sunlight falls upon the scene, one may notice certain glistening motes dropping into a little pan beneath their hands. This is the dust of diamonds, which is most carefully saved up to be used in the polishing, the final stage; and, whatever chippings or splinters are obtained here or elsewhere in handling diamonds, are pulverized in agate mortars for the same purpose.

At intervals the workmen pause to look at the diamonds, to see how they are getting on. We observe them at a little distance, and notice the adamantine luster of the facets. Already it is possible to pick out an uncommonly fine stone by its cold, steel-blue light.

The most interesting department of Coster's is the one where the polishing is done. Here, at last, you may look into the hearts of the diamonds freed from their grosser vestments. Here, if anywhere, the spectator is apt to be stirred with unholy covetousness. If he has a lady with him, she would be more than human if she did not sometimes cry out, "How splendid!" "Just too lovely for anything!" and ask the guide how much a pair of such diamonds would cost, pointing at a perfect beauty that would weigh ten carats, sure. Cases are reported in which husbands, at that stage of the rounds, have hurried up their investigations, suddenly finding that they have no time to "look it all through, my dear." And, even when they have torn themselves and the partners of their lives away from the scene of fascination, they have not heard the last of Coster's diamonds by a great deal. At any moment, anywhere, while looking at the marble or bronze effigies of a cathedral, or hunting among church-yard tombs for quaint inscriptions, or rapturously gazing at some Madonna which is the glory of a picture-gallery —when the mind ought to be filled with the most solemn thoughts—one may hear the question, "Weren't they splendid?"

"What, my dear?" says the dull being who never takes a hint.

"Why, those diamonds at Coster's!"

"Oh, yes, I remember—quite pretty." And then the insensate husband, perhaps, instead of pursuing the interesting subject, begs leave to recall the fair one's wandering attention to the beautiful carving on that ancient tomb, or the seraphic expression of the Virgin's eyes, etc.

It has been said that there is one way to stop a mouth which babbles too much of Coster's. A kiss will do it, without fail, if followed up by a gift of something in diamonds, according to the means or generosity of the donor. But this is doubtless the slander of a cynic, and repeated here only under protest.

The polishers are about twenty strong. They are mostly young fellows, who do not require glasses. Sharp eye-sight is the indispensable qualification for their work, They are all hanging over horizontal wheels which are driven at tremendous speed. Upon these revolving disks they are pressing something very forcibly with both hands. It is a stick with a diamond imbedded in the head thereof—the same that we have seen in the cutting-room. Sometimes the workman releases one hand, and takes a feather from a cup by his side. This has been soaking in olive-oil, in which there is an ingredient of diamond-dust. He lets a few drops of it fall on the flying wheel at a point near its center or axis of motion. The centrifugal force at once scatters the oil and the included dust all over the surface in a barely perceptible film. Its tendency is to be thrown off the edge of the wheel but this is prevented by a raised rim, which keeps it all somewhere on the disk. Without the application of this mixture the diamond would never get a polish.

As we stood looking down the line of the polishers, who in turn glanced from their work at us, the guide made a signal to one of them. He at once withdrew his diamond from the wheel, wiped it on a leather apron, and brought it to us for examination. It was a large stone—fifteen carats, perhaps—which had been polished enough to show its native worth. Its color was a yellow, so deep as to convert into a merit what would otherwise have been a great defect. Had the tint been that of straw instead of orange, its selling value would have been small. But as it was extremely yellow, even for a South African stone, connoisseurs would be sure to want it for their collections. There would, perhaps, be a competition for the treasure. Strange caprice of fancy which elevates a fault into a virtue!

Another signal from the guide brought forward a diamond of a very different sort. It was much more to my taste than the other. As the man put the stick into my hand, the end of it seemed to blaze. It shone so vividly that its size could not clearly be made out. Apparently it was larger than the yellow one. But the guide informed me that the polished surface of this stone was much the smaller. Its finer water imparted the wonderful brilliancy I had noticed. From its facets leaped coruscations that dazzled the eye like gleams of lightning. It needed no expert to tell one that here was a diamond of the rarest quality—something that might fairly be claimed to stand first on the list of those twenty-odd grades into which the white stones are divided by the dealers. I could not refrain from touching it with the tip of a finger before the guide could warn me. The contact, which was but for an instant, blistered the skin, so great was the heat caused by the friction of polishing. It was a pleasure to know that this peerless gem—about eight carats when finished—would be worth far more to adorn the neck or bosom of beauty than the bigger yellow one of the rare shade, destined only for the cabinet of some whimsical male collector.

After the exhibition of this perfect diamond to our wondering gaze, anything of lesser splendor would have failed to please. So we bade farewell to Coster's, after paying a visit to the graceful steam-engine which supplies the motive power for all the disks that are kept whirling on the busy second floor. There are other floors of the same establishment where other work is done. There is a great safe down in the basement, which is opened for you, disclosing boxes and bags holding treasures to the extent of as many million dollars as you choose to imagine. Every well-regulated visitor at Coster's is pleased to pay the complimentary fee expected of him, when he knows that it goes to the benefit of the workmen; for, if his eyes have been open to anything besides diamonds, he must have noticed intelligence, sobriety, and honesty written in their faces. Then he understands that at Coster's there is a better guarantee for the security of diamonds against theft and loss than if an overseer stood watching each squad of men with pistol in hand.

APPENDIX.

CONSTITUTIONAL GOVERNMENT FOR RUSSIA.

(SEE CHAPTER XXVIII.)

It is a matter of common report and belief, in Russia, that the experiment of a constitutional government would have been made on the accession of Alexander III, but for the opposition of his ministers. His father was strongly disposed to establish a representative body of the people, and a responsible ministry. This reform would have been a crowning of that edifice, the building of which was cut short by his murderers. The present Tsar desired to carry out this inherited scheme, but before acting deemed it prudent to take the collective opinion of his cabinet. This fact shows his readiness to receive advice on important questions. He mentioned his own preference, but declared that he would be guided by a majority opinion. This was adverse to the proposed change. So ended, for the time being, a movement of the greatest significance.

The Tsar is said to be the strongest man in his dominions. Mythical stories are told of his ability to straighten out horseshoes with his naked hands, and double up silver pieces between his thumb and finger. Those who know him testify to his high personal courage. The seclusion of which we hear so much is, after all, only nominally observed. The careful precautions against Nihilists are adopted by the chief of police, who charges himself with the safety of his master. Alexander III attends military reviews and public ceremonies of church and state. He goes where duty calls him. He is seen more often in the streets and parks of St. Petersburg than Queen Victoria in those of London. She, too, is guarded at such times by soldiers and policemen, and no one thinks the protection superfluous. The Tsar, in all his movements, is hedged about with no more restrictions than seem to be needed for the security of a man who is known to be pursued by a sworn band of assassins. If he is as strong and brave as reported, it would be strange if he lacked decision of character. Once resolved on conforming the imperial system to the more modern type, he may not again be dissuaded by any ministry from executing that beneficent design.

There is no doubt that, if unmistakable public opinion in Russia should call for this great change, it would be made. It remains to be ascertained if a majority of her people really want those constitutional forms for which the heart of civilized man everywhere is supposed to yearn. If so, Russia, fortunately, has the machinery at hand for the gratification of her longings. Every *Tir*, or commune, now possesses the full power of self-government in economic and strictly local affairs. The village elders, who are true home-rulers, are chosen by the people. In every province or department of Russia the same principle is illustrated on a larger scale. It is only in respect to imperial or political issues that the autocracy makes itself felt. The citizens of Moscow, for example, may do many things at their own expense for which we of New York are obliged to crave permission of the Legislature.

Accustomed to govern themselves within a certain range, the Russians could easily be fitted for participation in the higher duties which a constitutional government would impose upon them. A lower House could be evolved from the seeds of the *Tir*. An upper House could be created by the Tsar out of abundant existing materials. Thus, without any violent metamorphosis, liberal institutions might be introduced into Russia. They may come, as a spontaneous offering from the throne, sooner than their most sanguine friends in the empire now expect.

THE END.

www.ingramcontent.com/pod-product-compliance
Lightning Source LLC
Chambersburg PA
CBHW020540300426
44111CB00008B/734